"*Wisdom, Attachment, and Love in Trauma Therapy* provides a sophisticated and compassionate understanding of how trauma therapists experience, train, and contribute to the healing of their heroic clients. In this well-written and integrated book, Susan Pease Banitt conveys a conceptual framework integrating principles extracted from contemporary neuroscience, psychology, and philosophic orientations to emphasize the features of successful therapy. Through her personal experiences, she emphasizes the importance of the therapist being present and accepting of the client. Perhaps most relevant to the trauma therapist, she provides a deep understanding of the vulnerabilities of the therapist, who may be a survivor of trauma."

Stephen W. Porges, PhD, distinguished university scientist and founding director of the Traumatic Stress Research Consortium, Kinsey Institute, Indiana University, and author of *The Pocket Guide to The Polyvagal Theory: The Transformative Power of Feeling Safe*

"Susan Pease Banitt offers us more than a book; this is a mission statement on how many of us who work to bring healing to the wounds of trauma really feel about the state of our field. Pease Banitt, an expert at her craft, shares her much-needed voice as she teaches on one of the great clinical imperatives: it's the relationship that heals. Practical, useful and integrative, any clinician working in trauma healing ought to have a copy of this book to develop in the art of this work."

Jamie Marich, PhD, LPCC-S, LICDC-CS, REAT, RMT, author of *EMDR Therapy and Mindfulness for Trauma-Focused Care, Dancing Mindfulness: A Creative Path to Healing and Transformation, Trauma Made Simple, Trauma and the 12 Steps,* and *EMDR Made Simple*

"Susan Pease Banitt bravely challenges outmoded mindsets that have never served us as we work to heal trauma survivors. She asserts that our clients need to feel loved, that there is a place for touch in psychotherapy, that dissociated and later recovered memories are normal responses to trauma, and that we need sit in belief of what our clients tell us, including ritual abuse and trauma-based mind control."

Ellen Lacter, PhD, licensed clinical psychologist, registered play therapist, marriage and family therapist, past president of the California Association of Play Therapy, academic coordinator of the Play Therapy Certificate Program at the University of California, San Diego Extension

"In this book, Susan Pease Banitt is able to integrate psychosocial history, cultural diversity, interdisciplinary sciences, interfaith spirituality and good old-fashioned common sense. She synthesizes complex information in ways that make sense of clinical chaos without resorting to reductionism. Her work has very practical applications beyond theory and empowers healing processes for clients and therapists alike. Pease Banitt's brilliance stands out above the rest because her personal and professional lives are congruent and lived with a high level of integrity."

Ericha Scott, PhD, LPCC, ATR-BC, keynote speaker, creative arts psychotherapist, consultant, globally published researcher, and theorist in peer-reviewed journals

Wisdom, Attachment, and Love in Trauma Therapy

Wisdom, Attachment, and Love in Trauma Therapy focuses on the creation of the therapist as healing presence rather than technique administrator—in other words, how to be rather than what to do. Trauma survivors need wise therapists who practice with the union of intellect, knowledge, and intuition. Through self-work, therapists can learn to embody healing qualities that foster an appropriate, corrective, and loving experience in treatment that transcends any technique. This book shows how Eastern wisdom teachings and Western psychotherapeutic modalities combine with modern theory to support a knowledgeable, compassionate, and wise therapist who is equipped to help even the most traumatized person heal.

Susan Pease Banitt, LCSW, is a social worker and psychotherapist who specializes in the treatment of severe trauma and PTSD. She has worked in the field of mental health for more than four decades in diverse settings and teaches classes on healing from trauma in Portland, Oregon. She is the author of *The Trauma Tool Kit: Healing PTSD from the Inside Out.*

Wisdom, Attachment, and Love in Trauma Therapy

Beyond Evidence-Based Practice

Susan Pease Banitt

Routledge
Taylor & Francis Group

NEW YORK AND LONDON

First published 2019
by Routledge
711 Third Avenue, New York, NY 10017

and by Routledge
2 Park Square, Milton Park, Abingdon, Oxon, OX14 4RN

Routledge is an imprint of the Taylor & Francis Group, an informa business

© 2019 Susan Pease Banitt

Library of Congress Cataloging-in-Publication Data
A catalog record for this title has been requested

ISBN: 978-1-138-28974-1 (hbk)
ISBN: 978-1-138-28975-8 (pbk)
ISBN: 978-1-315-21377-4 (ebk)

Typeset in Goudy
by Apex CoVantage, LLC

Contents

Foreword

The meeting of two personalities is like the contact of two chemical substances: if there is any reaction, both are transformed.
            —Carl Jung, *Modern Man in Search of a Soul* (1933)

This book has the power to change the evolution of our profession. In the pages that follow, Susan Pease Banitt, LCSW, speaks to the budding movement of mental health providers who seek to integrate logic and intuition and to welcome psychotherapy as a science, an art, and a multidirectional process of healing.

I've often called this multidirectional process of healing *reciprocal transformation*, meaning that when two, or more, people come together in the efforts of healing, all are transformed. In relationship, deep wounds can emerge in the form of transference, countertransference, and enactments. The gentle practices of awareness, compassion, and presence can bear witness to the hurt and allow us to transcend it, facilitating what we have come to call healing experiences. As we build these 'soft skills' of awareness, compassion, and presence—ones that are difficult to measure but necessary for healing—we cultivate a field of healing within ourselves and extend it to our clients. As any wise, experienced clinician will tell you, clients have solid BS detectors and will not stand for feigned anything. In order to improve our own skills, we must look honestly into ourselves and cultivate the qualities that serve us, as well as our clients. This inner work on the part of the clinician is crucial, and developing awareness of our own coping strategies serves to improve the quality of our work. By acknowledging our own limitations, we can learn to transcend them.

When faced with the complexity of human experience and the enormity of human suffering, we, as caretakers and providers, can also become overwhelmed and lean on techniques and modalities to find comfort and to legitimize our work. When we cling to manuals, techniques, and trainers, we can miss the richness and opportunity that comes with deep listening—to ourselves and to those we serve—and in turn can skim over the depth of transformation that is possible when human beings connect. It is a tricky balance, then, to fill our toolkit with evidence-based practices and to fully trust the unique connection that each relationship offers. As Sue suggests here, when we learn the skill of using our whole self—brain and body, mind, spirit, and beyond, we become evidence-empowered instead of evidence-enslaved.

In the shift to evidence-empowered, attachment-informed clinical work, we integrate the benefits of modern science with the wisdom and ineffable power of human presence. Presence precedes connection, and connection is central to human development and the experience of healing, particularly as it relates to developmental trauma. Sue reminds us of this truth and guides us to reflect with wisdom on how our training, our cultural influences, and our own attachment patterns can impact the process of relational healing, in therapy and beyond. As we integrate awareness of ourselves and others, our scope of healing broadens.

Sue and I met years ago at a conference for the International Society for the Study of Trauma and Dissociation, where we were both presenting. As soon as I learned her full name, I exclaimed something brilliant to the effect of, "Oh, you're you!" and went on to explain that I had heard a recorded radio interview she had done. Suffice it to say, I already knew from listening that she and I were on the same page. She talked about yoga, indigenous healing, religious belief systems, and cultural competence. I could have exclaimed instead (and it would have been a bit more eloquent) "Soul sister!" as that's what I feel when I hear her speak, when we present together, and when I read this book.

Many years, conferences, and presentations have passed since that meeting, and Sue and I have had time and space to delve into conversations around the themes in this book. There is something about learning the depth and complexity of trauma work that helps you to see the challenges and, at times, dysfunction, of larger systems. Many 'master therapists,' as Sue describes them, will simply put up with these dynamics, pressures, and inconveniences. And yet, at this level leaders continue to emerge. Therapists like Sue who speak to the imbalances and inaccuracies that are popular have courage, heart, and the depth of conviction that can only come from years of experience. In speaking to the current challenges of systems and the field as a whole, these leaders pave a path of innovation and improvement, leaving a sense of greater ease, health, and integration in their wake. Perhaps you are already taking part in this positive evolution, and this book can support you in continuing to lead, or perhaps, it will ignite you to begin.

I chose my graduate advisor based on this very same capacity to transcend limitations in mental health culture and lead by example. When I arrived on a last minute trip to Cambridge in the fall of 2004, I'd planned to visit the Harvard Graduate School of Education and see how I felt there—if I could see myself studying in the library, connecting with the students, and learning from the faculty. The Risk and Prevention program, as it was called at the time, had been co-founded by Dr. Michael Nakkula, who had also written *Matters of Interpretation*, a reflective book about developmental counseling that deeply resonated with me. With anticipation, and without an appointment,

I knocked in Dr. Nakkula's office door—fifth floor of Larsen Hall, room 505. "Come on in!" I heard him holler. Astounded by my luck, I entered the office and proceeded to have a 40-minute conversation with one of the most grounded, attuned, empathetic, and available professors I've had to this day. As it turned out, he'd also been a Communications Studies major in undergrad, and we both loved the crisp fall weather. While those are the only two things I can recall us having in common, I left there feeling connected, seen, and celebrated, feelings that are all too rare in competitive academic settings. When I enrolled in the master's program the following year, I was eager to be guided by someone who walked the talk.

Years later, as a graduate of two of the programs Dr. Nakkula had contributed to creating, we were in the basement of Longfellow Hall—just across Appian Way from Larsen—with his wife (who was also amazing and taught in our program) and kids milling around. The occasion was bittersweet—he had accepted a position at the University of Pennsylvania, where he remains at the time of this writing. He stood up and gave a short and heartfelt speech, which was to be expected at such an event. He did, however, say something that I did not expect, and in doing so he broke a rule I was not even aware I was following.

"What we are doing here, really, all boils down to love."

Did my academic advisor just say the 'L' word? In front of other academicians? I wholeheartedly agreed and, once he said it aloud, I realized that I would have been embarrassed to say the same thing in front of the very same crowd. Of course, he was calm and even-keeled, never to be thrown by someone speaking the truth, even when the words came from his own mouth. At that moment, I learned that, despite all the words and measures, theories and methods I had studied, I was afraid to say the most important and central word in human relationship, the thing I knew was at the heart of the difficult work we were all doing: loving one another.

In this book, Sue helps us to recall and become increasingly comfortable with love as the basic truth of human relationship and attachment. In a gentle and inclusive manner, she reminds us of our humanity and our own vulnerabilities, encouraging those in human services to reflect on their own developmental processes and ways of relating as a foundation for deep healing work. She speaks with humor and with the evidence of a lifetime of practical experience in counseling and social work. She has, as I like to call it, time with human beings, which has allowed her to explore and reflect on what is most useful for each unique soul who crosses her clinical path. Reassociating the disconnect between masculine and feminine, Eastern and Western approaches, left and right brain, she reminds us that complex work cannot be boiled down to simple strategies but takes the ongoing effort of personal and communal development. It takes the practice of patience, presence, and love.

In the face of the challenge of interpersonal healing, we can swing to many ends of the pendulum: clinging to textbooks, or defiantly ignoring science in service of our own belief system; becoming rigid or numb to the suffering of others, or becoming consumed by the stories and experiences of those we serve. In the pages that follow, you will find the clarity that comes with having done the personal, professional, and experiential work. As Sue speaks to the need to honor science, ourselves, our clients, and our increasingly intercon-nected cultural contexts, she supports us in tuning the instrument of our own minds and hearts.

Thank you, Sue, for this offering, and to you, dear reader, I hope you enjoy.

Lisa Danylchuk, EdM, MFT, E-RYT
Author of *Embodied Healing: Using Yoga to
Recover from Trauma and Extreme Stress* and
*How You Can Heal: A Strengths-Based Guide to
Trauma Recovery*

Preface

Healing through relationship has been the central tenet of psychotherapy since its inception. Many of us were drawn to this field by the compassionate therapists we encountered, whose techniques were rooted in wisdom handed down from therapist supervisors to practitioners. Yet, since the early 1990s market forces, rather than wisdom practices, have come to influence psychotherapeutic techniques. The advent of managed care in mental health has emphasized what has come to be called 'evidence-based practice'. Even though there is a huge body of research showing that the quality of the relationship in psychotherapy trumps any theoretical modality, academic researchers focus on techniques and strategies in therapy because they are easier to measure (and therefore get funding for) than the intangibles found in the qualities and healing potentials of the therapeutic relationship. The traditional teaching foundations of good therapy: presence, compassion, patience, and wisdom have fallen by the wayside in the race for metrics. With ever-shrinking allotments of time for treatment available, we have a new generation of therapists who have much expertise in strategies and alphabet techniques (CBT, ACT, DBT, etc.) but not much guidance in the use of self. Many of these therapists are floundering or burning out, especially when it comes to that most difficult of therapies: treating patients with extensive and severe trauma histories.

Ironically, over the same time period, the American public has become very interested in wisdom teachings from Eastern traditions. Yogic and mindfulness practice is at an all-time high. Many people, especially traumatized clients (and their therapists), seek out alternative therapies to help manage their symptoms and gain a perspective that can be lacking in traditional mental health care or the reductionist techniques of 'behavioral health'. A whole new profession has sprung up to supplant traditional mental health services called Yoga Service, where yoga teachers, most of whom are not mental health professionals, are flocking to prisons, residential care facilities, hospitals, shelters and after-school programs to teach yoga-based stress reduction techniques to high-risk populations. They are having great success with highly traumatized people.

I have always gravitated towards work with highly traumatized populations, beginning with youth in residential care and shelters and inpatient units, moving to child protection work, medical social work, and eventually private practice after my twins were born, a period of over 40 years. In my first book, *The Trauma Tool Kit* (2012), I shared a bit of my journey as a trauma survivor and presented the multifarious modalities I used to help myself and others heal from chronic delayed PTSD. I have been working as a mental health supervisor in various incarnations (residential, child protective services, and clinical) since the late 1980s.

Currently, as a clinical supervisor for social work licensure in Oregon, I specialize in training therapists to do trauma-competent psychotherapy with traumatized and dissociative clients. The dearth of well-trained trauma therapists coupled with a decrease in services available for mental health inspired me to start writing and teaching on the subject of excellent clinical work with trauma patients. I am not a researcher. I am not an academic, although I do read many studies and journals to stay abreast of developments. I present and write with a clinical supervisor's eyes and ears with the goal of passing along any wisdom I have gleaned to future generations of therapists. Case examples are presented to illustrate theoretical concepts.

I have divided the chapters into three sections: Wisdom, Attachment, and Love. The wisdom section encompasses examples of clinical mastery, wise use of self, state-of-the-art neurobiological knowledge along with clinical implications and implementation suggestions, and, finally, theoretical wisdom with an emphasis on Althea Horner's early stages of ego development. The attachment chapters focus on fostering attachment, preventing traumatic attachment rupture in therapy, and repairing ruptures as they occur. Helpful qualities that the therapist may develop to engage clients and minimize ruptures are presented. The concept of love in therapy is explored through the development of different types of empathy, self-care (self-love) for the therapist herself, and, finally, a frank exploration of different kinds of love and the way they can manifest for better or for worse in therapy.

Let me note here that because most therapists are women, and most clients are also women, I have used female gender pronouns throughout the book. However, I have also used some male pronouns as well the nonbinary pronoun 'they' to promote flexible thinking and application for the reader. Like many therapist authors before me, I refer to the primary caregiver as 'Mother' throughout most of the book while recognizing that many men, gay and straight, cis and trans, are primary caregivers of children. All case material has been disguised to conceal identities.

I feel an immense amount of gratitude for all the clinicians that came before and shall come after me, those of us who dedicate our lives to helping others heal. The importance of mental health work cannot be overestimated. Mental health is not only the foundation of physical health, it also determines our level of functionality locally, nationally, and globally.

Many great therapists have been generous with me over decades: with their time, their kindness, their learning, and their writing. I am very grateful for organizations like the International Society for the Study of Trauma and Dissociation and the National Association of Social Workers and their conferences where I can meet like-minded supportive clinicians. I have been blessed with many fine supervisors, consultants, and peer healers to work with that have supported and informed my work. I want to acknowledge my husband, Peter Banitt, MD, who was an early supporter of my work and supports my vision of healing in the world, and my wise daughters, Maya and Larissa Banitt, who champion my work every chance they get.

My intention is that this book address a modern training deficit for psychotherapists, which is *how to be* in the therapy hour rather than *what to do*. This deficit becomes quickly exposed in the difficult and sensitive work of trauma therapy, in impasses, adverse events, or negative outcomes for clients with complex or developmental trauma. Research over several decades has shown that it is the quality of the relationship rather than any specific theory, technique, or evidence-based practice that has the most impact in the efficacy of treatment. Since attachment is the key to great trauma work, the need for practitioners to embody wisdom in the treatment room is acute. Wisdom practices abound in Eastern philosophies and religions, and it is helpful to draw on these teachings to conceptualize a wise use of self in the therapy of traumatized clients. This book brings Eastern wisdom and Western clinical techniques and research together to give the modern clinician an expanded ability to understand the effective use of wisdom, attachment, and love in the treatment of traumatized people.

Susan Pease Banitt, LCSW, RYT
Portland, Oregon

Part I
Wisdom

1 What Makes a Great Therapist?

People will forget what you said, people will forget what you did, but people will never forget how you made them feel.

—Maya Angelou

When I was in my early teens, I met the great family therapist and social worker Virginia Satir. I don't recall much of what she said. I remember that we were a small group of people in a cozy room with a lady who looked like she was surrounded by a bubble of light. Her unforced smile shone in her eyes as she looked about the room, talking. She spoke of pain and families and healing. I liked how I felt when I was with her; it was a new feeling of safety, of coziness, and something I didn't have a reference for at the time, wisdom. I felt that while I was in that space with her, everything was OK for the moment. She appeared stable and kind and thoughtful. She spoke of pain in a way that was not painful. Although I was not talking I felt as though I could have said anything to her. The moment became magical without being uncanny. Her intelligence revealed itself as ordinary yet, in its focus, extraordinary. She did not spout theorems or complicated vocabulary. Her communication arose simply and lingered in the atmosphere, instantly understandable. Without realizing it, I decided I wanted to be like her when I grew up, a master therapist.

Many clinicians have never heard of Virginia Satir. She is one of many wise therapists who appear, develop their practice and their theories, and then fade away with time or new thoughts. Some write books, and some do not. These therapists touch dozens of people; some affect thousands. They begin centers, or movements. Many practice quietly in their corner of the world. Maybe they guide a few blooming therapists along the way. If you are fortunate enough to meet a truly wise clinician, you will not easily forget them. Their being carries an essence of healing that is hard to quantify. Their presence transforms you. Once we have met such a person, who transcends the ordinary boundaries of the words counselor, clinician, therapist, we are moved to want to be like them. To watch them work is like watching a great magician, only instead of pulling rabbits out of hats, they pull people out of misery and despair with great skill.

How do we get there from here? You are reading this book right now because you want to know more, to do better, to help your traumatized clients and become a sage clinician. Maybe you are ambitious and competitive, ready to make your mark on the world; maybe you simply have a compassionate heart, or perhaps you have hit 'the wall' in your practice, that place where you know you can make a bigger difference with less effort but haven't figured out how to do so yet, especially with challenging clients. Well, buckle up 'cause Kansas is going bye-bye.

We all start as beginning therapists with the basics:

1. Start on time
2. End on time
3. Don't make the session be about you
4. Be present

Lather. Rinse. Repeat. Except it is not so easy, is it? To be fully present with another human being, to stay out of our own self-centered, or as the Buddhists would say, *self-cherishing*, thoughts. This practice is actually quite difficult, like a meditation. Perhaps good therapy is a meditation, and like meditation it may take a lifetime to perfect.

Left/Right Hemispheric Integration

As beginning therapists, we gain skills. Like a good piano player, we learn a piece one hemisphere at a time. In the left-brain side of our work, we digest theories, concepts, techniques; we write about them in school. We read and read. We integrate diagnostic concepts from the *Diagnostic and Statistical Manual of Mental Disorders* (DSM), whichever version we are on. We observe; we study; we deduce; we assess; we formulate. We treat the patient as an object for our study, and this treatment is *necessary* for this part of the performance. After all, how can we work inside someone else's mind when we have only a vague idea of their problems or how a mind even works? Left-brain skills ground our work and give us our professionalism and our licenses. I wouldn't want to take my car to see someone week after week with them mucking about inside with no idea of what the real problem was. Would you? That would be a tremendous waste of time and money that could be more damaging than helpful. And, we usually have forms we must fill out to show our left-brain competence. So. Many. Forms.

And yet, if our brains were like cars, once we had the diagnostic picture, we would know exactly how to treat it, and the treatment wouldn't vary much. In that case, why have humans do treatment? Why not computer programs? More reliable, less countertransference! Well, it has been tried. Somewhere, someone is working on an 'app for that'. Who knows? Maybe they will be successful. But I don't think so. There is another side to the brain![1]

A pianist's right hand has to operate absolutely independent of the left hand. This, in itself, is a minor miracle when you think about it. Sometimes when I present on this material, I show a clip of Martha Argerich playing a Bach partita on the piano.[2] When you play with only one hand, you get half the piece and a much less interesting listening experience, an incomplete composition. To play a Bach partita, two hands are playing different melodies that weave and clash, integrate and spring apart. Playing at this level requires an intense degree of neural integration only developed through hours and hours of painstaking practice, practice that is often as frustrating as it is rewarding.

The same principle that makes for a great pianist applies to being a great therapist. We are more than a collection of thoughts and theories. Great therapists work with their intuition, pattern recognition, and their own feelings (countertransference), sorting through decision trees and matching their observations with moment-by-moment choices of how to interact with a client. These choices include where to look, how to sit, how to breathe, when to stay silent, when to speak, how to modulate the voice, where to put emphasis, and when to articulate an observation versus when to ask a question and wait, how to use our facial expressions, and much more. Sure, we know many theories, many techniques, but how do we know when to use them? The neurological complexity of our task cannot be overstated. *Good therapy is called an art and a science.* We fuse our left-brain knowledge with gut feelings, the heart of compassion, and the ineffable intuitive knowing of the right brain. We have to practice each hand separately, sussing out both theories and our intuitive connection to our clients, and learn the music of healing before that beautiful moment when we can skillfully play our music with both hands. It may take many years of practice before we produce a masterpiece. This complicated process is why checklist therapy will never work for our most difficult cases. Procedures and checklists are tools, but they are not the art. They are dumb instruments that need to be in the hand of maestros. We are kidding ourselves if we think we can solve the problems of issues like developmental trauma with a prescribed protocol. In fact, my practice and the practices of many of my colleagues are filled with failures from such one-size-fits-all evidence-based approaches.

One more consideration is necessary to complete the musical analogy—a pianist can go out and find a lovely instrument on which to play their beautiful music. *The instrument we play in therapy is our own being, our own brain and gut, our own nervous system.* Like actors, we must first develop our bodily instrument before we may play well upon it. *We cannot commission someone to build us a beautiful, wise, and empathic brain; we have to build it ourselves.* This awareness separates mediocre therapists from truly wise ones. Our work will only be as good as our limbic instrument born of our own self and character development. This truth should be self-evident, but in case it is not, let us do a thought experiment. I could give two therapists the exact same protocol—maybe a CBT one or an exposure therapy one, or even a mindfulness script. Now imagine how the protocol is executed. One therapist has come from a weekend retreat, is blissfully centered, relaxed, and happy with their life. The other therapist has an anger problem and constantly gets annoyed with the people in their life; maybe they had a road rage incident on the way to work. Both clinicians have a great deal of self-control and education. But whom would you rather sit with if you were feeling vulnerable? How would the protocols be affected by the mien of the therapist? Scripts are easy to teach, but only modestly effective without a strong therapeutic alliance. Over the last couple of decades, there have been several studies and meta-analyses that consistently show the therapeutic relationship as superseding theoretical orientation or technique in the importance of a successful therapy. In this 2015 study, where a CBT protocol was used with psychotic patients, the authors concluded the following:

> The patients' perception of the therapist as empathic, genuine, accepting, competent and convincing is associated with therapeutic alliance in CBTp. Perceived therapist genuineness and competence are the most relevant predictors of patient-rated therapeutic alliance. Training and supervision should focus on increasing basic therapist qualities.
>
> (Jung, Wiesjahn, Rief, & Lincoln, 2015)

Doing therapy by protocol is relatively simple but is only really effective if the therapist takes on the task of being the therapy by their very essence and presence.

In the intermediate stage of clinical work, we have mastered many theories and techniques. We have worked hard to get to know ourselves. Perhaps we have a good grasp of our own countertransference to our patients' transference. We have several years of supervision, and hopefully several years of our own therapy under our belt. We have a modicum of competence.

Let's look at competence in the model of the four stages of competence (Adams, 2017):

1. Unconscious incompetence—the ordinary person as counselor may or may not give great advice but has no knowledge of the pitfalls of relationships or deeper structures in the psyche. This person has little to no insight into their own mind. Pre-beginner stage.
2. Conscious incompetence—ideally this stage emerges during graduate school or during licensure supervision. It may manifest whenever a therapist works with a new population at any point in one's career. It is a very uncomfortable stage in which people either feel like quitting or become invigorated by the challenge (or both). Beginner stage.
3. Conscious competence—the intermediate stage where one has an adequate set of tools and a good idea when and how to apply them. This stage requires a lot of conscious focus, integration, and practice. It can go on for years, and many clinicians never really transcend this stage due to their own unhealed issues, fragmentation, or lack of interest in learning how to 'play with both hands'.

4. Unconscious competence—the clinician has now fully integrated their knowledge with their way of being. Like a trained dancer, any misstep becomes part of the dance and the audience is unaware of a problem in the choreography, because really at this stage of competence, there are no problems that cannot be turned towards healing. The two hands play together consistently, and it can feel like magic. Instead of conducting therapy, therapy is conducting us, and there is a quality of flow and bliss to the work.

An advanced clinician has not only mastered the fourth stage of competence (understanding that mastery is less of a destination and more of a process), but has also incorporated their work into their entire being. Like my experience with Virginia Satir, wisdom radiates in the therapy regardless of the therapist's specific words or actions. The more challenging our clients' issues, the more necessary it is to develop these qualities in oneself if we want to be successful and bring the maximum amount of healing ability to the therapy.

Being vs. Doing

When I assembled my first talk on wisdom and advanced practice for trauma clients, I found it difficult to find overarching models of wisdom in the West that were not religious. In fact, if you Google the words 'Western Wisdom', the top finding is a website of sayings from the Old West, like "Polishing your pants on saddle leather don't make you a rider" and "Don't name a cow you plan to eat." Of course, the West does have its philosophers and thinkers as well as some truly great therapists. But to get to the essence of wisdom teachings for therapists and healers, I found it helpful to turn to the teachings of the East: Hinduism, Buddhism, Taoism.[3] These cultures are so ancient that the mind boggles trying to comprehend the longevity of these awarenesses and teachings. What really separates the East from the West in terms of wisdom, philosophy, and even theology are the concepts of Being vs. Doing.

My second-year supervisor had his own mantra for me, "Don't just do something, sit there." He scrawled this mantra on my process recordings and repeated it on a regular basis in supervision. Like any young person in America, I was a doer. We are taught to 'do' in school from the time we hit kindergarten until we graduate our professional programs. Schools do not really teach us how to 'be'. Even the focus in therapy has shifted from more of a 'being' modality, such as psychoanalysis, to 'doing' modalities, i.e., 6- to 8-week evidence-based protocols that 'git 'er done'. Problem is, evidence-based protocols are generally based in research that only looks at effects 3 months, 6 months, sometimes 12 months out of the study. It is not cost effective to conduct studies over long periods of time, and academic departments need to 'publish or perish'. I am not opposed to peer-reviewed research; studies can be helpful with some caveats. *Studies are limited in their usefulness and generalizability, especially for folks in private practice settings who may be seeing highly complex cases over long periods of time.*

Let's look at some of the differences between evidence-based (doing) vs. wisdom-based (being) practices. Evidence-based practices are very recent, whereas wisdom-based practices are ancient. In Chinese medicine, a treatment is not considered vetted until it has been studied for about 200 years—a vastly different timescale than our peer-reviewed studies, most of which do not look at effects past one year! The idea that the practitioner's quality of being is an essential part of healing the patient is thousands of years old. Ayurvedic practitioners from India, Chinese medicine practitioners, and medicine people from indigenous tribes all had to qualify themselves through their character, calmness, and steadiness of mind over a long period of time before they were accepted as students or apprentices. In addition, there needed to be a level of moral or spiritual attainment evident to be accepted into training. By contrast, college student admission often favors the 'go-getter' and prefers accomplishments to insight, morality, or wisdom. Some of the wisest students I've met take fewer AP classes and do fewer extracurricular activities to maintain their mental health and peace of mind. They do not get into the 'top' schools. The morality (and mental health) of the student is often assumed in psychology programs. When problems arise with a clinical student's behavior, they are often dealt with retroactively rather than proactively. With a financial need to accept and keep students, some programs do not have the luxury of weeding out poor practitioners even if they want to.

Modern research studies look for relatively short-term changes in small measurable outcomes, and it is best if those changes happen rapidly. Western, and especially American, culture takes a short-term rather than a long-term view, and we like to see immediate results from our work. Eastern medicine is suspicious of super-fast changes and looks for permanent changes over a long period of time rather than short measurable changes that may fade quickly or have unintended negative side effects. Of course, with the body, short-term fixes such as surgeries, antibiotics, or even anti-psychotics can produce brilliant results. When working with the less-definable mind and nebulous interconnected systems, such as the hypothalamic–pituitary–adrenal (HPA) axis, Western medicine stumbles a bit. If you have worked with traumatized clients, you are well aware of the failures of Western medicine to adequately address the sequelae of HPA axis damage from trauma such as autoimmune disorders, obesity, insomnia, and digestive disorders.

A big distinction of the different methodologies of assessing the effectiveness of various treatments between East and West lies in the research itself. The typical client in my practice or yours probably would not qualify for a research study. There are so many exclusion criteria! A team of researchers, including Edna Foa, PhD, a leading voice in the treatment of PTSD, conducted a study on prolonged exposure (PE) therapy that was published in 2013. Exclusion criteria for that study are described below:

> Participants were excluded if they (a) had a history of schizophrenia, bipolar disorder, or cognitive dysfunction; (b) had a history of alcohol or

drug abuse or dependence within the previous 3 months; (c) met criteria for mental retardation or pervasive developmental disorder; (d) had a medically unstable condition that would interfere with participation or biological measurements; (e) had an ongoing intimate relationship with a perpetrator; (f) presented with serious suicide risk; (g) were pregnant; (h) were taking psychotropic medications or medications that could interfere with HPA axis functioning except maintenance serotonin-specific reuptake inhibitors; or (i) were employed in positions that altered patterns of sleep wakefulness.

(Zalta et al., 2013)

Therapists in private practice, hospitals, and community agencies do not have the luxury of handpicking clients with these kinds of exclusion criteria. The criteria listed above would rule out nearly all of my trauma clients over several decades of practice! Another problem is that clients exclude themselves from studies. Journal articles may or may not reflect that reality. There are many folks who walk out of treatment studies once the terms are explained to them. So if 150 people inquire about the study, but half leave because they do not like the sound of prolonged exposure, for example, and the half that stay gets great results, did PE really get that great of a result? And is that result relevant to a typical clinical practice?

In contrast, Eastern and indigenous healers rely on observation, oral tradition, and written treatments that have been passed down through generations to inform their healing practices. These cultures knew about epigenetic learning long before we did. Native Americans encourage their people to consider the effects of their actions for seven generations. Chinese medicine practitioners and even naturopathic doctors consider the effects of the ancestors on their patients' health. They encourage healers to emerge from generation to generation within families, and children in these families are taught healing principles at a young age. It is not unusual to meet a medicine person in these cultures who can cite many generations of healers before them and whose knowledge is encyclopedic.

Medicine people and shamanic practitioners rely on ways of knowing that are not testable in university laboratory settings and thus are not research friendly. Their practices depend on mind fields that are free of doubt and skepticism; in fact, faith and trust are important conditions of their healing practices. The West talks about 'neutrality' in research, but in these cultures the idea that minds are 'neutral' would be nonsensical. Practices such as shamanic journeying, clairvoyance, ceremony, and spirit communication depend on right attitude, a deep ability to traverse one's own mind and imagination, and rigorous training in abilities that are not easily measured by Western standards. In the end, these are ancient wisdom-based cultures that actively cultivate wisdom in their people as opposed to intellectual cultures that are merely focused on facts.

The Tao of Therapy

The *Tao Te Ching* is a unique document in all of history in that it espouses wisdom in a text devoid of religious or spiritual practices. The Tao is defined as the abiding principle of the universe, or as some say, merely as The Way. This evocative stanza from the *Tao Te Ching* illustrates the non-doing of being:

> The Master acts without doing anything and teaches without saying anything. Things arise and she lets them come; things disappear and she lets them go. She has but doesn't possess, acts but doesn't expect. When her work is done, she forgets it. That is why it lasts forever.
>
> (Mitchell, 2009)

In the Tao, a master of wisdom is described as someone having the following qualities:

CAREFUL: as someone crossing an iced-over stream
ALERT: as a warrior in enemy territory
COURTEOUS: as a guest
FLUID: as melting ice
SHAPEABLE: as a block of wood
RECEPTIVE: as a valley
CLEAR: as a glass of water (Mitchell, 2009)

These qualities struck me as the same qualities I have encountered in what I would call master therapists. In contemplating these attributes, I realized that the wise therapist knows that she has them or wants them, and cultivates them carefully. If we flip these qualities to their opposite we come up with what we shall kindly call the, ahem, non-wisdom therapist.

Not careful = Careless
Not alert = Preoccupied or Dissociated
Not courteous = Rude
Not fluid = Rigid
Not shapeable = Opinionated
Not receptive = Reactive
Not clear = Opaque or Confusing

I am sure we all know at least one clinician who embodies more qualities from the latter list than the former. Getting a degree does not guarantee character. Wisdom lies in knowing we all are just as capable of being the non-wise therapist as we are of being the wise therapist. We know that pleasant and unpleasant qualities lurk in our minds ready to come out at any time. The more we rehearse our unpleasant qualities outside of the therapy hour, the more likely these qualities will manifest inside a therapy session. Knowing this, master therapists cultivate vigilance and self-awareness as a daily practice, not only as an attribute to be turned on in our therapy offices. If we notice that unpleasant qualities arise and obstruct our ability to provide great therapy (and we will!), we are obligated to take action to change these habitual reactions. We can do this through supervision, through our own insight-oriented therapy, and through various mindfulness practices. As therapists, we know that we literally create and re-create our brain from moment to moment over the lifespan. We get to choose what kind of brain we want to create. If we do not choose consciously, we will choose unconsciously. Working with traumatized clients will push all of our buttons. We will have plenty of opportunity to be triggered and to find out where we lack wisdom. We then have the opportunity to work through these qualities, which is both a curse and a great blessing for one in pursuit of wisdom.

Masters of Attachment

So far, we have defined mastery in therapy as achieving the fourth stage of competence: unconscious competence, as well as having developed a healing quality of being as a therapist. The master therapist incorporates wisdom, self-knowledge, and an empathic presence so impactful that it supersedes the 'doing' or mechanisms of any particular therapy technique or theory. One could say that the master therapist has perfected their ability to create the conditions where clients can safely attach and heal.

Dan Siegel, clinical director at the UCLA School of Medicine and the executive director of the Mindsight Institute, is considered by many to be a modern master. He has written several books about attachment and healing from trauma and also about the dynamics and neurological underpinnings of relationships, a field he coined 'interpersonal neurobiology'. Siegel defines good caregiving with four S's:

Seen
Soothed
Safe
Secure (Siegel, 2016)

When he discusses good caregiving, he is not just talking about therapy but any caregiving relationship: parent-child, lovers, friends. For him, maintaining a safe and secure attachment between individuals is the necessary foundation for healing the mind.

If we examine the history of modern psychology, we will find that many of the master therapists (both men and women) put attachment first in their work with clients. How they made these attachments and described them theoretically differed by personality, temperament, and intellectual conceptualization. They all put attachment as a primary goal of the therapy. These therapists assumed that the relationship of the patient to the therapist or analyst recapitulated elements of the earliest parenting and attachment experiences of the client and over time repaired them with corrective experiences. Here are some of the psychology of attachment's greatest hits. Each describe an aspect of traditional maternal function.

SIGMUND FREUD: called even-hovering attention the necessary posture of the therapist

ALFRED BION: used the term 'maternal reverie' to describe the containing and organizing presence of the mother on the infant

DONALD WINNICOTT: described the 'holding' environment that recapitulated an ideal mother-infant relationship within the therapeutic relationship and facilitated healing

HEINZ KOHUT: in studying and developing the idea of the narcissistic personality described the corrective necessity for empathic attunement and mirroring by the therapist

CAROL GILLIGAN: her seminal book *In A Different Voice: Psychological Theory and Women's Development* emphasized the necessity for relational therapy and healing

CARL ROGERS: gave us a way to talk about the necessary posture towards our clients as "unconditional positive regard" again recapitulating an ideal attachment scenario

VIRGINIA SATIR: emphasized the need for the therapist to be fully human and aware of the needs of mind, body, and spirit in the client

TARA BRACH: in her work as a Buddhist psychologist gave us the foundational ideas of mindfulness and radical acceptance of the client

SUE JOHNSON: in Emotionally Focused Therapy shows how the basic need of the human personality in relationship is for attachment and that it is the therapist's job to be highly attuned to the inevitable dance of attachment ruptures and repairs in working with couples and individuals.

The 'L' Word

Each of these clinicians is brilliant in their speaking and writing. Some of them are (or were) master teachers. But none of that matters to clients. The prerequisite for clients to enter fully into their healing work is the feeling of being safe, secure, and cared for. In other words, they need to feel loved. Yes, I said it, the 'L' word. Lack of love through abuse and/or neglect is what has gotten our clients into dysfunction and trauma, and the remedy for reconnection is love. I have always wondered why therapists do not talk more about the healing power of love as a necessary ingredient of therapy. Of course, I've heard lots of things over the years, lots of ideas about love in session:

- fears that love and sex get confused and acted out
- love is a loaded term that people understand differently
- love is indefinable and therefore not clinically useful

These are all relatively true. I think we are mostly afraid to name what love is and have trouble defining it. It even embarrasses some of us. But love is a wisdom term and belongs in our lexicon. What could be more relevant to a person's life than to learn to love and be loved?

I do not usually quote the Bible, but I am a literary geek, and I believe that one of the most beautiful and practical descriptions of love in all literature is from I Corinthians 13: 4–7. This passage is so popular, it is a staple of weddings and can be found on all manner of posters and cards. This passage defines what love is and is not in very simple terms. To show how relevant this definition is for therapists, I am going to substitute the words 'the therapist' or 'she' for 'love' in this famous verse.

> [The therapist] is patient and kind; [she] does not envy or boast; [the therapist] is not arrogant or rude. [She] does not insist on her own way; she is not irritable or resentful; [the therapist] does not rejoice at wrong-doing, but rejoices with the truth. [The therapist] bears all things, believes all things, hopes all things, endures all things.
>
> ("Bible Gateway", 2016)

In the book bravely titled *A General Theory of Love*, the three authors, all psychiatrists, make a similar argument. They attempt to define love as a necessary neurobiological process of the human being. When human children are thwarted in love or deprived of it, mental, and sometimes physical, illness ensues. In the therapy hour, they argue that the therapist needs to provide the necessary conditions of loving repair through limbic resonance—the emotional and attachment brain circuits that promote love within and between people. They say,

> Because our minds seek one another through limbic resonance, because our physiologic rhythms answer to the call of limbic regulation, because we change one another's brains through limbic revision— What we do inside relationships matters more than any other aspect of human life.
>
> (Lewis, Amini, & Lannon, 2000)

How do we operationalize love in therapy, in a professional way? How do we love our clients without falling in love with them or needing them to love us back? Love, in this context, is a verb, not a noun. Fostering attachment through caring is an important component of any treatment, so essential that to many people (or cultures) the idea of caring and treatment are redundant. First of all, we need to cultivate our own open heart. Cynics and misanthropes make terrible therapists. Going back to I Corinthians 13, we can ask ourselves, are we patient, kind? Are we irritable, resentful, rigid, or controlling? Do we think we are better than they are? Do we have spaciousness in our being for another whole human being, not just a set of diagnoses?

We need to realize that we have never met a mere human being. Each person is a vast universe. Some parts of their being will be more likable than others, more available for connection. We may feel aversion to some of their behaviors or thoughts, but if we cannot find something to like about them or love about them, how can we really be helping? The master therapists I have met are humble. They do not set themselves above the client no matter the diagnosis or disability, and so they treat their clients with utmost dignity and courtesy.

It is 1980, a time when many programs use electric shock therapy and other aversive behavioral techniques as 'therapy' for autistic children. It is my first week on the job as a childcare worker at a residential program that houses severely autistic and psychotic youth. My supervisor calls me into his office to introduce me to one of my two 'primaries', children that I will be forming relationships with during my shifts and following for as long as I work there. As I walk in, I see an adolescent girl standing in the hallway. She appears slightly agitated, twisting back and forth at the waist with her feet rooted to the ground looking up. She repeats a nonsensical phrase, "A fan keeps you cool in the summer." He calls this girl into the office to meet with us. She sits down heavily and stares out the window with her bright blue eyes and a flat expression. I had worked with autistic kids before, but they were a lot younger than this teen. My supervisor proceeded to carefully introduce us and explain to my primary who I was and why I was there. I wasn't sure she understood anything he was saying. She does not speak or look at me but twirls her hair and looks out the window. At one point, she looks me up and down out of the corner of her eyes. He asks her who I am, and she calmly answers, "Susan is my new primary." He finishes up the interview, and I am astonished. He treated this young woman calmly and as a peer yet understanding her need for pacing and processing. There was no arrogance on his part, and it was clear that she rose to the occasion and accepted the changes on the unit calmly. It was a beautiful and dignified conversation, and I hadn't really seen an interaction like it before, even though I had already worked four summers with autistic and psychotic populations.

So many things moved me about this conversation. My supervisor had absolutely no ego in this interaction and no need to 'control' or 'manage' this teen. He clearly saw her as a fellow human being and afforded her respect and dignity (and love) in the interaction. She rose to the occasion beautifully by calming down and focusing as best as she could. He could have been talking to his sister, a person on the street, his boss; the interview was remarkable for how ordinary it was. Perhaps (hopefully) in this time, 35 years later, this type of interaction is usual for autistic youth, but at the time it was remarkable and has informed my work ever since. On that unit, there were many aggressive outbursts, but the great thing I learned there was that when I approached those kids with respect and dignity, they usually returned the favor. The counselors who lost their patience, were control freaks, or became easily frustrated had to deal with many more unpleasant behaviors from the same youth.

The Myth of Us and Them

In the beginning of my career on the East Coast, there was a popular idea afloat that analysts could achieve a state of perfect mental health free from neurotic functioning, a state that they called 'fully analyzed'. In order to achieve this state one had to shell out thousands of dollars for a training analysis that lasted several years until one resolved all mental and neurotic conflicts in a perfect state of awareness from which they could dispense a perfect therapy. Yikes! Only someone very ignorant of the human psyche (or very narcissistic) could come up with such a fantasy goal and imagine they had attained it.

I will admit that for a minute I thought this was something to actually aspire to, and then reality set in. I never did meet that mythical clinician who was so perfect as to be free of psychological flaws, and I'm sure I never will. The human mind is a vastly complicated labyrinthine structure full of twists and turns comprising both the most angelic aspects and the basest of potentials. In Hindu scripture, the mind is compared to a fly that will land as easily on the most delicious food as on animal excretions. The Eastern psychology of mind considers the mind the repository of complexes accumulated over many lifetimes and hundreds of experiences ranging from uplifting to traumatizing. Jung added the idea that perhaps our minds were not only our own, but part of a vast collective unconscious uniting all the experiences of humanity. To heal our own minds completely in these paradigms we would have to address all the traumas of this life, all the traumas and complexes from previous lifetimes, and our connection to all the universal traumatized minds that interpenetrate our own. Psychoanalysis may be valuable, but it is not that powerful. That is why healing practices in India involve many and varied practices, symbolized by the god or goddess holding multiple tools. In fact, Hindu scripture dedicates itself to enlightenment by focusing on the return of the mind to oneness, free from the fragmentation of traumas.

In the West, we now have a new breed of clinician, who may or may not ever have had any of their own therapy. Relational aspects of therapy have fallen to the wayside, a casualty of the need for evidence-based procedural practices of short duration. In the meantime, patients take psychiatric medication of long duration—the exact opposite approach to treatment that we had in 1980 when medication was supposed to be of short duration and psychotherapy lasted years rather than weeks. Much therapy now consists of testing for diagnosis, with evidence-based procedures as therapy. The therapist just has to be educated enough to complete their checklist diagnosis and therapy and, voila, treatment happens. That is all well and good until it is not, and the clients come rotating back through a few months later, perhaps having picked up a couple of new problems, one of them being attachment failure in therapy. In a system where there is no overarching accountability, patients can easily fall through the cracks, and clinicians can imagine that they are doing a good job, ironically enough, without any real evidence.

Today, instead of having the 'fully analyzed' therapist we have the myth of the 'fully educated' therapist. Sure, we have to get CEUs for our licenses, but often problems or relapses in treatment are attributed to the clients rather than the procedures or clinicians. *They* are the problem. *They* get labeled as unmotivated, noncompliant, combative, difficult, hysterical, resistant, and so on. *We* are just doing our job, probably with an overcrowded caseload in an agency that restricts the number of sessions and even, in some cases, dictates the diagnosis. Get our own therapist or supervisor? Hah! With what income and time are we supposed to do that?

Here's the thing. We ARE them. According to an article in *Psychology Today* magazine (Epstein & Bower, 1997), 75% of therapists have struggled with serious issues in the last three years, and most of those issues have to do with relationships. One study cited in the article found that female psycho-therapists were more likely than other professional women to have a history of family dysfunction, parental alcoholism, childhood abuse (up to 2/3) and/ or a history of psychiatric hospitalization. Most male and female therapists (over 60%) admit that they might have suffered from clinical depression at some point in their lives. Research on suicide is scanty, but what little there is indicates that both psychologists and psychiatrists are at higher risk of suicide than the general population. This is not necessarily bad news! Many of us go into this field because we are trying (consciously or unconsciously) to solve problems of our own suffering or the suffering of those close to us. Understanding the territory of suffering and healing can make us excep-tional healers, but only if we have done our own work of self-healing.

Academic language can reflect and perpetuate 'us and them' thinking. I spent years deciphering abstruse psychoanalytic concepts and texts for classes and research at the beginning of my career; as a result I am fluent in psych-speak. Freud's seminal book *The Ego and the Id* (Freud, 1961) is practically unread-able by today's standards, but it did inspire me enough in high school to pick psychology as my major. With the exception of Freud, who lived a very long time ago in another country, I do not see the reason why our modern academic language needs to be so inaccessible to the average reader. There is almost a cult of psychological academia that has formed around language that only the 'insiders' really understand. Like a hazing, academic language establishes who is inside and outside the circle of knowledge, and it has a slightly male flavor. It is the language of our journals and our textbooks. I am not a fan. Perhaps it is the fact that I was raised in an advertising household where short copy was good, and pithy was better, or maybe because I'm still stinging from that comment by my high school English teacher about my writing sounding like Polonius (you were right, Mrs. Malosh!). In any case, it seems to me that academic writing is the first place that the US and the THEM get established. THEM (sic) would never talk like US.

But isn't that the problem? We go to school and have to learn new psychological concepts that we translate into 'academese' ("Academese", 2017) so that we can understand our weighty reading, and, then, when we see clients we are faced with two choices. Either we can continue to speak to our patients in therapist speak or we can learn how to translate things back into a common language for them. If we do not translate, we do not 'meet the client where they are at'. If we do, we risk being seen as having less status, perhaps, than our peers. This dynamic is more at play in the middle two competency levels. When we are even a little bit insecure about our skills and assessments, we might be tempted to pad our opinion with the use of fancy language and vocabulary. When we have reached a fully integrated competence, there is really no need to create a status through language, at least with clients. We can only explain things simply when we have fully digested them. At middling levels of competency, we may not even be able to explain what we are doing in plain language to ourselves, much less to our clients.

One last element feeds the us and them dynamic, and that concerns the therapist 'mystique'. The aura of power and mystery around therapy has been fed, to a certain extent, by books, radios, movies, and TV. It has also been cultivated by the profession itself. We lack transparency as a field and as practitioners. Therapists have subtle ways of letting patients know that they are not in on the 'secrets' of therapy when they join us. We expect our clients to know the culture of therapy without teaching them about it, which results in a subtle shaming of the client. For example, how many of you tell your patients that your sessions are 50 minutes long, even though they have booked an hour? Or do you just expect them to know? How many of you are open to answering reasonable questions about your training and life circumstance? Do you explain to them the significant cultural differences in a therapeutic conversation and relationship or are they just supposed to know that we don't touch, don't answer questions, and that the switch to let us know they are there is in the waiting room? Knowing something our clients don't and then expecting them to figure it out reinforces the power dynamic in the room in our favor, and recapitulates the all-powerful stance of a parent. Our patients can be triggered by these surprising dynamics, and we call it transference. I'm not sure that's fair.

In Service to Attachment

Take a moment and think about all the people and systems you have to answer to as a clinician. If you are like most of us, you may have obligations to the following: a supervisor who may or may not be your administrator or even a mental health professional, your agency, insurance providers, the state, your profession, team members, your own family, yourself, and your clients. You may also be answerable to a board, to funders, to partners, to donors, or to a publisher. Your job may scream complexity. Even if you are in a solo practice, there are still several of these parties that you need to consider in your work.

Add to this mix the occupational probability that you are a people pleaser, and you are not independently wealthy. In other words, you need to keep this job while keeping everybody happy. Does your head hurt yet?

Without a guiding light, one can get lost in the morass of competing needs and demands. Some days we all do. I do. But having survived and thrived over four decades in human services, let me give you a tip. Keep your eyes on the prize: your clients. I would love to say to you that this will be enough. It won't be. There will be some days when you will be forced to choose allegiances; there will be days when your agency will not let you do your job. You may be tempted to skimp on services to satisfy the demands of a supervisor or an insurance company or a colleague. If you end up giving in too many times, compromising your attachment with clients in favor of appeasing people at work, you will quickly find the juice draining from your enthusiasm for the work. At worst, you may end up feeling traumatized yourself. On those days, you will need extreme self-care, a topic we will discuss later in the book.

Your clients desperately need you. They may die without care, especially if they feel no one cares about them. Choose attachment for them as a priority in your work. If you place your clients' needs for stable and secure attachment first, all other decisions will flow from that priority. And it may piss some

It was the early 1990s and managed care was becoming a driver of psychiatric treatment in facilities all over the country. I had 10 business days to diagnose, treat, and safely place severely mentally ill children from 3 years to 12 years old from a locked inpatient unit. As the psychiatric social worker, I met with the mother of one of the children. She wrung her hands as she described to me the abrupt way her insurance company was dumping her son out of care that he needed. In social work fashion, I joined with her and encouraged her to keep 'going up the ladder' of her insurance company until she found someone that could help her retain her services for her ill child. I gave her tips for negotiation, some buzzwords that would get some attention. A few days later, the head psychiatrist approached me, "Why did you tell that mother to make waves with the insurance company? We are in talks for reimbursement with them!" I assured him that I knew nothing about these talks, but that if I had, I would have done the same thing, because my job was to be a social worker, not a hospital negotiator, and patient advocacy was not only within my scope of practice but also in my Code of Ethics. He didn't like it and made some comment about my being 'holier than thou'. I wasn't trying to be; I was trying to do my job. In the end, he could grumble, but he couldn't really threaten my job.

people off, not gonna lie. But your career is a marathon, not a sprint. Keep making choices that feed your soul even if you take some heat for it. Otherwise you may need to pick another career in a few years.

What if I had caved? What if I had gone back to that parent and told her to keep her head down? What would that have done to our working alliance, to her kid? Would that defeat have defeated her? It certainly would have ruptured our attachment. I would have become one of THEM. Her child could have died without services. I am not, by the way, trying to trash this psychiatrist, whom otherwise I liked and respected quite a lot. He was in a role doing his job. *And I was doing mine.* This dynamic is a necessary part of checks and balances in a psychiatric system. We all need to serve our roles with the highest integrity.

Paradoxically, for maximum effectiveness we want to serve the attachment needs of the therapy without becoming attached to the results of the therapy. Some people get confused thinking that attachment means one of the Buddhist or Hindu hindrances to enlightenment. Attachment to outcome, in Eastern philosophies, clouds our thinking by getting our ego to focus on success and failure. Our ordinary ego is fed by success and injured by failure. If we operate from an egoic place in our work (or in life), we can never truly feel content because so much of what happens is out of our control. We do not want to be in service to egoic attachment. In fact, we would ideally practice some form of selfless service or karma yoga, as it is called in India—the idea that we are entitled to our actions but not to the fruits of them. Another way of saying this is we show up, do our work to the best of our ability, and then let it go. All we can control in the moment, any moment, is ourselves. This is wisdom. Achieving that level of nonattachment consistently as a therapist constitutes maturity and mastery and, for most of us, many years of practice! It differs from the type of relational attachment we are making with our clients, an emotional bond of attachment created by safety, security, and trust.

Trauma Competence

As if being a good therapist wasn't a hard enough task, in order to help our traumatized clients we need to become trauma competent therapists if not trauma specialists.[4] My husband is a cardiologist. No primary doctor in their right mind would consider trying to treat the at-risk cardiac population without assistance unless they had no other choice. The interventions have become too sophisticated, and there is a whole body of knowledge built around this specialty. They refer and defer to a cardiologist for patients with cardiac disease.

So why treat psychological trauma any differently? PTSD and related disorders are also life threatening, complex, and difficult to treat. It requires years of practice, study, and supervision to become really adept at treating this at-risk population. Yet, we see generalist therapists with minimal to no trauma training treating these disorders quite often and with mixed results.[5]

Part of the issue is that trauma is actually quite a new field. The term post-traumatic stress disorder was only first coined in 1973. Another issue is the lack of formally recognized specialization in the field of psychology. My husband had to do a three-year fellowship above and beyond his three-year residency to become a cardiologist. He is required to take exams every few years that qualify him to be board certified in cardiology. As of now, we do not have such exams for the field of mental health, although I think they would be an excellent idea. Any doctor can theoretically (and with a license) practice any kind of medicine, but with a board certification the consumer knows that they are getting a highly trained specialist. It may be a good idea to consider referring our highly traumatized clients to highly trained clinicians, become a highly trained clinician ourselves, or at the very least, seek out regular supervision and consultation with supervisors who are trauma experts.

As a highly trained trauma therapist, the first thing I want a newbie to know is this: trauma ruptures attachment. Always. Trauma collapses our ability to trust in safety from people, from our environment, from the God of our understanding. As therapists who work with traumatic stress, we need to understand how profoundly difficult it is for our clients to safely attach to us as treaters. If we put anything as a priority before our connection to our client, whether it is agency policy, treatment protocols, or paperwork, we risk endangering the foundation upon which any successful treatment rests. Because new clients will not disclose their relational traumas before they have some trust in us, it is unlikely that we will know much about their traumas or how their trust in people was previously severed. We need to understand this truth from our first session. Great therapists become adept at fostering attachment in early stages of treatment. They are keenly aware of pitfalls in relationship building where their client may lose faith in them and work to avoid them.

And here lies the rub and the main difference from a field like cardiology. Our clients, themselves, may not know they have had childhood trauma until they are well into mid-life and/or until they have had several years of therapy. We do not (yet) have instruments that can peer inside brains like an echocardiogram can look inside a heart and tell us for certain that our client has suffered trauma, or what kind of trauma it is that they have been subjected to. Buried traumas lay like landmines in a patient's brain and psyche until they are stepped on and explode. Herein lies the rock and the hard place. If the memory of trauma emerges too early in the patient's awareness, they get destabilized and can be at risk for completing suicide, severe substance abuse, or having a psychotic break. If the traumas never come to surface, the patient will have to suffer the effects in their minds, bodies, and relationships throughout the lifespan.

Because traumas affect the entire body/mind mechanism, they may present as any number of psychiatric disorders. Consider generalized anxiety disorder (GAD), for example, as a common precursor or prodromal, if you will, manifestation of PTSD. When longstanding GAD blooms fully into PTSD, and the PTSD is successfully resolved, often the GAD resolves as well. This phenomenon of a disorder being secondary to unresolved PTSD may be true for many categories of psychiatric disorders—attentional disorders, dissociative disorders, and mood disorders come to mind. With the Adverse Childhood Events Study research, we are finding that there are, in fact, many psychiatric disorders that correlate to trauma: ADHD, depression, bipolar disorder, and personality disorders, to name a few (National Center for Injury Prevention and Control, Division of Violence Prevention, 2016).

Master therapists with their finely honed neural integration, knowledge, limbic regulatory abilities, wisdom, and deep understanding of attachments and the human condition have always made ideal trauma therapists because the most fundamental need of the trauma client is for safe and secure attachment with their treater. The primary tasks of these wisdom therapists are service to their clients, keeping an open mind to understand the complexities of healing, staying up to date with new information in healing, and the willingness to continue to grow and evolve their own practice down to the foundations of their own self.

Notes

1 For those of you neuroscience sticklers, I want to acknowledge that the left brain/right brain distinction may be more metaphor than literal reality, but stay with me, it is an important one.
2 You can see it here: www.youtube.com/watch?v=7mFDXNODNyc
3 I am not alone in this assessment. Buddhist practices such as mindfulness and Hindu practices like breath work and yoga have rapidly made their way into mainstream awareness and therapy practices in the last several years.
4 I am not a big fan of the term 'trauma-informed' for clinicians as it has become such a catchall term. Some therapists I know are calling themselves 'trauma-informed' after a weekend workshop or a couple of books. I prefer referring to trauma specialists who have a great deal of training and the certificates to prove it.
5 A large proportion of my practice consists of folks who have been through two, three, or more therapists. Many are disillusioned by their previous faulty therapy experiences or even downright despairing. Relational work becomes even more important with people who have felt failed by previous treaters.

References

Academese. (2017, May 25). Retrieved August 1, 2017, from Wiktionary: https://en.wiktionary.org/wiki/academese

Adams, L. (2017). *Learning a New Skill Is Easier Said Than Done*. Retrieved November 27, 2017, from Gordon Training International: www.gordontraining.com/free-workplace-articles/learning-a-new-skill-is-easier-said-than-done/#

Bible Gateway. (2016). *I Corinthians 13*. Retrieved July 27, 2017, from Biblegateway. com: www.biblegateway.com/passage/?search=1+Corinthians+13&version=ESV

Epstein, R., & Bower, T. (1997). *Why Shrinks Have Problems: Suicide, Stress, Divorce-Psychologists and Other Mental Health Professionals May Actually Be More Screwed Up Than the Rest of Us*. Retrieved August 1, 2017, from Psychology Today: www.psychologytoday.com/articles/199707/why-shrinks-have-problems

Freud, S. (1961). *The Ego and the Id* (The standard edition of the complete psychological works of Sigmund Freud ed., Vol. 19). (J. Strachey, Ed., & J. Strachey, Trans.). London, UK: Hogarth Press.

Jung, E., Wiesjahn, M., Rieff, W., & Lincoln, T. M. (2015). Perceived therapist genuineness predicts therapeutic alliance in cognitive behavioural therapy for psychosis. *British Journal of Clinical Psychology, 1*(54), 34–48.

Lewis, T., Amini, F., & Lannon, R. (2000). *A General Theory of Love.* New York, NY: Random House.

Mitchell, S. (2009). *Tao Te Ching: A New English Version.* New York, NY: HarperCollins.

National Center for Injury Prevention and Control, Division of Violence Prevention. (2016, April 1). *Violence: Adverse Childhood Experiences.* Retrieved October 17, 2017, from Centers for Disease Control and Prevention: www.cdc.gov/violenceprevention/acestudy/index.html

Siegel, D. (2016, April). *Disorganized Attachment, the Mind and Psychotherapy.* Paper presented at the meeting of the International Society for the Study of Trauma and Dissociation, San Francisco, CA.

Zalta, A. K., Gillihan, S. J., Fisher, A. J., Mintz, J., McLean, C. P., Yehuda, R., & Foa, E. (2013). Change in negative cognitions associated with PTSD predicts symptom reduction in prolonged exposure. *Journal of Consulting and Clinical Psychology, 1*(82), 171–175.

2 Neuroscience and Trauma-Informed Practice

PTSD is a whole-body tragedy, an integral human event of enormous proportions with massive repercussions.
—*Susan Pease Banitt,* The Trauma Tool Kit *(2012)*

Masterful therapists strive to be on the cutting edge of emerging scientific knowledge that informs their practice. Knowledge is dynamic, not static; it grows, morphs, disintegrates, incorporates, and reintegrates. Just as we must continually update our operating systems and software on our computers, so must we upgrade our minds with new practices while keeping abreast of the latest theories.

In the spirit of updated knowledge and continual growth, this chapter will present some of the latest neuroscience findings at the time of this writing (2017). As a clinical supervisor, both of second-year MSW students and for post-graduate licensure, I have found that understanding theory is only (the left-brain) half of the knowledge needed for treatment. Application (right-hemisphere thinking) comprises a more difficult task and is why therapist licensure requires several hundred hours of post-graduate practice with supervision. So, after each theoretical section there is a discussion on application directly relevant to clinical practice with suggestions for marrying knowledge with action.

ACE Study

In 1985, Dr. Vincent Felitti was running an obesity clinic for Kaiser Permanente in San Diego when he became stumped by patient results. The clinic helped people lose weight in large amounts, but about 50% of participants would suddenly drop out after losing significant amounts of weight with no explanation. In an effort to assess why patients were leaving, Dr. Felitti conducted interviews with the dropouts. A slip of the tongue on his part provided a clue. Instead of asking a patient, "How old were you when you became sexually active?" he asked, "How much did you weigh when you became sexually active?" She answered, "Forty pounds." And then added, "It was when I was

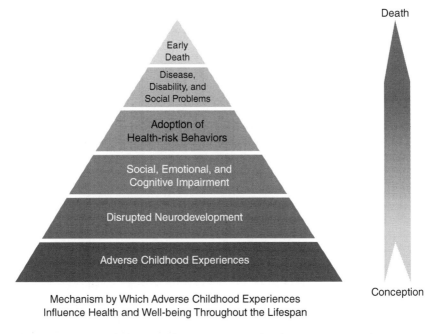

Mechanism by Which Adverse Childhood Experiences
Influence Health and Well-being Throughout the Lifespan

Figure 2.1 ACE Study (Centers for Disease Control and Prevention, 2014)

four years old, with my father" and started to cry. Several more client interviews yielded similarly distressing answers. Dr. Felitti began to realize that
patients were gaining weight—not slowly over years as some thought, but suddenly, after traumatic events in childhood. In fact, most of the 286 people
interviewed had been sexually abused as children (Stevens, 2012). It dawned
on him that distressing childhood events were perhaps a major cause of mental
and physical problems in adulthood.

Through Kaiser Permanente, Dr. Felitti joined forces with the Centers for
Disease Control to conduct research on this question: did adverse childhood
events cause problems in mental and/or physical health as people aged? From
1995 to 1997 they enrolled over 17,000 patients in their study. The ACE
(adverse childhood events) study did not look at the number of difficult episodes in childhood but at *the number of* **categories** *of adverse events that people
were exposed to in their childhood.*

The categories are:

1. Recurrent physical abuse
2. Recurrent emotional abuse
3. Contact sexual abuse
4. An alcohol and/or drug abuser in the household
5. An incarcerated household member

6. A household member who was chronically depressed, mentally ill, institutionalized, or suicidal
7. A mother who was treated violently
8. One or no parents
9. Emotional neglect
10. Physical neglect

Notice that there is no metric for psychopathology, no diagnosis involved. The patients answered a questionnaire to come up with their ACEs score. The data crunching began, and it continues to this day. There are dozens of charts and articles generated that are available to view on a number of websites. Recently the documentary movie *Resilience* (Brook Holston et al., 2016) was released to focus on the ACE study and its beneficial effects on community medical care and education.

As you can see, the ACEs can be roughly divided up into abuse issues versus household challenge issues. This finding supports a traditional social work 'person in the environment' approach to treatment, a focus on the broader circumstances of a person's life growing up as opposed to a specific focus on pathology and symptoms. Each area of mental health treatment has their biases, preferences, and one could even say temperaments (with, of course, a great deal of overlap). Psychiatrists are trained to focus on neurobiology and pathology; counselors focus on relationships and mental health diagnoses; marriage and family therapists focus on relationships; and social workers focus on all of the above plus social justice and community advocacy. Traditional mental health treatment has neglected great swaths of trauma-inducing events in people's lives, and in a sense has 'blamed the victim' for labeling the results of these woundings as psychopathology. Collectively, doctors and therapists are beginning to wake up to the pervasiveness of trauma in both childhood and adulthood. In 2011 alone, the National Institutes for Health allotted 5.55 billion dollars to projects that involved research in neuroscience (Society for Neuroscience, 2016).

Mental health professionals, and all of our society, have been heavily influenced by the legal system in our assessment of trauma. Unless we are trained otherwise, we tend to assess pathology and distress along the lines of what is recognized in the legal system as distressing. Let me give you an example. If a stranger sexually assaults someone, the stereotypical 'stranger in the bushes' rape, they are more likely to get a severe sentence than a date rapist, who may be more likely, in turn, to get a severe sentence than a sexually abusive family member (who often is not prosecuted or sentenced at all). In the article 'Rape and the Criminal Justice System', the authors state, "Afraid that losing cases will look bad on their records, prosecutors are excessively reluctant to prosecute acquaintance rapists." They elaborate:

> In a stranger rape, the possibility that the parties misunderstood each other's signals does not arise. As a result, the woman's character and all the controversial issues of appropriate sex roles and behavior in dating

situations ordinarily are not issues. Toward the victim of a stranger rape, the public usually feels compassion, with a correspondingly severe attitude toward the rapist.

(Bryden & Lengnick, 1997)

Because stranger rapes are more likely to get convictions and longer sentences, the general public assumes that these events are more traumatizing. Unless therapists are educated otherwise, they will make the same assumptions. In fact, people can be far more traumatized over a longer period of time by sexual abuse from a parent or intimate acquaintance that doesn't rise to legal definitions of sexual assault than in cases where stranger attacks do meet that definition. *The ACE study shows that there are many types of adverse events in childhood that don't even involve any abuse or criminal events.* But they still cause traumatic neurological cascades in the developing mind and body that affect people for years afterwards and even over the entire lifespan.

The ACE study results have been astonishing and are revolutionizing health care and community care with far-reaching impacts in education, community mental health, the justice system, and treatment of chronic medical conditions such as substance abuse, heart disease, and obesity. *People who scored 9–10 were dying on average 20 years earlier than people who scored 0–1.* The CDC has documented a dose-response relationship to the number of adverse events recorded and the amount of physical, emotional, and social issues people had later in life. In other words, the higher the ACEs score, the more difficulty people had with physical health, mental health, and functioning in society in general. Here are just a few of the problems a score of 4 or more ACEs predicts: smoking, alcoholism, depression, heart disease, drug abuse, the need for anti-anxiety medication, hallucinations, and problems with the law, as well as early teen sexual behaviors and pregnancy. In order to understand how so many disparate dimensions of human experience can be affected by ACEs, we need to dive into neuroscience.

Clinical Application:

- Understand that diagnosis is not the be-all and end-all of trauma assessment. Your clients do not have to have PTSD to be traumatized. The ACE study may be a better tool than the *DSM* (American Psychiatric Association, 2013) with which to assess levels of trauma in the body/ mind—especially developmental trauma. Ideally, you will use both of these tools for diagnosis and assessment.
- Include the ACEs questionnaire as a regular part of your intake or assessment forms or procedures.
- Educate your staff and supervisees about the importance of this study as part of trauma-informed care. Help them understand that the mind IS the body, and that all psychological trauma has physical consequences.

HPA Axis

Over the last 10 years or so, much research attention has focused on the hypothalamic–pituitary–adrenal axis as a major system affected by traumatic stress. This structure connects the autonomic nervous system to the neuroendocrine system. If it is injured or disabled in some way, people develop a myriad of problems with health and behavior.

The hypothalamus sits in the brain and 'talks' to the pituitary gland by creating hormones and sending them over to the pituitary gland. If you recall high school anatomy, you may remember that the pituitary gland functions as a 'master gland', directing other important glands such as the thyroid and adrenal glands through secretion of hormones, which, in turn, secrete *their* own hormones. The system is complex and hierarchical. The adrenal glands produce cortisol, the fight or flight hormone. You could think of this system as consisting of the CEO (hypothalamus), Vice President (pituitary gland), and Managers (downline glands such as adrenals, thyroid, parathyroid, etc.). They constitute the neuroendocrine or hormonal systems of the body.

What function does the neuroendocrine system serve? Take a look at Figure 2.2. What is the first thing that jumps out at you? For me it was that the components of the neuroendocrine system are all such disparate, seemingly unconnected functions. The second thing I noticed was that all of my

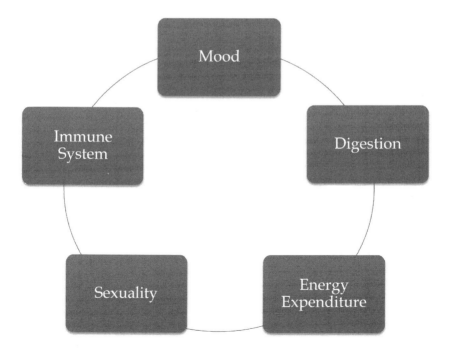

Figure 2.2 HPA Axis Functions

trauma patients had complaints in these areas of functioning. In fact, the more extreme their trauma history, the more likely it was that they were under some kind of medical care for complaints related to this chart. If you take a quick look around the HPA axis wheel, you will notice that symptoms manifest as disturbances of 'too much' (hyper) or 'too little' (hypo) and sometimes a chaotic vacillation between the two cycles (e.g., bipolar disorder, digestion, sleep cycles). Like Goldilocks, every organic system is looking for that range of 'just right' functioning. Trauma throws every system off the axis of optimal functioning and into a certain amount of chaos, where the body is constantly playing 'catch up' to find equilibrium.

Let's go through this chart.

Mood: The most common moods that present in therapists' offices are anxious and depressed moods. Less common are mixed, rapid cycling or some kind of euphoria (mania). I have yet to meet a trauma client that doesn't complain of mood problems.

Digestion: a huge area that covers every process from the mouth to the colon. One could also include signaling for hunger and thirst. Clients either are too hungry or fail to register hunger. Digestion is often sluggish with feelings of bloating. Meals are unsatisfying, rendering a common human pleasure a source of loss. Celiac disease and irritable bowel syndrome can be triggered. Blood sugar levels can become inconsistent. Obesity is common. If we go back to the ACE study, we will find that obesity, abdominal pain, and diabetes increase with the ACEs scores.

Energy Expenditure: One of the most common complaints of people that have been through traumatic stress is either an abundance of energy (hyperactive, hypomania) or a feeling of being emptied of all drive and energy (hypoactive, depressed). These can be chronic states as in chronic fatigue disorder or rapidly shifting states where there are certain times of the day people feel really keyed up and wired followed by a crash where it is difficult to function at all. This pattern can also show up in sleep symptoms where clients complain of insomnia, sleeping all the time (hypersomnia), or being awake but feeling like their brain is still asleep (brain fog).

Sexuality: is defined by the Oxford English Dictionary as "the capacity for sexual feelings" (Oxford University Press, 2016). Most therapists see the obvious connection of sexual abuse to altered sexual function. What is a little less obvious is the application of hyper and hypo functioning of the HPA axis to sexuality from nonsexual traumas. According to this chart, **any type** *of traumatic disturbance along the HPA axis may result in hypersexuality (e.g., promiscuity, unsafe sexual practices) or hyposexuality (low libido, low desire).* It would be interesting to see more research looking at how nonsexual traumas impact the HPA axis in the area of sexuality.

Immune System: Hyperfunctioning immune systems result in autoimmune diseases such as rheumatoid arthritis, psoriasis, asthma, Hashimoto's syndrome (hyperthyroid), lupus, and Type 1 diabetes. There are over 80 types of autoimmune diseases that affect about 5–8% of the population; women are disproportionately affected (Brower, 2004). Hypoimmunity or immunodeficiency results in lack of resistance to infectious diseases, slower healing of injuries, and, in some cases, cancer.

Prior to the awareness of the HPA axis' role in the body, clients presenting with the above syndromes were often labeled as 'factitious' or 'malingering' by psychotherapists and psychiatrists. Through the ACE study, doctors and therapists are now starting to recognize that these disorders may have their roots in trauma and will often appear alongside trauma, especially in adults with traumatizing childhoods.

Clinical Application:

- Assess patients with a history of trauma (not just mood disorders) for dysfunction along the HPA axis, which corresponds to vegetative symptoms: sleep, appetite, energy levels, libido, and mood.
- Work collaboratively with the patient's medical doctors. Create a team approach even if you are working in private practice. Your trauma patients will always have a disturbance along the HPA axis that warrants medical care. Make sure they get it. Do not fall into thinking that processing the trauma psychologically will heal these physical issues any more than stitching up a knife wound will take away the psychological trauma of a violent attack.
- Use techniques in sessions and prescribe homework that works directly with calming down the HPA axis: breath work, mindfulness, grounding exercises. Consider being trained in a complementary therapy such as Reiki, yoga, or tai chi or recommending these classes to your clients.
- Teach sleep hygiene. Without sleep, our clients remain in a state of disturbance where they cannot heal. If sleep disturbance is severe, refer for medical treatment.

Amygdala Override

You are walking down your favorite nature path and a snake appears. You jump to the side of the path; your heart pounds, and you don't remember making the decision to jump. As it turns out, the snake is merely a stick. To the amygdala, that doesn't matter. Potential snake was good enough reason to hijack your motor responses and higher cortical centers.

The amygdala, the almond-shaped gland in the center of our brain, functions as an emergency response center. Once the amygdala detects danger, it has the ability to shut down planning functions in the prefrontal cortex ("is it a snake; should I jump?") and take over motor responses (by jumping you to the side like a fast zombie). And this is a good thing. Otherwise, certain personality types might still be debating whether the object in question is a snake or a stick while the snakebite is underway. The more trauma a person has undergone, the more sensitive the amygdala becomes to threat in the environment. Once the amygdala has taken over judgment and motor functions (it's just doing its job), our clients' behavior becomes unpredictable and idiosyncratic. Anything can happen, from violence (fight) to leaving a session suddenly or even firing us (flight) to dissociation or withdrawal (freeze).

A 40-year-old schizophrenic woman self-referred to my private practice (a highly unusual occurrence). In my attempt to get her into a local care program, I was mandated to do a trauma assessment against my preferences. After the second question of the assessment, she curled up in a ball on my sofa and stopped speaking. It was unclear what was happening, as I had not known her for very long. I felt a mild sensation of panic flow through and out of me at the sudden catatonic demeanor of my client. Was she regressed? In another personality compartment? In a psychotic episode? I decided to start speaking to her in a soothing voice, reminding her that she was sitting on my sofa in my office and that she was safe, grounding her in the details of the now. After about 30 seconds, she popped her head up over her knees, and with a smile asked, "How'd you do that?" As quickly as she went into amygdala hijack, she came out of it. The rest of the session passed uneventfully.

Clinical Application:

- Until we have done the work of mapping triggers with our client, we run the risk of inadvertently setting off the amygdala response. And, unless we have done the work of mapping our own triggers, we risk going into a reverb effect with our client: their amygdala response sets off our amygdala response, which sets off theirs, which sets off ours, *ad nauseam*. Know your triggers, and help map your patient's triggers from early in treatment.
- Create a strong, safe, and grounded environment to work in. Have a safety plan[1] and rehearse it. The safer you feel, the more grounded you will be. The more grounded you are, the more grounded you can help your client become, especially in a time of crisis.
- Develop your tools for first recognizing and then pulling people out of an amygdala hijacking. If you work in crisis intervention, this may be a

no-brainer, but most therapists do not have to work consistently with crisis intervention skills. Do not try to fight fire with fire. Raising your voice, a hard stare, or threatening a client in amygdala hijack will create escalation that could result in violence towards you or your facility. Neuroscience says calmer is better—a calm brain is an organized and predictable brain.

Autonomic Nervous System

The autonomic nervous system consists of the sympathetic and the parasympathetic branches. The sympathetic system creates what we commonly know as the fight or flight response. It provides an activation of our body that promotes our survival as a species and prepares us to encounter stressful situations in our body. The parasympathetic system uses a different set of nerves to calm down and regulate the body and serves the functions of 'rest and digest' or 'feed and breed'. Together they provide a homeostatic mechanism so that the body stays in balance throughout the activities of life. One may dampen the function of the other but they are always operative. You can think of them like hot and cold water always mixing together to create a certain temperature, depending on what is needed in the environment.

Sympathetic Nervous System

When folks are subjected to either a single intense trauma or a series of stresses over time, the sympathetic nervous system (SNS) activates to provide the physical resources to meet the challenges of that situation for the purpose of physical survival. The human body was not meant to live in a state of chronic sympathetic arousal, yet that is how many of our trauma clients live and have been living long before they meet us. To truly understand the condition of our clients and to help them understand their bodies and behaviors, we need to be able to understand the effects of SNS arousal. After my own bout with PTSD, this theoretical construct took on a very lifelike reality. Living in chronic sympathetic overdrive, as our traumatized patients do, is an extremely difficult and debilitating condition that can end up having permanent negative health effects on the body.

Sympathetic system activation has these effects on the body:

Eyes: increases the pupil size and pulls muscles of eyes towards peripheral vision (the better to see oncoming threats by increasing depth and breadth of visual acuity).

Digestion: decreases the amount of saliva in the mouth and overall slows down the digestive system, thus diverting energy for a fight response. It also stimulates the production of white blood cells in the bowels just in case of a perforation.

Metabolic: frees up stored fuel in the body quickly to mobilize energy, especially glycogen from the liver; inhibits the production of insulin, which is used to promote food storage (a parasympathetic function).

Circulatory: increases heart rate and increases blood pressure by constricting blood vessels to get blood and oxygen to the organs quickly. Also decreases blood flow to extremities to focus on organs. Increases blood clotting—again preparation for perforation injury.

Respiratory: increases rate of breathing to promote oxygen delivery and helps lungs take in more air by expanding volume through dilation.

HPA Axis: mobilizes the hypothalamus, which creates a cascade of job-specific hormones designed to make the body battle ready, including cortisol, epinephrine, and norepinephrine. These hormones increase alertness, release energy, and prepare the body for a rapid response to injury.

Urinary System: decreases urine production in the kidneys (water retention); relaxes bladder and inhibits sphincter for retention of urine until a safer moment.

Tracking these nervous system reactions in the physical body helps the therapist understand how the stress of the trauma is impacting the everyday functioning of the client. It also helps make troublesome behaviors meaningful

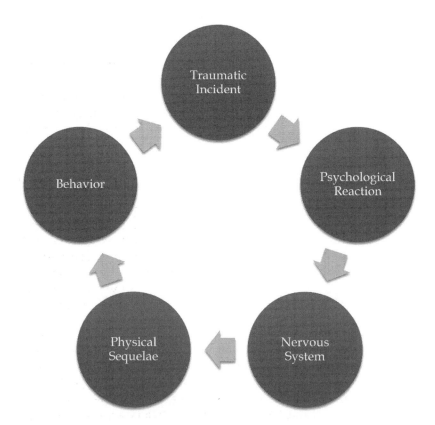

Figure 2.3 Cycle of Trauma

and solvable if we know that some fallout of trauma is not just psychological but also physical.

Figure 2.3 demonstrates how a loop can be created from traumatic stress and its manifestations in the body. Trauma begets trauma. A traumatic reaction leads to a psychological reaction, which activates the sympathetic nervous system. The sympathetic system outlined above creates specific and predictable reactions in the physical body. These physical changes then can lead to behavioral changes in the client. Often these behavioral changes are judged harshly leading to another traumatic incident, and round and round we go.

For example, maybe we have a stressed teenaged client with a trauma history. They are failing school and, after some interviews, we realize that they have blurry vision and trouble concentrating. The blurry vision can be a symptom of chronic sympathetic overdrive from overdilated pupils and the muscles of the eyes constantly pulling peripherally, making it hard to converge on small print. These physical symptoms lead to an inability to read for very long periods of time, write papers, or have good comprehension. This student then maybe is labeled as 'lazy' or a troublemaker. Feeling like a failure, shamed, and criticized, the teen spirals further down into depression or might be acting out. If we can see the involvement of the sympathetic system in the beginning of this cycle, we can help the patient advocate for themselves physically, a very empowering stance, and a road that is less taken with the way most psychotherapy practices are currently functioning. If our theoretical client gets help with mindfulness-based stress reduction or even some vision therapy, their study problems can resolve, their self-esteem can increase, and they might be able to start making their way forward. This type of intervention creates space for healing their deeper issues instead of spiraling down into further stress and despair.

Parasympathetic System

In the parasympathetic system, the effects of sympathetic activation are neutralized and reversed. Parasympathetic stimulation returns the organs to a normal (noncrisis) mode of functioning. The stomach starts digesting food; peristalsis returns. The heart rate slows; muscle tension drops. The neuroendocrine system ceases pumping out amped-up hormones. Peripheral scanning with the eyes relaxes in favor of convergence (close-up) work. When their sympathetic system's hypervigilance releases, our client can start to feel safe again.

In the last few years, I have added Reiki as a complementary therapy to the work I do, especially with traumatized clients. Reiki is a deeply relaxing method of healing shown to help relieve stress and depression (Baldwin, 2011) that can be done with either hands on or hand off the client. (The client is always fully clothed.) Reiki can be done with the patient in a therapy chair or on a massage table. When I am doing a Reiki session, I know when my client's parasympathetic system becomes dominant because I can hear the stomach start to gurgle—an embarrassing moment for them at first, but always a good sound to hear, because the body does not lie! If the digestive system is active, the parasympathetic 'rest and digest' system has become dominant and inhibited, at least for the moment, the sympathetic fight or flight response.[2]

Clinical Application:

- Our job as therapists is to help clients connect the dots for their healing and coping skills. Linking physical symptoms of trauma to 'disabilities' or problem areas in functioning helps empower our clients to take action and interrupt the negative spiral. We need to connect the dots from incident to psychological reaction to physical manifestation to the behavioral consequence and unwind this cascade by addressing both physical and emotional causes of distress.
- Become a Sherlock Holmes and apply the chart in Figure 2.3. Do a thorough assessment of the physical complaints of your client and correlate them to nervous system functioning.
- Consider the ripples outside of your office.[3] For instance, how does sympathetic overdrive lead to a risk for heart disease? If your client is a first responder, for example, and also has a history of personal trauma, you may want to be proactive in helping your patient keep track of their cardiac health and make appropriate referrals.
- Find ways to activate the parasympathetic system in session. There are so many modalities—even just listening to relaxing music for a few minutes can help! Give homework for your clients to learn to turn on their ability to 'rest and digest'!

Polyvagal Theory and Dissociation

Until recently, we have not had a good way to explain the phenomenon of dissociation and dissociative disorders in traumatized patients. There have been many academic fights about even the existence of dissociative disorders. Several years ago, I heard a prominent psychiatrist say to an audience of over 2,000 people at a trauma conference that he had never seen a case of dissociation! I would say that he probably has never recognized a case of dissociation.

As a clinical supervisor, I find the weakest clinical area of every therapist I supervise is dissociative disorders. Many therapists are taught little to nothing about the prevalence of dissociation and how to assess for it. Dissociation is hard to spot because behaviorally it manifests more as an absence than a presence: absence of affect, absence of memory, absence of process. It is possible that the field of psychology has been blind to dissociation because we have tended to put more faith in what is observable as a presence (affect, memory, process). Up until recently, we had no concrete scientific way to explain dissociation as a neurological or biological phenomenon. Enter Dr. Stephen Porges.

Dr. Porges goes beyond the sympathetic vs. parasympathetic definition of the autonomic nervous system as outlined above. He discovered that humans actually have two main branches to the vagus nerve that are involved in parasympathetic response. One of these branches, the dorsal vagal complex (DVC), is an older evolutionary structure that has existed in neurology since the time of reptiles and amphibians, through the evolution of primitive vertebrates, and still exists in most vertebrates, including humans. The DVC is unmyelinated and mostly provides regulation to the organs beneath the diaphragm. Its older evolutionary function can be seen in animals such as the turtle, whose DVC evolved to provide an adaptive defense of freezing under stressful circumstances. Under extreme duress, the same animals might faint or even die from a stress reaction.

Because freezing was not a great strategy for the survival of mammals with a more complicated neural structure, higher vertebrates evolved a myelinated vagus branch called the ventral vagal complex (VVC). The VVC provides for a more nimble and nuanced response to stress through the sympathetic response outlined above but also by facilitating social affiliation and cuing. It provides regulation to the organs above the diaphragm, including the limbic system inside of the brain (Wikipedia, 2017).

Trauma always pushes us into more primitive defensive structures. Mammalian defensive systems fail in the face of extreme trauma. The very setting of trauma often deprives us of social help in the face of violence or injury. When people get help immediately after a devastating event, they are much less likely to develop PTSD or dissociative disorders. We know this as a culture, and that is why a response to disasters comes from both the government and nonprofit sectors. When we cannot flee, when we cannot get help, when we cannot fight off an attacker, the more primitive DVC steps in as a last ditch (although ancient) defensive structure of the body: the freeze or dissociation response. We become psychologically and physically frozen. In extreme cases, we may faint. I do know of at least one case where a child actually died from a fear response during an assault.[4]

When people have a critical level of trauma in their system, they can become stuck in a chronic state of DVC activation. Some of the signs are:

- Isolative behaviors
- Averse to new experiences
- Flat affect
- Digestive issues: obesity, irritable bowel syndrome, anorexia
- Low tolerance for low frequency sounds
- Does not like to be touched/held
- Memory issues
- Dissociates frequently

It is important that we understand these phenomena as states, not traits, even if they have persisted for a long time. They manifest because the client does not feel safe. The more evolved mammalian circuits are not able to take care of the extreme fear that is running in the background of the nervous system.

To elicit functioning from the VVC or higher mammalian vagal circuits, the therapist needs to have the ability to engage those circuits herself and use them on behalf of the client (Howes, 2013). In fact, one could see this entire book as a guide to using engaging the VVC—access to the limbic brain and heart—for the therapist and client.

Clinical Application:

- The theory may be complicated but the clinical needs are simple enough. As Dr. Porges himself puts it, "The most successful trauma therapists are those that enable their clients to negotiate and navigate a sense of safety" (Eichorn, 2015).

- Engage your higher mammalian self, consciously, in session. In other words, don't meet your client with a reptilian flat face! Friendly, but not staring, eye contact, smiles, and an overall welcoming, caring, and transparent demeanor go a long way to creating safety even before the patient sits down for their first session. I once knew a neurologist who kept a picture of a smiling monk on his desk. He was not Buddhist; he just derived great comfort from seeing the monk's warm expression. Be the monk!

- Do a physical or mental walk-through of your treatment space, from the time the client pulls in the parking lot to the moment they sit down in your office. What is the environment like that they have to walk through to get there? How safe is it? How safe does it feel for someone with a trauma history? Are there loud noises (like street work)? How is the lighting? Are there long stretches of empty corridor they have to walk through to get to you? How can you warm up any part of the physical space that doesn't feel safe and welcoming? Ask your clients about their preferences.

- Do focus on social supports for your client. Porges describes social support as a necessary "neural exercise." If they are not yet capable of forming stable attachments, can they join some kind of group that will help them activate the VVC, such as a chorus or an improvisational comedy group?

- Develop your ability to see which vagal state is activating in your client. A client in the shutdown reptilian vagal system needs heightened safety and security. They need a soothing voice and tender expression. Confrontation in this state is contraindicated. If they are in the higher mammalian circuits, they can tolerate a little more challenge and excitement in session. Notice when your own behavior initiates a change in vagal state and work gently with that.

- It is a little strange that our profession has evolved into a place where people are very reluctant to touch each other, just because of a few bad apples. Against a sea of lawyers saying otherwise, I am going to say here that I think there is a place for safe and nurturing touch in clinical practice, but as with all else we do it needs to be boundaried and documented. A handshake, a hug with permission, or Reiki with permission to touch are powerful modalities that help people move towards healing. If an immobilized 4-year-old moves into a higher vagal circuit and wants a hug or to sit on our lap and color on an inpatient unit, what are we doing to them, to their developing brain, if we deny such basic human need? Let us revisit these discussions in our treatment centers and practices.

Memories, Fragmentation, and Dissociative Strategies

Neuroscience is an emerging field. The brain is a vast and complicated organ. We have only begun to plumb its depths. Nowhere is this truer than in studying the phenomenon of dissociation. We barely understand the process of making and retrieving memories, much less how memories are repressed and split off to the degree where different ego states and personalities are created. It seems that the brain employs a kind of 'divide and conquer' strategy to manage overwhelming traumatic events. But before we jump into some theoretical neuro-modeling, let us look at what we do know about memories and the hippocampus.

The Hippocampus

The hippocampus has many jobs. One job involves converting short-term memories into long-term memories. It also helps us navigate our environment spatially. These two things at first glance do not seem related, but consider that our memories consist of a narrative that happens in time and space. We can deduce some of the function of the hippocampus by what happens to the individual's abilities when it is impaired. We know that in Alzheimer's disease the hippocampus is compromised, which results in short-term memory loss; in early stages, the person with Alzheimer's may remember events very clearly from early childhood but forget their grandchildren.

Sitting in the limbic brain, the hippocampus looks remarkably like a seahorse, hence its name which, translated from Greek, literally means, 'horse' and 'sea monster'. Several research studies have established that the hippocampus changes shape and loses volume after a trauma, and that it changes consistently to the kind of trauma it has experienced (or processed?). In other words, people who were subject to physical abuse had the same type of shrinkage in the same area of the hippocampus, whereas veterans of war had shrinkage and volume change in a different yet consistent area of the hippocampus. Due to its high levels of glucocorticoid receptors, the hippocampus is extraordinarily sensitive to the hormone cortisol. Put another way, it doesn't like stress and responds to stress with neuronal atrophy. The good news is that research has established that certain medications, such as fluoxetine, seem to increase the volume of the hippocampus back to pre-trauma levels. The hippocampus has the amazing ability to generate new neurons as part of its regular function. There is a great deal of research currently being done on the function of the hippocampus.

Clinical Application:

- Conduct formal mental status exams at the beginning of treatment or whenever new traumas emerge to assess memory and cognitive function.
- Be aware that memory issues affect anyone in an educational setting and take measures to help them accordingly. Get learning disability status as needed so that clients may be able to have longer test times and resources.
- Consider referring for medication that will help to restore the function of the hippocampus.

Memory Fragments and Reassociated Memory

The brain seems to have a divide and conquer strategy to cope with memories that could derail functionality in the mind and body, especially in the early years when the whole brain is still quite plastic. People who have had one or more severe traumas often have those memory components stored in different compartments. When a traumatic event hits in early childhood, the brain separates the components of the memory to help prevent the child and the brain itself from becoming overwhelmed and nonfunctional. When clients engage in the memory retrieval necessary to fully heal traumas, we will encounter 'memory fragments'. These fragments break out into the essential components as seen in Figure 2.4: the narrative of the event, the input of the five senses during the event or sensations, and the feeling state of the individual at the time of the event.

When a client is processing historical trauma, they usually will encounter only one out of the three fragments at a time; the other two parts of the complete memory are segmented off. Often the clients do not know that they are experiencing memory fragments; they just feel crazy and anxious and/or depressed. Because we need all three components for a memory to feel 'real', the patient will often disavow these fragments as artifacts, imaginings, and

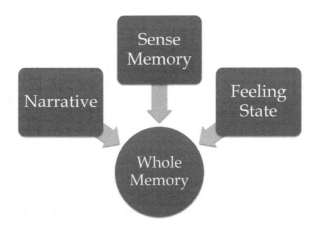

Figure 2.4 Memory Components

non-memories in the beginning of treatment. When even two of the three components reassociate, the client will feel as if they have 'discovered' a new memory, but really the components have been there all along, just disassembled like a puzzle on a table. This fact brings into question the idea of what a 'recovered memory' actually is. In the media and elsewhere, recovered memories are always assumed to be whole and an entirely new cognition to the client rather than a putting together of pieces that are already somewhat in consciousness. In this model, memories are never really lost in their entirety; they are just scattered. I have come to prefer the term reassociation for this process, as it is the opposite of dissociation.

What do these isolated memory fragments look like? Narrative fragments are pieces of story without sensory input or a feeling state. A client may say, "I know I was molested but I don't know how or who did it" or they may just know that something terrible happened to them in childhood but have no details. They might have a narrative that says they were different before and after an event, even if they don't know exactly what the event was. Their narrative might come from the police or hospital, especially if drugs were involved and their senses were impaired. When a client discloses a deeply held narrative for the first time, it is common for the feeling state to manifest shortly after or during the disclosure, a feeling state that they may not have consciously felt before. Hearing oneself speak the truth for the first time is a powerful and often devastating experience! Usually a client has had this narrative in their head for years, unspoken. In the presence of a trusted other, they feel safe enough to begin to reassemble the memory. Reassociating memories can take weeks to months. During this process, it only makes sense that there are significant neurological changes afoot as parts of the brain start to connect with each other for the first time.

Sensory fragments show up routinely in a patient's associations, if we are astute enough to notice them. These are often, but not always, visual snapshots of a scene in the client's head. *Clients do not relate to sensory memory fragments as part of their history.* Because daydreams and imaginings are visual images with no personal narrative or internal feeling state attached, clients relate to these fragments as imaginings or daydreams. They often think they are making the whole thing up. But unlike daydreams, these images (or other sensory inputs) are powerful and persistent; they have lingered for years in the client's mind and are consistent, more like a recurrent nightmare than a daydream. Although we are discussing visual memory fragments, please note that a significant number of people are abused in darkness, with their eyes shut, under the covers or in other places where a visual component is not part of the experience, so it is common for sensory memory fragments to pertain to one or more of the other senses: auditory, smell, taste, or kinesthetic.

There has been some professional discussion about whether sensory memory fragments can show up in the dreams of clients before they are integrated as a real memory. Normally dreams do not represent actual experiences but are a complicated synthesis and purging of our waking life in REM sleep. However, since it is now accepted that full-on flashbacks can be nightmares, it stands to reason that traumatized people might, in fact, be able to dream traumatic memory fragments. In some cases, dreams have been the first place that these memories have presented themselves.

Feeling state memory fragments manifest as somatic flashbacks. *Any recurrent feeling state that cannot be explained by events happening in real time is probably a somatic memory fragment.* Sometimes we call these states 'overdetermined', 'drama', or an 'overreaction'. These feeling states are usually dysphoric. Fear and anger seem obvious enough. Other common somatic memory fragments include feelings of intense loneliness, terror, abandonment, humiliation, shame, grief, and helplessness. It is possible that, for some people, what we may diagnose as depression or an anxiety disorder is really a persistence of disassociated somatic memory. Anxiety and depression often lessen or resolve when memories are fully reassociated and processed.

Let's apply this model to the case of Little Red Riding Hood, an unfortunate minor who became lost in the woods and was attacked by a vicious predator who killed and impersonated her grandmother before taunting and attacking her. A hunter found RRH, as we shall call her, at her grandmother's house covered in blood. When RRH returned to civilization, she had a great deal of anxiety, an obsession about wolves, and missing time.

RRH presented as an otherwise normal little girl who was clearly traumatized. Her main symptom was an olfactory hallucination. She smelled forest odors when she was not in the forest, and those smells filled her with a feeling of foreboding.

When RRH came to therapy she may have said, "I see a picture of a wolf in the woods in my mind, but that doesn't feel like a real memory (or my memory), and it doesn't make sense to me. What was I doing there? Did that even happen?"

This is a visual sensory memory fragment. Remember, our brain doesn't register memories as 'real' unless they have all three components: narrative, sense, and feeling state.

Alternatively, RRH could come in and say that she knows that something bad happened at her grandmother's house, although she cannot say exactly what that was. She knew her mother gave her baked goods to take to her granny that morning and that she was found at her grandmother's house by the hunter. She feels a vague sense of guilt and remembers chasing a butterfly. Everything in between feels very fuzzy and unreal to her. She feels 'fine'.

This is a narrative memory fragment. With narrative memory our clients 'just know' or feel strongly that something bad happened but cannot give sensory evidence or a coherent narrative, just enough narrative to have the framework for a memory.

Or RRH could just come into therapy in a state of panic and anxiety and not know why she is feeling that way. She has developed a phobia of ears and teeth and has a strong dysphoric reaction to anyone that calls her 'my dear'. She can deduce that these feelings relate to her missing time and being found by the hunter, but they do not actually *feel* connected. The panic and dysphoria are feeling state memory fragments lacking narrative context and sensory input. In this fragmentation scenario, RRH may have been previously diagnosed with panic disorder.

She could have one, two, or three of these symptoms and not know that they are at all associated with each other if enough time has elapsed after the incident. She may define herself as an anxious, overreactive, and sensitive city girl with a poor memory and weird obsessions. Without a narrative from the hunter (let's say she just stumbled out of the woods on her own) and if she was sufficiently young (let's say under 6 years old), she may not even know or remember that she was ever attacked.

Clinical Application:

- Ask gentle reassociative questions when a possible memory emerges. How do you feel about that image you keep seeing in your head (sensory to feeling state)? What do you see in your mind's eye when you think that someone hurt you in school (narrative to sensory)? Do you have a story that comes to mind or a period of time associated with this feeling of profound loneliness (feeling state to narrative)?
- Believe your client before they believe themselves. Know that any persistent image, state, or thought is a clue to what happened to them. Discount nothing.
- Keep an open mind to the unfolding story, and know that identifying memory fragments can take months to years. Be patient.

Dissociation Through Self-Fragmentation

There is another way the brain protects itself and the person from catastrophic memories. If a person is young enough, generally under about 7 years or so, the brain, instead of compartmentalizing memory fragments, may completely compartmentalize memories as self-fragments or partially compartmentalize them as ego states. Memories in self-fragments are stored *in toto*; the self is split up into discrete parts that contain the memories for the organism without burdening the core self with undigestible memories. These self-fragments (also called 'parts' or 'alters') are frozen in time at a specific age that is not the current age of the client.

Sometimes the fracturing is incomplete, resulting in discreet ego states that are associated with certain memories. These ego states become subsets of self-states. The memories associated with them are more readily available than when memories are completely walled off as alters, but they are still compartmentalized and repressed. If you look at Figure 2.5, you will see that 2/3 of this self is compartmentalized through ego states that are associated with memories and 1/3 of the self has split off into a completely discreet self-state that holds a separate history (or memory), shown by the space between this section and the rest of the self.

THE TRAUMATIZED SELF

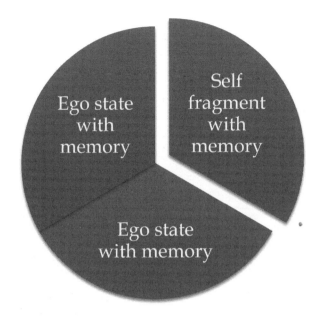

Figure 2.5 Self-Fragments and Ego States

The completely separate self-fragment with memory exemplifies the diagnosis of 'dissociative identity disorder' (DID), whereas the compartments that are somewhat discreet but not altogether separated would be more representative of 'other specified dissociative disorder' (if there were no completely separate self-fragment in the organism as shown below) or may indicate certain personality disorders (Shapiro, 2016).

Clinical Applications:

- Assess for degree of dissociation and the likelihood of DID with a test such as the Dissociative Experiences Scale (DES) (Trauma-Dissociation. com, 2017)
- Be aware that the prevalence of DID is about 1–3% of the general population and higher in clinical populations (International Society for the Study of Trauma and Dissociation, 2011). Therapists will definitely see clients with DID in the course of their practice.
- Take your time with a thorough assessment while being careful not to destabilize your patient. The average time it takes to diagnose a person with DID is 6 years.

Polyfragmentation and Engineered DID

Over 20 years ago, I was made aware of a subset of patients with DID who did not develop DID organically but as a deliberate creation through trauma-based mind control. These clients present differently from those with organic DID and have different needs to be met in therapy. From early childhood, they have been subjected to a form of human slavery where their minds have been systematically fractured with traumatic experiences and then rebuilt in such a way that they could be programmed and controlled over the course of their lifespan by handlers. The people with engineered DID challenge even the most sophisticated and experienced trauma clinicians, because part of their programming is to avoid detection and foil treatment with therapists. The groups[5] that 'train' these people consider them expensive assets and will not let them leave or heal easily. They surround the programming and parts with various 'booby traps' that can derail therapy, confuse or distract the therapist, and disable or even kill the client. It is a very specific subspecialty in trauma treatment, one that requires a great deal of education and support to do well.

Up until recently, very few clinicians had ever heard of such a possibility or were aware of the reality of these mind control groups. As a member of the International Society for the Study of Trauma and Dissociation, I have access to a Special Interest Group (SIG) called Ritual Abuse Mind Control and Organized Abuse (RAMCOA). This group was created in 2008 and now boasts around 150 international members, most of whom treat people with engineered DID. Some of therapists in this SIG, which is run as a listserv, are also survivors of these groups. The wealth of information from the generous and genius therapists on RAMCOA has been indispensable for my clients and my practice.

One clue that you might have a case of engineered rather than organic DID on your hands could be the intense feelings of being deskilled and inadequate that arise in you as you are treating one of these clients. They puzzle and confuse even the most experienced of therapists until their multiplicity is recognized as engineered. Another sign might be the sudden appearance of self-harm, compulsions, or 'crazy' behavior after patient disclosures. These people have trip wires layered into their programming that are set to 'go off' whenever a therapist gets too close to a hidden truth or when the client remembers something new. These booby trap programs can look like:

- sudden suicidal impulses out of nowhere, especially ones that are 'supposed to look like an accident', as one client told me
- scrambled words or word salad in a client that has no history of schizophrenia
- an abrupt nonnegotiable firing of the therapist when the client is making progress
- pseudoseizures—episodes that look like grand mal seizures or dropping into a semi-conscious state with no EEG evidence of seizure activity
- feelings of being electrically 'shocked' at different places on the body
- recurrent and constant migraines

- an unexplained compulsion to return to a previously abusive environment that they have successfully left, such as an abusive family of origin
or spouse, especially at certain times of the year such as Halloween.

The DID in such a client is supposed to be hidden, and they will have a
fairly successful (for a while) 'front' or 'shell' personality. This front personality holds a semblance of consistency while switching personalities happens
'behind the scenes' as it were. Florid DID in these criminal groups is considered a sign of programming failure and is vigorously 'discouraged'. Polyfragmentation is a word that refers to the fact that there is often fractal splitting
of the splits, multiplicity within multiplicity. An alter can contain more ego
states and more alters, as can those alters within and so on. This presents
a very complicated neurological and psychological picture, and there are
often many physical sequelae to engineered DID. As with all of our clients,
the keys to healing lie within our benevolent and caring relationship with
these folks.

Clinical Applications:

- If you suspect someone like this on your caseload, I would recommend
getting consultation at the outset with a clinician that has extensive
experience with ritual abuse and mind control.
- Two excellent resources for information are the website www.endritu-
alabuse.org run by Ellen Lacter, PhD, and the seminal treatment book
Healing the Unimaginable: Treating Ritual Abuse and Mind Control (Miller,
2011). You will need to know what they have to offer.
- If your client tells you about ritual abuse, believe it. Ritual abuse is real.
Do not be put off by media propaganda that it does not exist. I have many
colleagues who have, as I have, encountered ritual abuse and mind control in their practices. Some of these colleagues are survivors of it. Ritual
abuse is alive and well in many communities. Intergenerational cults that
practice violent sex magic (either real or feigned) are breeding grounds
for mind control slave recruitment from various government agencies,
military factions, and criminal organizations around the world.
- Learn about some of the common mind control programs and triggers.
This knowledge helps us spot these clients sooner. As with any diagnostic
work, pattern recognition is key.
- There are not enough specialists to go around. Know that, as one mind
control survivor told me, a great therapist who is skilled in attachment and
the art of therapy is the best antidote for a lifetime of control and abuse.

Notes

1 I cannot stress the need for a safety plan enough. Chapter 9 addresses safety in the
workplace in depth.

2 Patients report that this relaxation response lasts anywhere from several hours to three days, a significant amount of relief for clients that have sometimes been in sympathetic activation for months on end when they arrive at therapy. Other commonly reported effects of Reiki are deeper sleep, better digestive function, and a feeling of well-being.

3 Social workers are trained to consider the person in the environment, but other mental health disciplines do not necessarily have the same training. But the consequences of trauma are so far-reaching; can we really afford not to make these considerations?

4 It is ironic that the system meant to protect the organism can also kill the organism. Researchers call this the 'vagal paradox'.

5 I do not have the time and space to delve into who these groups are, their modus operandi, and reasons for existing in this book. There is a wealth of information and disclosure on the internet and in several autobiographical books written by survivors of these programs, many of whom have gone on to become therapists. I would also recommend the books of psychologist Alison Miller for both clinicians and survivors.

References

American Psychiatric Association. (2013). *Diagnostic and Statistical Manual of Mental Disorders* (5th ed., DSM-5). Washington, DC: American Psychiatric Association.

Baldwin, A. L. (2011, Fall). *Reiki, the Scientific Evidence*. Retrieved August 7, 2017, from Center For Reiki Research: www.centerforreikiresearch.org/Downloads/ReikiScientificEvidence.pdf

Banitt, S. P. (2012). *The Trauma Tool Kit: Healing PTSD From the Inside Out*. Wheaton, IL: Quest Books.

Brook Holston, K. P. (Producer), Bradwell, J. (Writer), & Redford, J. (Director). (2016). *Resilience* [Motion Picture]. USA: Brainstorm Media.

Brower, V. (2004). When the immune system goes on the attack. *EMBO Reports, 5*(8), 757–760.

Bryden, D. P., & Lengnick, S. (1997). Rape in the criminal justice system. *Journal of Criminal Law & Criminology, 87*(4), 1195–1197.

Centers for Disease Control and Prevention. (2014, June 14). *About the CDC-Kaiser ACE Study—the ACE Pyramid* (N. C. Centers for Disease Control and Prevention, Producer) Retrieved December 1, 2017, from Centers for Disease Control and Prevention: www.cdc.gov/violenceprevention/acestudy/about.html

Eichorn, N. (2015). Trauma Treatment From a Global Perspective: A Conversation with van der Kolk, PhD, Stephen Porges, PhD, Joseph LaDoux, PhD and Ian Macnoughton, PhD. *Somatic Psychotherapy Today, 5*(4), 24.

Howes, R. (2013, October). *Point of view wearing your heart on your face: The polyvagal circuit in the consulting room*. Retrieved August 7, 2017, from Psychotherapy Networker: www.psychotherapynetworker.org/magazine/article/160/point-of-view

International Society for the Study of Trauma and Dissociation. (2011). Guidelines for treating dissociative identity disorder in adults, third revision. *Journal of Trauma & Dissociation, 12*(2), 115–187.

Miller, A. (2011). *Healing the Unimaginable: Treating Ritual Abuse and Mind Control*. London, UK: Karnac Books.

Oxford University Press. (2016). *Sexuality*. Retrieved October 2, 2016, from Oxford English Dictionary: https://en.oxforddictionaries.com/definition/sexuality

Shapiro, R. (2016). *Easy Ego State Interventions: Strategies for Working With Parts*. New York, NY: W.W. Norton & Company.

Society for Neuroscience. (2016). *Science Funding Resources*. Retrieved September 28, 2016, from Society for Neuroscience: www.sfn.org/Advocacy/Neuroscience-Funding/US-Funding-Priorities/Neuroscience-Funding-Through-NIH

Stephen Porges, P. R. (2015). Why the Vagal System Holds the Key to the Treatment of Trauma. In *Frontiers in the Treatment of Trauma*. Storrs, CT: National Institute for the Clinical Application of Behavioral Medicine.

Stevens, J. E. (2012, October 3). *The Adverse Childhood Experiences Study—the Largest, Most Important Public Health Study You Never Heard of—Began in an Obesity Clinic*. Retrieved September 13, 2016, from ACES Too High News: https://acestoohigh.com/2012/10/03/the-adverse-childhood-experiences- study-the-largest-most-important-public-health-study-you-never-heard-of- began-in-an-obesity-clinic/

Trauma-Dissociation.com. (2017). *Dissociative Experiences Scale—II*. Retrieved December 2, 2017, from Trauma-Dissociation.com: http://traumadissociation.com/des

Wikipedia. (2017, July 24). *Polyvagal Theory*. Retrieved August 7, 2017, from Wikipedia: https://en.wikipedia.org/wiki/Polyvagal_theory#The_ventral_vagal_complex

3 Ego Development and Traumatic Defenses

It's a joy to be hidden but a disaster not to be found.

—D. W. Winnicott

Egoic. Defensive. Resistant. Who wants to work with a client like that? Anyone? Anyone? We use these terms inside of our profession to describe processes in the mind that are supposed to be neutral. The problem is that in the 'real' world, these words connote negativity and are more likely to be hurled at a partner in the middle of a fight than to communicate understanding. Although we as therapists are trained to take a more neutral stance, I find that therapists cannot help falling into negativity, at times, with clients that they find difficult. Often our so-called 'difficult' clients have extensive trauma histories and high ACEs scores. Traumas have consistently disrupted and corrupted early ego development throughout their difficult childhoods. Relational ability becomes compromised, ranging from tenuous to nonexistent due to extreme and chaotic dysregulation. During a successful course of trauma-based psychotherapy, these deficits in ego structure are exposed, identified, regulated, and healed relationally in the therapeutic attachment.

Ego Development

Ego has gotten a bad rap recently. In spiritual circles 'ego' is conflated with 'egotism' or selfishness and is something to be avoided or rejected, as it supposedly separates the person from a state of blissful union with the divine. Originally, though, the word 'ego' came into use in the West via Freud. This ego matures along with the brain. It mediates between the internal world (id, in traditional Freudian theory) of the person and the external world we call 'reality'. If we have a body, we need to have an independent ego in order for the body to live. For example, hunger arises in the body and informs the mind. The ego's job is to provide all of the necessary steps for feeding the body: working to get money, going shopping, preparing food, etc. All of these steps entail highly complex tasks for the ego, especially in modern civilization. One has to be reasonably stable emotionally, be intellectually focused, and have good planning skills to execute these steps, which correspond to competent executive function in neuroscience.

In the formative years of early childhood, there is no functioning ego. Mother[1] provides the functions and the model of the ego. When baby is hungry, Mother provides food; when upset, she soothes; when sick, she takes care of him. Nature has designed humans to be the most dependent of species because of our large brain and relatively helpless bodies when we are born. *How* Mother cares for the child is as important to the developing ego as *what* she does. If she treats baby as a lovable person while she takes care of him, the developing ego in that child will be steeped in a loving feeling towards himself and others. Loving-kindness seems to be an organizing force in the ego/mind. We can see how disorganized a child becomes who has been mothered by someone with an unhealthy or deficient ego.

Object relations theory tells us that how the caregiver behaves towards the child deeply imprints upon the child's mind and is taken into the developing personality as an 'introject'. This introject informs the developing person about their worth as an individual while also giving them a template for how to behave with others. Many of our traumatized clients not only lack positive maternal (and paternal) introjects, but actually have abusive or neglectful ones.

A client in her early 30s comes to therapy for premenstrual dysphoria. During the course of her therapy, she finds herself very worried about her safety in the presence of her therapist. She begins to have dreams about the therapist coming to therapy naked, or abusing her sexually in sessions. As this client explores her history she realizes, at first with surprise and then with acceptance, that she has no memories of feeling comfort from either parent, both of whom abused her in various and violent ways. Any rare kindness she experienced from adults happened at friends' houses or in school. Initially she cannot feel attached to anyone or any animal. She only feels connected to trees. Yet she forms enough of an attachment in therapy to continue to attend her sessions. Over many years, she develops feelings of connection with the animal world. Initially, when she dreams of animals, the dreams are tainted with a toxic feeling. One day, after several years of weekly sessions, she proudly announces that she had a dream about a mother whale and a baby whale that was loving and maternal, and she could feel the warmth of that connection.

This client was able to eventually let go of her negative introject, represented in treatment by the abusing therapist in her dreams, and embrace her first conscious positive maternal introject in the form of a mother and baby whale love bond. This major piece of ego repair took several years to accomplish, but, once established, became a permanent part of the client's mind and reality.

What is the ego exactly and how does it come into being? I have spent a lot of time asking myself, "What attaches?" "What develops?" In some ways, the mystery of the origin of the ego is a topic better suited for philosophy or even metaphysics than psychology. Is there a primitive, immature but intact structured self that we are born with, analogous to the immature body that grows and develops? Or is the immature ego/self in a state of fragmentation that coalesces and gains organization around attachment, as Kohut postulated in the 1970s? Is the self a closed 'autistic' structure as the ego psychologists suggest, or is our primitive ego in a state of undifferentiated communion with energies, thoughts, and experiences of others?

Cultures that believe in reincarnation do not see the infant's mind as the *tabula rasa* that Western cultures do. In Paramahansa Yogananda's famous *Autobiography of a Yogi*, he reports being able to remember his infant mind:

> The helpless humiliations of infancy are not banished from my mind. I was resentfully conscious of not being able to walk or express myself freely. Prayerful surges arose within me as I realized my bodily impotence. My strong emotional life took silent form as words in many languages . . . Happier memories, too, crowd in on me: my mother's caresses, and my first attempts at lisping phrase and toddling step. These early triumphs, usually forgotten quickly, are yet a natural basis of self-confidence. My far-reaching memories are not unique. Many yogis are known to have retained their self-consciousness without interruption by the dramatic transition to and from "life" and "death".
>
> (Yogananda, 1998)

In the first postulation of ego, it is a structure or, maybe a better word would be, template that is innate in the human being. This structure is given life by being attached and in relation to other objects (people—in object relations theory). The ego develops along the lines of its likes and dislikes and the quality of attachment to others in its world. In this model, extreme trauma can 'split' or fragment the original ego, what some might call the 'core self'. The most abused clients may describe having parts of all ages, including dead baby parts, as a part of their self-structure.

Another view, put forward by Kohut in the 1970s, was that the infantile ego was actually fragmented from the beginning and evolved into greater cohesion with reality and people in its world as development progressed with a good-enough mother (primary caretaker). In this model, Mother helps the baby's diffuse consciousness to safely focus on her as a point in reality in a loving matrix. Psychopathology in the personality and trauma then manifest as a 'failure of cohesion' of a healthy ego structure.

Although paradoxical, it is possible that both theoretical approaches have validity. If we look at neurological correlations to the developing ego, we see that the brain of children under 7 years old is highly plastic. There is an inherent essential structure, but it is highly malleable and undifferentiated with many possibilities not only for growth but also for pruning growth when the child gets to a certain age. Between birth and adolescence, the brain is in a continual process of synaptic or axon pruning. We literally 'use it or lose it'. A loving and attuned parent can help this system organize and function well, while an abusive or neglectful parent can disrupt neurological functioning and the burgeoning ego. It helps to listen to the language of our patients who will describe a 'fracturing' or 'breaking apart' of the self (split self) as well as a feeling of chaos and deficiency of groundedness in the self (lack of cohesion).

Horner's Stages of Ego Development

In my very first week of work at the League School of Boston, a residential program for autistic and psychotic youth, I walked into a training held by then director Barbara Schaechter, LICSW. She had put two things on the chalkboard. The first was this sentence: "All behavior is meaningful." The second was a timeline of early childhood development and self-cohesion from Althea Horner's book *Object Relations and the Developing Ego in Therapy* (Horner, 1975). This timeline outlined in great detail the developmental stages of the child ego from birth to 3 years of age, and the psychological deficits that were enfolded into the developing ego if the child's needs were not met in that time period. During the 70s and 80s, Horner's model was taught extensively on the East Coast and other places. To this day, she remains the only therapist I am aware of who has outlined so many stages of ego development so clearly in the young child and related those stages to casework in psychotherapy. As my wise director knew, all behavior is meaningful and explainable in adults and children when we understand the ego deficits incurred in early childhood through trauma and other adverse events, in relation to the stage of development operating at the time of the event.

The Undifferentiated Self (Birth to 5 Months)

According to Horner, the baby starts off in a state of what she called "normal autism". Because of advances in the understanding of autism, I have renamed this stage of ego development the 'undifferentiated self'. Attachment seeking is hardwired into the infant brain and begins immediately. If you put a newly born baby onto its mother's stomach, it will begin to move upward to the breast. This behavior is called 'breast crawl' and was first described at the Karolinska Institute of Sweden in 1987 (The Mother and Child Health and Education Trust, 2016). Horner describes clinical issues of this stage as a failure to attach, possibly due to neurological factors.

In the 1970s, when Horner was writing her book based on her colleagues' discoveries, the field of trauma did not exist. Child sexual abuse was considered exceedingly rare. Pediatricians were told that the rates of incest were one in one million and that they would probably never see a case in their entire career! Widespread acknowledgment of various kinds of child abuse—physical, sexual, emotional—did not gain attention until the mid- to late 1980s. The literature of that time almost never mentions traumatic abuse as a cause of harm to the child's development.

We now know that trauma hugely disrupts neurodevelopment and attachment. The age at which trauma and subsequent attachment disruption occurs dictates what kinds of relational problems the client will have and informs therapists where we need to focus our attention in repairing these attachments.

Infants are subjected to any number of abuses. Our clients only know about those abuses if someone tells them, if they have scars, or if there is a medical history available to inform them, which, in most cases, there is not. In the 1980s, the Child-At-Risk Hotline in Boston routinely received reports of infant abuse—ranging from falling out of windows, to burns (accidental and deliberate), to shaken baby syndrome, to rape (rare, but real). What Horner and her colleagues did not yet know was the prevalence of child abuse and neglect in the psychiatric population. In her writings, issues of abuse are rarely brought up. She focuses on parenting from an attunement and presence perspective. And while it is true that an unattuned parent can be distressing to a child, severely abusive or neglectful parents can be magnitudes of order more disruptive to the attachment process.

Symbiosis (Culminates Around 5–6 Months)

During these first crucial five months, the baby is designed by nature to secure attachment with the parent in a way that can feel like a blissful fusion. The young child does not yet have a sense of difference between mother and self and a minimal sense of mother and other. Stranger anxiety does not set in until about 8 months of age. When this symbiosis is disrupted, even for very short periods of time, the infant is designed by nature to act to restore the attachment as quickly as possible. If the child cannot, the world becomes a very strange and frightening place.

Tronick's Still Face Experiment in the 1970s showed beyond any doubt that even very young infants acted with urgency to reconnect with their mother upon seeing their mother's still and unresponsive face. In the videos, we can see a child whose caretaker is instructed to still her facial expressions become shocked and saddened and then move through several stages to try to regain attachment including the following stages:

- **Reaching**: The baby reaches out physically and with facial expressions to attract the parent's attention.
- **Protest**: The baby will make noises and escalate to screeching or crying trying to push the parent in into reconnection.

- **Turning Away**: If the attempts to reconnect fail, the baby will turn away from the disturbing parent's face.

The experiments always end here for obvious ethical reasons. One can see that the child was headed into a place of shutting down, detaching, or even dissociating. As Tronick says, "We need loving contact like oxygen. We really do not have many ways to deal with the pain of disconnection at any age" (Johnson & Tronick, 2016).

During this crucial stage of development, the mother and baby engage in what is called mutual cuing. The mother shapes the baby's behavior by responding positively to certain cues, and the baby shapes the mother's behavior when she is not responding to the baby's needs by protesting or pushing. This dance is crucial for establishing a beginning trust in attachment that is foundational for the baby's perception of basic benevolence in the world. If the mother cannot or will not respond appropriately to the baby's bids for attachments and needs, or if the baby is abused during this time, a pattern of what she called 'defensive detachment' might set up. In the trauma world, we might call this dissociation.

If attachment fails at this stage, Horner describes a set of behaviors in the child or adult client that sound a lot like our modern diagnosis of reactive attachment disorder, "indiscriminate friendliness with an inordinate craving for affection with no ability to make lasting relationships," or antisocial personality, "the inability to keep rules, lack of capacity to experience guilt . . . the failure to develop the affectional bond that goes with attachment." She also describes a situation where the child can have "multiple, unintegrated attachments that are paralleled by a failure of the integration of the self-representation" (Horner, 1975) caused by inconsistent caretakers. This description sounds like the beginnings of dissociative identity disorder. A parent who is an inconsistent and chaotic target of attachment can make the child vulnerable to psychosis, or a false self that is tenuously connected to an isolated and unrelated core self. In all of these cases, the client develops extreme defensive detachment as a core character structure.

Clinically, the main focus with a client with this history (and maybe the only focus for years to come) is on creating a safe cocoon where the innermost detached parts of the client's self can 'hatch' into the light of day and attach to a safe and caring therapist, as would normally happen in the next phase of development. Horner states, "The issues of attachment and detachment in the clinical situation will be central to the treatment of all patients for whom these have been developmental issues" (Horner, 1975).

Hatching: The First of Three Stages of Separation/Individuation (5–10 Months)

With the advent of locomotion (crawling and, in some instances, walking), the child begins to leave the blissful symbiotic cocoon and explore moving away from the Mother. The awareness of separation slowly dawns on the child's developing mind, culminating in stranger anxiety at around 8 months of age, where the child becomes aware that:

1.   she needs the Mother, and
2.   Mother is different than other people.

Horner's developmental view of the ego at this stage is that it is fragile and vulnerable to feelings of dissolution or nonexistence. If the child cannot locate and connect with Mother when she needs to, she may feel like her very self is dissolving and the world is literally coming to an end—a very disturbing state indeed! Horner relates this intolerable emotional state to the development of borderline personality disorder.[2] The baby will merge with the mother's energy and body through cuddles and breastfeeding in order to gain comfort and restore a sense of order and regulation in her self, body, and psyche. If the parent is inconsistent, neglectful, or abusive, or if the child is subjected to overwhelming stimuli such as pain in the body, the child cannot be comforted and brought into harmony in their body/mind. This inability to neuroregulate will follow these kids into adulthood and all their relationships, until they have the corrective relational experience that they are always seeking. The therapist provides both the container and the object for this corrective interpersonal experience.

Horner describes the main clinical failure of therapeutic work with the person here to be empathic failure. *The intense rage our borderline patients feel when we do not understand them (or they feel we do not understand them) is a result of the borderline panic that erupts when they feel their fragile ego dissolving and disappearing.* These clients literally feel like they are fighting for their lives and their sanity. This dynamic is different from ordinary dissociation and the concomitant feeling of unreality. Perhaps the self-mutilation that is common to this disorder is an attempt not just to become grounded but to *establish a sense of existence through pain to counteract the terror of nonexistence.* Suicidal feelings may not be an attempt to escape or to manipulate the provider, but to *establish congruence with a sense of nonexistence.*

When this type of client feels threatened in the therapy by abandonment, whether it is because the therapist has misunderstood them or is physically absent, a client in this panicked state will vigorously engage all the strategies for reattachment including the push/protest stage. To us it may feel like the client's behaviors comprise an unwarranted overreaction or drama. They may look manipulative or like they are acting out, but they are not. They are trying to survive. To the person suffering this sense of impending dissolution, separation (either physical or emotional) feels like a matter of life and death, sanity or insanity, or even worse, existence or nonexistence.

Practicing Period: Second of Three Stages of Separation/Individuation (10–18 Months)

By 10–18 months of age, nearly all children will have begun to walk upright. This accomplishment facilitates a huge jump in autonomy. At the same time, a child's language will reflect a beginning sense of self with a vocabulary of 'wants' and 'don't wants'. This language is both verbal and nonverbal. At the most basic level, the child shows the parent (and herself) what she wants by moving towards it and what she doesn't want by moving away. She no longer needs to wait for her parent to pick her up and carry her short distances. Children of this age actively engage their environment, sorting out what is what for themselves. Parents tend to underestimate the abilities of this age.[3] Without locomotion, we really cannot know what is going on in the young child's head (and maybe they cannot either).

Horner describes the clinical issue at this stage of development as an inflated sense of self, or grandiosity. The child has more ideas in her head than she can safely execute. Rudimentary cause and effect thinking through exploration has begun, giving the child an expanded sense of their own capacity but without actual mastery. The child still needs constant supervision. Horner describes how the child of this age can feel a sense of magical omnipotence connected to both the elation at the sense of walking and the merged connection to the mother's power to provide for the toddler's needs. For example, the toddler walks over to the refrigerator, pulls on the handle, and the mother opens the door for her and grabs her sippy cup. Magic! Bliss! The child feels powerful and good.

A child in the practicing period will continue to develop a healthy sense of self and of their own basic goodness as long as that is what is mirrored back to the child from the parent. If the parent is abusive, the child is made to feel helpless and humiliated and risks developing a core sense of 'badness'. The mother can feel both a sense of relief and a sense of abandonment at this stage. A very disturbed parent who develops a psychotic transference towards the child cannot tolerate even the most rudimentary bids for independence and will feel abandoned by a child walking or crawling away from them. Or they can feel completely overwhelmed by the child's 'demands', which are merely expressions of biological and developmental needs: hunger, thirst, diapering, affection, need for intellectual stimulation, etc.

A physically or sexually abusive parent as well as an extremely neglectful parent can shatter and/or arrest the toddler's tenuous sense of self, resulting in ego fragmentation and a sense of extreme helplessness. One can imagine that the grandiosity of this stage could become perverted into an overwhelming sense for the child of magical badness and power, rather than goodness. The child is left then with the choice to identify with this grandiose badness (possible beginnings of sociopathic character) or reject it, if they can, by splitting it off of awareness into an emotional part or even a fully developed personality fragment (the beginnings of DID and other dissociative disorders).

Rapprochement: The Third Step in Individuation and Separation (18–36 Months)

Any parent who has raised more than one child knows that children can develop in very different ways. Some babies stand right up at 9 months of age and start walking. Others have prolonged periods of crawling. The timelines presented here are guidelines that vary by circumstance and genetics, not hard and fast rules. With that in mind, sometime around 18 months of age the child's awareness of being a separate being from her mother starts to crystallize. By this age, Horner concludes, the child has had its omnipotent feelings and overconfidence deflated any number of times, making the child vulnerable to feelings of shame. The child starts to clearly see that power resides with the caretaking parent and that their own power is limited. It is an important moment where parenting intersects with child development. As Horner says, "The good-enough mother of this period will make it possible for the child to divest himself of his delusional power without undue anxiety or shame" (Horner, 1975).

There are many tasks associated with this age. As we have noted earlier, the very beginnings of the ego rest on want/don't want or, as Buddhists might say, desire and aversion. In the rapprochement period many ego functions develop, forming the core of the personality. These include:

1. identification with the caregivers and introjection of caregiver qualities,
2. tolerating ambivalent feelings, and
3. libidinal object constancy.

The first—identification with caregivers and introjection of their qualities—is a largely unconscious process that informs our relational choices and personality traits throughout the lifespan. Straight cisgender girls tend to identify with their mothers, and straight cisgender boys tend to identify with their fathers.[4] People say, "the apple doesn't fall far from the tree." Without psychological insight and awareness that is true. Nature does seem to hardwire us to incorporate our same gendered parent's behaviors and qualities. As I tell my trauma clients, "if you loved how your family of origin interacted, great, go with 'chemistry' and your hardwiring from your family. But if you were traumatized by them and they traumatized each other, you are going to have to rewire your personality through awareness and hard work to counteract the choices your unconscious mind will want to make."

Sometimes the identification with the parent is consciously rejected ("they were mean and I'm not like that"). *Despite this conscious rejection of the undesirable quality (meanness), the child still unconsciously takes in the quality of that parent as an introject that is alien to who the client feels themselves to be.* For example, a sweet and loving client may have a very mean internal voice with which she berates herself. She has consciously distanced herself from the mean parent's behavior and contained the mean introject from acting upon outside objects (other people), but the meanness remains in the form of emotional violence towards herself.

Ambivalence characterizes toddler consciousness. One of the great developmental tasks of the 2-year-old is learning to tolerate more than one feeling at a time without completely melting down. Toddlers can lose it because they want all the ice cream flavors, or because they are not sure what room they want to be in, resulting in the tantrums they are so famous for. This behavior is completely normal for this age. Dealing with competing desires and aversions is no small task, cognitively or emotionally! If the parent is loving and holds a secure attachment container for the child, the child will naturally mature through this stage. When they are grown, they are able to take many points of view and hold different ideas together in the same space in their head—a skill necessary for problem resolution and relationship repair. But if complications of abuse and shaming affect this process, the child may become severely impaired in their ability to work through and resolve ambivalence—an impairment that can persist throughout a lifetime. Adults who cannot tolerate ambivalent feelings tend to see the world in black and white, their decision-making impaired by lack of nuance and frustration tolerance. These folks tend to disrupt attachment when their loved object does not live up to their sense of how things 'should' be. They can develop a narcissistic personality.

The ability of the child to tolerate ambivalent feelings is contingent on the ability to develop libidinal object constancy. What is libidinal object constancy? Piaget described 'object permanence' as the cognitive achievement of knowing that objects remain the same and do not disappear whether they are in or out of sight. Libidinal object constancy is the ability to hold a consistent image of the loved one in one's heart and mind through time and space. An adult with libidinal object constancy has internalized an image of the good parent (Freud, 1992). They can be present to their relationships even when those relationships are temporarily unsatisfying. They know at a deep level that they are loved and that people do not 'disappear' when they are not present. They feel loved and loving, caring and cared for. The task of libidinal object constancy begins in the rapprochement period with a 'good enough', emotionally present parent. If the primary parent is inconsistent, punishing, or abusive, the child can vacillate between fearing, raging at, and envying the parent. They may develop a very deep sense of shame interpersonally and not be able to feel that the world is a benevolent place or that anybody is ever 'there for them'. This type of client may not be able to hold onto any sense of caring connection during therapy breaks, such as vacations. This type of client may need a picture or voice message from the therapist over vacations. Or they may need a 'transitional object' such as a stuffed animal.

To have a separate secure identity, the child must know that there is a loving parent in their corner, consistently there for them no matter what. Most of our clients have not had this type of parenting experience, so we need to become the 'no matter what' parents, returning again and again with them to the basic 'holding environment' of unconditional positive regard during therapy sessions.

Ego Defenses

In the world of medicine, defenses are understood to be necessary and desirable. We call the body's defensive system the immune system. For the mind, the word 'defensive' has become an unpleasant term associated with arguments and war. We call someone 'defensive' when they are not listening to us, or when we do not like what they are saying. But if we look at ego defenses as the immune system of the self, we can see that ego defenses are as necessary to the safety of the healthy mind as the immune system is to the healthy body.

Sigmund Freud laid the groundwork for the concept of ego defenses, and his daughter Anna Freud developed the first lists of ego defenses and their definitions in her seminal book *The Ego and the Mechanisms of Defense* (Freud, 1992). George Vaillant, MD, a Harvard Medical School psychiatrist and professor, realized that not all defenses were created equal. He saw that some defenses were more pathological than others. Clinicians in the Harvard teaching hospitals, myself included, were encouraged to consider one of our goals in treatments with patients to be moving them up the ladder of ego defensiveness from more pathological defenses such as projection and denial to less pathological defenses such as altruism and humor, as shown in Figure 3.1. For

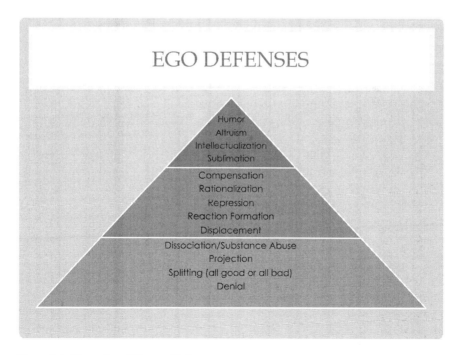

Figure 3.1 Hierarchy of Trauma Defenses

many of my clients this system worked well, but there were always clients that stubbornly remained at the bottom of the pyramid. In the last decade of work, I came to realize that those patients embodied the most traumatic experiences, and my view of this pyramid changed forever.

The very definition of psychological trauma asserts that traumatic events threaten the integrity of the sense of self. In many cases we hear trauma survivors say things such as,

> *My mind is broken.*
> *I feel shattered into a million pieces.*
> *I don't know who I am anymore.*
> *I can't go on living like this.*

All of these statements represent the inability of the ego to cope with the enormity of trauma that has been experienced by the client. The ego is literally overwhelmed by the trauma, and it fails, not as a moral failing, but as a structure. It gives way like a building overcome by a gigantic tsunami.

As I worked with traumatized clients, it struck me that using the pathological model of ego defenses was unkind and not strengths-based. I noticed that the greater the severity and duration of trauma experienced, the more likely it would be that the ego's 'immune system' would have to resort to stronger defenses, defenses that had been labeled 'pathological' by clinicians in a time before the advent of trauma awareness. *The greater the trauma load, the more likely we are to find people using defenses at the bottom of the ego defense pyramid.*

Consider this thought experiment:

> *You are in a prisoner of war camp where there are a variety of methods of abuse, coercion, and torture. For some things you can use your higher level defenses. You might deal with the pain of starvation by sharing your food (altruism) or laugh off the lack of hygiene (humor). As the events in camp get more intense, you may have to resort to the middle level defenses. Knowing that you can't attack your guards you might vent your anger on another camp mate (displacement) or try to develop some new skills during your time in the camp (compensation). But under extremely adverse conditions such as painful torture, none of these defenses is going to be nearly enough to help with the traumas you endure. Eventually you will resort to attempts to mentally escape through denial or dissociation, or finding substances that will alter your cognition. No one laughs their way through a torture session.*

Our clients have experienced significant episodes of extreme abuse and trauma, most often in their developmental years. Our clients are all Harry Potter, 'the boy who lived'. Their deployment of the most extreme defenses was necessary to survive the unsurvivable. Many people cannot live with the pain of a torturous and traumatic childhood, and end their lives either consciously or unconsciously. *Our clients made it through, not in spite of these 'pathological' structures, but because of them.* These defenses have been their best friends, but, like the body when the immune system overfunctions, new kinds of problems arise along with these defenses. In the body, an overactive immune system provokes autoimmune disorders. For trauma survivors, old survival strategies and vigorous defense systems prevent them from having the loving connections with other people that they so desire—a frustrating condition for both patient and therapist. Let us consider these most intense ego defenses in a bit more depth.

Denial

We talk about denial as if it is one thing, one ego defense. Denial is actually a complex of largely unconscious mechanisms of the mind. At its most basic level, denial is an inability to digest experience through acceptance. This lack of acceptance keeps our clients turning their wheels for months to years fighting reality, fighting awareness, and fighting feelings. It is exhausting for them and for us. It is also worrisome, as sometimes our clients put themselves or others in harm's way due to their level of denial about their behavior. For example, if a parent is in denial about a perpetrator in the family, they may inadvertently expose their children to danger at the hands of that family member.

When I was writing *The Trauma Tool Kit* (Pease Banitt, 2012), I described denial through its opposite—acceptance. Acceptance is a key to healing from traumatic events. Acceptance, or nonresistance, as some people call it, must come before the abreaction and integration of self-fragments that split off during intense traumas.[5] Denial puts us in prison and tosses away the key, sometimes for decades. I have a healthy respect for denial, as all therapists must. Premature awareness of memories can lead to a total breakdown in functioning, psychosis, or suicide. The body is very wise, and denial is part of the emergency protection system of the body/mind system. Like a circuit breaker, denial throws a switch that keeps victims from completely burning out their circuits of functioning and will to live.

Even though we talk about denial in the singular, denial can manifest in several ways that incorporate other defense mechanisms (see Figure 3.2). Denial can be broken down into four types or strategies—again bearing in mind that there is very little conscious choice as to whether a client denies their experience or how they deny it. If you look at the structure of the figure, one can imagine that the sides of the triangle interface with conscious reality. Three of the types have some exposure to the outside world, that is, some conscious components. But the innermost variety is completely encapsulated inside the unconscious mind of the patient—far from seeing the light of day.

Ignoring History

We see this type quite commonly with friends and acquaintances, or in certain very structured types of therapies. It may be the type of denial that is the most conscious, although still unconsciously driven. In the past, folks who wanted to actively ignore their history or didn't consider it relevant to their current

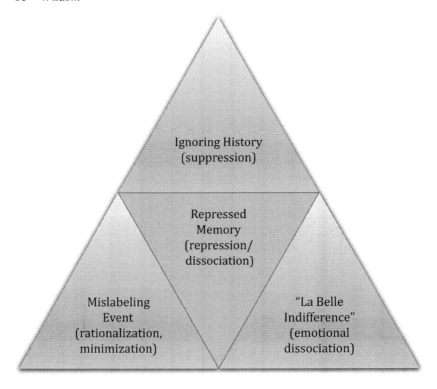

Figure 3.2 The Four Types of Denial

issues used to stay out of therapy altogether, back when therapy was defined as diving into the past to understand the present. In modern treatments such as cognitive behavioral therapy, PTSD symptoms and anxiety can be worked with directly without confronting a person's history.

A common statement associated with this type of denial is "I don't want to go back there." A person with this defensive structure will say this while still denying that there is, in fact, a 'back there'! Which leads us to another fact about the mechanism of denial—it is always full of paradoxes, inconsistencies, and discrepancies. A wise supervisor used to call this phenomenon 'bumps under the rug'—surefire indicators of a trauma history that may yet be unripe for processing.

Psychodynamic therapists might call this style 'suppression', a semi-conscious or conscious choice to avoid dealing with a painful reality, as opposed to 'repression', which is a completely unconscious mechanism. In other words, this type of client is at least aware that there is a 'back there', even if they don't want to or feel like they need to deal with those memories. You cannot reason with this type of denial. Even if the client has read many self-help books and watched hours of Oprah, they will have convinced themselves that processing memories is of no use whatsoever, and they will often try every other kind of self-help therapy available (including self-medication) before choosing to work on past events with a psychotherapist. One sees these people, who try to heal while ignoring their history, more often doing extreme sports, changing up their diets, or walking on hot coals than talking in a therapist's office.

Mislabeling Events

These clients can describe exactly what happened to them and still not be able to acknowledge the event. By refusing to name the event, or just by not 'connecting the dots', they attempt to minimize and rationalize away their experience.

> *A client in her mid-40s comes in for weight loss issues. In the course of telling her history, she reveals that when she was in her early 20s her husband of 3 months shoved her under a chair and forced her to have sex with him. This behavior upset her very much and hurt her physically, but because of her religious upbringing she felt like it was 'her duty' to give him access to sex. She acknowledged that after this experience they 'grew apart' and she began to gain a tremendous amount of weight. She was very surprised when her therapist labeled this event a rape.*

Mislabeling can be used by perpetrators and by victims. The first task for court-ordered sex offenders at my agency was to describe what they had done to their victims in an accurate way, without minimization or rationalization. This task proved exceedingly difficult. *Victims often mislabel interpersonal traumas as children because of the way their perpetrators talk about the trauma to them in the course of grooming or abusing them.* Thus physical abuse becomes 'teaching a lesson', humiliation is 'discipline', and incest becomes 'special time' or 'doing the child a favor'.

Our legal systems influence these labels and conversations. People tend to conflate the legal severity of an offense with emotional severity. If we value emotional damage as an injustice that needs restitution, this makes sense. Sadly, the courts are always several steps behind the psychologists in awareness of what constitutes victimization and emotional damage. In court, we can end up with a judgment where a perpetrator of incest who caused emotional damage over a long period of time spends much less time in jail than an adult stranger rapist who had one offense. Common behaviors that cause horrendous psychological problems and trauma, such as a sexualizing stepfather who may look but not touch, do not have a crime associated with them at all—at least not one that is easy to take to court. 'Peeping Toms' are known in general society as a stranger offense, not as a familial phenomenon. *If our society cannot name these traumas, how can our victimized clients?* Our culture helps us name what happens to us.

Unlike the first category of people that decide they do not want to look at their history, this group knows that something is wrong in their history, and they want to figure it out. Because they do not have the right cultural labels for their experience, they may overlook important traumas for years until an astute therapist labels them or until the culture begins to recognize and name the offense.

La Belle Indifference

Freud identified this type of emotional dissociation when he worked with clients with paresthesias, what we now call conversion disorders. It was common in his time for people to suddenly become blind or lose the use of a limb for no medical reason. A hysterically 'blind' person would blink normally if their eyes were approached but they would deny being able to see anything. What Freud found fascinating about these cases, and what made them stand apart from other types of medical illness, were these patients' remarkably casual attitude about their disability and those associated with the disability. They did not seem to care in the least that they had become blind or lame, and they did not care how it affected the people around them. He labeled this attitude *la belle indifference*, which translates from French as 'the beautiful indifference'.

I have only seen conversion disorder with la belle indifference a couple of times in decades of practice. In modern times, it is a relatively rare condition. Both times the clients were teenagers. What is much more common is to see people with a trauma history exhibit a type of 'devil could care less' emotional dissociation about their traumatic events. These clients are fully aware of their history. *They label the traumatic events correctly but have little to no affect related to the trauma.* They may deny that they were traumatized or that they need help at all, and they deny that their emotional dissociation affects their relationships.

> *A middle-aged man who spends most of his time in spiritual yogic practices is telling me about his family history. He says that his father was violent with all the kids in his family and that several times this man punched him so hard that he somersaulted into a wall 'like a cartoon character'. His face does not change expression, does not look sorrowful or angry as he tells me this story as one might imagine. In fact, he looks amused. He says, "I probably deserved it."*

Without access to our feelings, it is hard for us to discern the reality of what has happened to us. In the case above, this person was using a mechanism to avoid negative emotions that the spiritual teacher, Ram Dass, coined as 'spiritual bypass'. Spiritual bypass is defined as the use of spiritual practices that induce pleasant blissful states to avoid rather than engage with reality, not unlike drug use. The problem with spiritual bypass, as with all forms of avoidance, is that trauma symptoms persist in the body/mind until full healing is achieved. Until the trauma is recognized and dealt with, there is the ever-present risk of unconscious trauma reenactment in relationship.

Another cause of emotional dissociation can be the inability to actually feel one's emotions, a condition called alexithymia. This condition is not the same as autism or other disorders that can cause dissociation from feelings. With alexithymia, people cease to feel much at all, not only their traumas but also positive feelings such as joy, contentment, and happiness. People with alexithymia tend to think logically and have a constricted imagination. Alexithymia appears to be a stable personality trait and may be related to emotional neglect in childhood (Aust, Alkan Härtwig, Heuser, & Bajbouj, 2013).

Finally, there is a type of emotional dissociation that most therapists will readily recognize. Some clients have processed their trauma so many times that they cease to have any emotional connection to the event. They may never have connected to their authentic reaction at all. This phenomenon can happen after a criminal event. The client becomes desensitized to telling her story over and over to various detectives, judges, etc., without actually processing the emotional content. Emotional dissociation or la belle indifference can also be a function of having survived over a long period of time in a literal or figurative 'war zone', such as a situation of years-long domestic violence. When these clients testify in court, emotional dissociation can be a liability. Many times jurors have not believed victims because of the flatness of their affect as they tell their story.

Some therapists have not been trained in how to connect emotions in the body with patients' stories. A fully cognized trauma needs to be integrated with the body. In many cases, therapists themselves are stuck in a 'talking head' approach to therapy or their own life. A client cannot really integrate their story and their emotions until there is a great deal of trust and attachment between them and the therapist.

As a treater, I do not initially ask for the client's trauma story in depth unless there is an issue of protection (an elder, a child, etc.). I wait until they are truly ready to dive into the truth of what happened to them body, mind, and soul, a process that they initiate with me when they are ready. In fact, I will often stop people from telling their story in the beginning of treatment, especially when they are doing so out of expectation of 'how therapy is supposed to go' or if it seems they are trying to please me. At the first sign of the joining of emotion to memory, I support their integration but always without force.

Repressed Memories

In a traumatic event, the body brilliantly divides and conquers overwhelming traumatic memories into component parts in the brain, essentially fooling the brain into thinking that what occurred wasn't real. These dissociated memories are not internally recorded as part of the victim's history and self-structure. If the victim is under about 7–8 years of age, the brain is highly plastic and easily creates dissociated memories or even alternate selves in which to house dissociated memories, as in dissociative identity disorder. Dissociation compartmentalizes these memory components and helps us forget or minimize them to reduce their impact on the system (i.e., to help us stay alive). I have worked with 5-year-olds who cannot successfully dissociate horrible memories. They try to kill themselves. The repressive/dissociative mechanism is essential for survival and is most likely an evolutionary function.

Repression minimizes or eliminates any remnant expression of the trauma in consciousness. This system of forgetting is not unlike hacking up a body and burying the parts in different places all over the county where they are unlikely to be sensed, found, or assembled. There is a snapshot picture here . . . a feeling state there . . . and a questionable narrative that the client has trouble believing. (Could my father be a molester? Nah . . .) *This division results in the client's inability to recognize memories as memories, functionally repressing them even if components of the memory never actually disappear over time.* Most of my clients have not fully repressed their memories, although this can and does happen. Most just do not recognize their memory fragments as real. **Trigger warning for following example**.

A woman comes in complaining of severe PTSD. She reports that she knows she was raped around 4 years of age, and she has the scars to prove it. She doesn't know why she has become more symptomatic lately. There is much she doesn't remember. After two years of building (and testing) our relationship, as well as exploring support and healing around PTSD symptoms, the client is ready to tell me something new. She wrinkles up her face in distress: "I don't know why I have such bad thoughts in my head. I must be a bad person to have such bad thoughts in my head." I ask her if these are new thoughts. She says no. They have been there all along, since she was a small child. I encourage her to tell me. Hesitantly she tells me about being taken into an underground structure that is very scary, very evil feeling. She talks about a crazy man doing bad things to her and other children. There are cameras and many other people standing around. She feels frozen in place and tells about the scene in a very unemotional voice. All of a sudden she comes out of the memory. Her face crumples up and she begins to cry softly, "It's so sad, so sad." "That can't be real. Can that be real? Am I crazy? Why am I making up bad things?" We talk about her very real emotional response to the scene. When she had the isolated picture in her head, there was no emotion connected to it, but now that she has shared it with her therapist she begins to experience deep grief and horror. I point out that unless she is a very accomplished actress it is unlikely she could conjure up such a real 'fake' reaction to a 'fake' memory or fantasy. Incredibly she connects so strongly to this comment that she laughs and nods her head. What she has been through is not OK, but in this moment she is OK. She is believed. She is safe.

This client actually had dissociated memory components that were never repressed (the picture of what was happening) along with feelings that were fully repressed (sorrow and horror). Up until the moment she told me about the 'bad thoughts', those components had remained separate, but they spontaneously fused in the presence of a compassionate witness. This is the magic of psychotherapy—to have a consistent and caring person listen skillfully to unbearable stories.

Ego repair lies at the very heart of wisdom therapies. To understand child development is to have the master plan to the mind and personality. To know how trauma impacts development and how it impacts the client in the here and now is to have the keys to the kingdom. You have a schema for personality development and you have the defensive structures erected by trauma, now what? Once you walk through the gates and get a look at the defenses, how do you form the attachment so necessary in therapy to the successful resolution of deep traumas? It takes two to attach. Chapter 4 addresses the necessary steps to create a solid therapeutic alliance with the highly traumatized client.

Notes

1 Please note that the author intends 'Mother' to represent any gender and any number of people involved in the early bonding and primary caretaking of the child. The combination of carrying a pregnancy to term, breastfeeding, and the constant contact of early childhood provides the traditional definition of motherhood at this stage, but is, obviously, not the only option available to parents who may be of any gender and for whom pregnancy is only one way to bring a child into one's life. In Western life, completion of this combination with one person has become a rarity, but for the purposes of writing, it will be treated as such.
2 Previous to the label of borderline personality disorder, this condition was known as borderline psychotic disorder, due to the intensely distorted interpersonal transference that would develop in relationships that were not grounded in reality. This type of patient was seen to dip and out of psychotic functioning in their relationships depending on how much support they had internally and externally.
3 I was surprised to see my 15-month-old stand in front of a series of cars in a parking lot shaking her head 'no' at each car until she got to her car, where she nodded an emphatic 'yes'.
4 We do not have much research as of yet on how LGBT individuals unconsciously identify with their parents. I hope to see more investigation into LGBT development in the coming years.
5 Usually. But I have also seen people come to full acceptance in the midst of abreaction and memory integration. Healing is a spiral, not a line, and stages do not follow hard-and-fast rules.

References

Aust, S., Alkan Härtwig, E., Heuser, I., & Bajbouj, M. (2013). The role of early emotional neglect in alexithymia. *Psychological Trauma: Theory, Research, Practice and Policy, 5*(3), 225–232.

Freud, A. (1992). *The Ego and the Mechanisms of Defense*. London, UK: Karnac.

Horner, A. (1975). *Object Relations and the Developing Ego in Therapy*. Oxford, UK: Rowman & Littlefield.

Johnson, S., & Tronick, E. (2016, February 4). *Videos*. Retrieved February 19, 2017, from Dr. Sue Johnson: Creating Connections: http://drsuejohnson.com/videos/

The Mother and Child Health and Education Trust. (2016, February 21). *Initiation of Breast Feeding by Breast Crawl*. (T. M. Trust, Producer). Retrieved February 17, 2017, from Breast Crawl: www.breastcrawl.org/science.shtml

Pease Banitt, S. (2012). *The Trauma Tool Kit: Healing PTSD From the Inside Out*. Wheaton, IL: Quest Books.

Winnicott, D. W. (1965). *The Maturational Processes and the Facilitating Environment*. New York, NY: International Universities Press.

Yogananda, P. (1998). *Autobiography of a Yogi*. Los Angeles, CA: Self-Realization Fellowship.

Part II
Attachment

4 Fostering Attachment in Psychotherapy

Love cures people—both the ones who give it and the ones who receive it.
—Dr. Karl Menninger

Therapists are great at spouting theory, justifying our work with an evidence base. We have lots of information, and we need to have it. But, that is actually the easy part. What is hard? Application. We need to combine skills from different parts of the brain: knowledge with attunement in order to help the client create meaningful and lasting changes. If we cannot get clients to connect to us, we will be of little help to them no matter how much we know. Disconnected therapists run the risk of becoming little more than a talking head, a 'shrink'.

The term 'shrink', or 'headshrinker', is not a compliment. Wise therapists find themselves in the business of expansion, not contraction. We want our clients to get a bigger picture, enlarge their sense of self and agency, and reach for new opportunities in life. Shrinking heads through intellectual analysis can reduce the client's faith in their own capacities. Poor trauma therapy creates an unhealthy dependence born on the hope of a connection that is never quite achieved. We all learn better and grow faster when we have a genuine warm connection with our teacher, caretaker, or therapist. Like the masters in Chapter 1, we want to create the warmest possible container for our clients to grow in. We need to offer intellectual analysis wrapped in the milk of human kindness. The truth is, we have nothing solid to offer our clients without a benevolent and sustaining foundational attachment in therapy.

According to Herman's three-stage model (Herman, 1997), the first stage of trauma treatment is safety and stabilization. Many therapists jump right into the work of trauma recovery without taking the time to focus on building the foundational attachment in the therapy that constitutes the first step of stabilization. This step can be quite lengthy, and can be considered ongoing throughout the life of the therapy relationship.

We can see in this example how the client stabilizes as she forms an attachment to her therapist and then is ready to enter into Herman's second-stage

It is the mid-1980s. A 23-year-old client comes in for therapy worried that she is pregnant and is conflicted between her Catholicism and her knowing that bearing a child at this time in her life would compromise her mental health, no matter the outcome. She reports an exaggerated startle response and depression. Relieved to find she is not pregnant, she stays in therapy to deal with her depression and anxiety because she likes the therapist and finds it relieving to have someone to talk to. During her first year, she explores many of her fears about therapy and the therapist. Towards the end of the first year, she begins to have a series of terrifying nightmares, representative of profound trauma from childhood. At this time, she comes in and announces that she has decided to 'commit' to therapy. It has taken her nine months to come to a place where she feels can actually begin the work of therapy in earnest. To her, the dreams signify a readiness to explore the traumas of her past within the nascent connection to her therapist.

trauma work: remembering and mourning. This phase is also known as 'working through', trauma processing, abreaction, or 'feeling and releasing'[1] (Pease-Banitt, 2012). It seems obvious to say that clients attach along their own timetable, and that attachment is an internal, organic process that can proceed with varying speeds, but the practice of mental health in the new millennium does not support this awareness. Length of therapy is dictated by insurance approval. Agencies that constantly fight for financial survival cannot afford to give generous treatment packages. Psychotherapy (if we can even call it that now) is measured in weeks rather than months or years. Yet, trauma, by definition, encompasses relational damage. If our trauma clients have complex trauma, and most of them do, we are looking at years of profound relational damage that can only be turned around by developing a genuine caring and therapeutic relationship over a period of time that is more likely to be years than weeks. This process, like a pregnancy, cannot be rushed. The client above needed nine months just to feel like she could trust the therapist enough to begin therapy. Nine months is not such a long time in treatment, despite insurance reimbursement schedules. One client, a survivor of mind control and torture, needed nine years to develop consistent trust in their therapist.

First Sessions

By the time traumatized clients arrive at our office, they have already made an assessment about us based on our website, our pictures, our writings, and word of mouth. They take an enormous risk in coming to us at all. They entrust to us their most shattered sense of self, their deepest traumas, and their fragile hopes for recovery. All trauma patients have attachment damage from previous relationships. Many have also been let down by medical as well as psychiatric facilities. The betrayal of these clients by well-meaning but trauma-ignorant systems creates yet another level of relational wounding in their psyche.

The client gleans much information about the therapist in the first few minutes of a session. Their awareness of the therapist's qualities begins with the space. Is the space warm and comfortable? Accessible? Does the client have clear directions to the building's parking and transportation? Do we provide an orientation to the building and practice? How is the lighting on the way in? Are there any unsafe spots where folks could be triggered or endangered, such as a dark bathroom located at the end of an empty hallway? Are there handicap accommodations? Is there a separate entrance and exit? There doesn't have to be, but if there is, the client may want to know ahead of time. Is the space clean and cared for, or are the plants dying and the carpet needs vacuuming?

How we greet our client matters. We can be stiff and formal or warm and welcoming. We can smile or not. We can dress in fancy expensive clothing, revealing clothing, or plain clothing. *We demonstrate our warmth and attunement to the client, or lack thereof, upon first sight.* Traumatized clients know immediately if we do not like them or feel scared by them. They will probably worry about rejection and abuse throughout the duration of therapy, even if they know we care about them.

Rogerian congruence and transparency[2] in the therapy session alleviates anxiety in clients with a traumatized neurobiology (Geller, 2001). Relationally anxious clients need to have some idea of what we are thinking and feeling in order to feel safe to do the work. If our client smiles at us and we do not smile back, what have we just communicated in terms of attunement? In terms of equality of power? Of friendliness? We need to be forthcoming in answering questions to empower our clients without violating their boundaries or our own. If we advertise ourselves as a trauma specialist, we need to be prepared to answer why and how that is to the satisfaction of our consumer, the client. They have a right to know. Too often therapists take the rule of opaqueness to mean they do not have to answer even basic questions about their practice. Clients can see this type of therapist as a threat or even as predatory.

Let us take a moment to acknowledge that some therapists are, in fact, predatory. They are few, but they are out in the community practicing until their license is challenged. We may be in denial about this reality, but our clients, who have suffered multiple betrayals, are not. The field of therapy does not have a corner on psychological functionality (would that it were so!). Some therapists have personality disorders. New therapists may need training before they are ready to take on clients with heavy trauma histories. Some therapists actually have intent to harm. I once evaluated a survivor of cult and child pornography abuse who reported that their criminally involved mother was a licensed therapist in the community.

Competent trauma therapists encourage a match assessment by their clients. If a therapist is narcissistically injured or defensive when a new client has some questions about their qualifications, perhaps a highly traumatized clientele is not the population for them. We should never assume that we are so good, experienced, or famous that our clients do not have the right to ask us to demonstrate our credentials. Trauma therapists should be prepared to answer these questions:

- **To which professional organizations do you belong?**

  Professional groups provide leadership, advocacy, and ongoing education to their members in specific areas of practice. Consider joining the International Society for the Study of Trauma and Dissociation (ISSTD), the Institute for Traumatic Stress Studies (ISTSS), the American Professional Psychology Division 56 (Division of Trauma Psychology), or others to maintain your highest level of knowledge and training.

- **Do you have any special certification or training in trauma therapy?**

  One form this can take is specialized supervision over a period of time (such as in licensure supervision or a fellowship) with a supervisor who is a trauma expert. Another is through certification programs, such as the one offered by ISSTD. They offer a 72-hour Certificate or 100-hour Advanced Certificate in Complex Trauma and Dissociation.[3] Or you can apply for a specialty certification for training and experience already accomplished. The American Academy of Experts in Traumatic Stress certify practitioners in a number of traumatic specialty areas including crisis response, children, etc., based on career accomplishments and the number of years of trauma work.

- **Do you understand and treat PTSD and/or dissociative disorders?**

  While technically we are qualified as mental health professionals to treat any disorder in the *DSM 5*, full and transparent disclosure requires that we acknowledge our level of expertise in any given area. If a client asks this sophisticated question, one can assume that they are looking for a higher than average level of knowledge from their practitioner. We need to be totally honest about our level of training and competence. Examples of good answers would be, "Yes, I'm trained in PTSD but I do not have a great deal of experience with dissociative disorders," or "I am working with a supervisor to help me understand and become more expert in this area." If you are one of the minority of therapists out there that 'do not believe in dissociative disorders', please do not treat these clients. You may end up doing more harm than good.[4]

- **Have you experienced PTSD? Have you been in therapy?**

  These are totally fair questions. Like me, you may have been trained to deflect such personal questions in order to maintain 'neutrality' with statements like, "tell me why you want to know" or "what would it mean to you if I have or haven't?" Until my own experience with PTSD, I thought these were reasonable responses. I no longer do. PTSD and dissociative disorders are such extreme conditions that they alter a client's reality. If you have experienced these conditions, you already know where your client is; if you have not, there are not enough words that can convey the experience. Your client may want you to understand in a visceral way, or they may not want you to. That decision is up to them, not us. Allow them to create their own safety by choosing the type of therapist that works best for them. Prior to PTSD, I would have worked with any therapist that I liked and felt was knowledgeable enough. After the emergence of PTSD, I could never work with a therapist who had not had at least a taste of that experience; the gulf of understanding is too vast to bridge in order for me to feel helped. If the therapist has trauma that they are actively repressing, they may unconsciously discourage client disclosure to protect their own sense of self. So, please answer the question in an appropriate way. All of my clients, for example, know that I have suffered from PTSD (it is a matter of public record), but they don't know how or why. Revealing that you have been in treatment is important to clients as well. There was a time when nearly every therapist was in their own therapy. This is no longer the case; very few of the students and social work candidates I have supervised have had much time 'on the couch'. Our clients deserve to know if we understand what their side of the room feels like and whether we have done our inner work.

Congruence with web presentation is important. If we are smiling and warm in our picture online but cold and unsmiling when the client arrives, we are going to freak them out! Try to keep your website current and reflective of you and your practice as it is now. Our traumatized clients are hypersensitive to incongruity and are consciously or unconsciously scanning the environment for evidence of danger and betrayal. Don't give them more reasons to be worried.

One of my early supervisors, the venerable Stephen O'Neill, LICSW, BCD, JD, used to say, "Your patient will tell you everything you need to know about them in the first five minutes." Wise therapists know how to observe carefully during beginnings. They make no sudden moves, literally and metaphorically. Everything, every movement, every word, every facial expression, means something in the therapy hour. We therapists get to put on our Sherlock Holmes hat and discover our clients through attunement, observation, and connection. When done well, this can be a fun dance where our client feels deeply seen, heard, and understood.

Trauma clients often want to spill all the beans or spill no beans early in therapy depending on their ego defense styles. Clients test our ability to be the 'good mother' early. They need to know if we can contain them when their traumas explode out of control, or if we can move them out of frozen psychic immobility when they are stuck. Early sessions demonstrate our capacity (or lack of capacity) to elicit information in a way that harmonizes and strengthens the internal functioning of the client while optimizing neurofunctioning. If we can strengthen and soothe our clients' neurobiology by regulating their pace of disclosure without being bossy or oppositional, we will pass muster and create the beginnings of a warm, effective container for the work.

Sometimes we get into a first session and really do not like what we see. Don't waste your client's time! If you realize that you have an intense countertransference reaction—scared, disgusted, repulsed, or just feel like you are not up to the task, you are obliged to let your client know as soon as possible that you do not feel qualified to treat them, and make the appropriate referral. If you decide not to treat a client, go out of your way to not shame or humiliate them and always take ownership of the situation. You can say something like, "I am not sure I am the best person to help you with _____. My colleague _____ specializes in cases like yours." Avoid the temptation to make them bad or wrong in this type of situation. Remember, the clients we do not want to treat are another therapist's bread and butter. There is no such thing as a bad client, only a bad fit.

Therapist Attachment Styles

Every person comes to the career of mental health with vastly differing relational skill sets. Therapists styles of attunement and attachment manifest in the therapy hour. If therapists have received depth therapy and supervision, they may be able to identify their own styles and hindrances to forming solid attachments with clients. In the current climate of mental health treatment, though, I fear that many therapists have skipped this essential understanding of themselves in favor of more mechanistic treatments. Because modern supervision often pays more attention to administrative duties than insight (if one receives clinical supervision at all), it is possible that many newer therapists lack the self-awareness of previous generations of therapists.

All treatments take place in the milieu of relationship, however objective we fancy ourselves to be. Through the lens of attachment work we find that there is no neutral ground. We have our own attachment styles that interact with our clients' attachment styles. In the model presented below we are on the grid, not outside of it. In fact, the very fantasy of being 'objective' may reflect a dismissive-avoidant pattern of relational thinking. In order to engage in an authentic relational way we need to let go of the ideas of objectivity and a static reality. Every interaction we have with our clients gives both of us an opportunity to shift. Relationships move; they dance. We start in one place with our dance partner and move to another, together. When we can join our clients where they are on the dance floor of relationship, this therapeutic movement gains grace. In order to join them we need to know where we are in the dance, ourselves.

The British psychoanalyst John Bowlby (1907–1990) developed a theory of attachment based on his observations of infants and their parents (usually mothers). He noticed that the child developed certain styles of attachment based on the responsiveness of the parent. These styles became ingrained in the personality and formed the basis of attachment in all subsequent relationships, especially romantic and intimate ones. The initial basic styles of attachment described were secure, anxious, and avoidant. Hazen and Shaver (1987) developed a questionnaire that helped people assess these styles by marking which one they felt described them best:

A. I am somewhat uncomfortable being close to others; I find it difficult to trust them completely, difficult to allow myself to depend on them. I am nervous when anyone gets too close, and often, others want me to be more intimate than I feel comfortable being.
B. I find it relatively easy to get close to others and am comfortable depending on them and having them depend on me. I don't worry about being abandoned or about someone getting too close to me.
C. I find that others are reluctant to get as close as I would like. I often worry that my partner doesn't really love me or won't want to stay with me. I want to get very close to my partner, and this sometimes scares people away (Hazen & Shaver, 1987).

In 1998, Kelly Brennan, Catherine Clark, and Phillip Shaver expanded on this work by developing the Experience in Close Relationship (ECR) questionnaire. The ECR measures relationship attachment along two axes: anxiety and avoidance. In addition to Bowlby's secure, anxious, and avoidant categories, they have added the complexity of mixtures as developed by Richard Fraley (Fraley, 2010), seen in Figure 4.1.

Combining the two axes of avoidance and anxiety now gives us four attachment styles: secure (low avoidance, low anxiety), preoccupied (low avoidance, high anxiety), dismissing avoidant (low anxiety, high avoidance) and fearful-avoidant (high avoidance, high anxiety).

In her Strange Situation Study researched with babies and mothers, Mary Main described a style of attachment that she labeled 'disorganized' which would correspond to the fearful-avoidant category. The Strange Situation involved the mother leaving her child in a room with a researcher and then returning to the young child. She and her colleagues observed that sometimes the young child would exhibit behaviors indicating that their mother was frightening to them. Children, left alone, normally want comfort from their parents when they return. If the parent is frightening, they are caught in an unresolvable paradox of high anxiety and high avoidance yet needing comfort. These children would exhibit mixed diverse behaviors that were confusing and

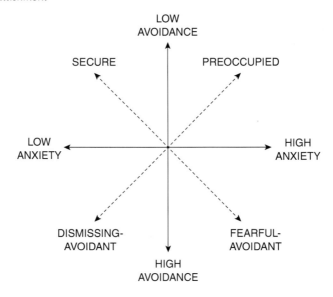

Figure 4.1 Attachment Styles

then scary to the researchers when they realized how frightened, disorganized, and in some cases, dissociated, these children were. Surprisingly, she found that from 8–15% of the children in her research fell into the disorganized category.

By definition, very few trauma clients fall into the secure category. Trauma ruptures attachment. Always. It is the nature of trauma to sever connections of the heart, mind, and spirit. Scary abusive parents cause various degrees of attachment disruption in their children. Even if we have grown up in a secure family environment, traumas can disrupt attachment in other ways. Environmental catastrophes disrupt the security felt in nature; court cases gone awry can ruin a person's faith in government; spiritual abuses rupture faith in God. To reestablish any sort of attachment is to create a healing space in the mind and a focal point of hope for repair.

But what happens when the therapist has their own attachment problems? It might be ideal if therapists would obtain what is called by Dan Siegel, MD, 'earned secure attachment' (a fifth attachment style) before practicing therapy (Siegel, 2010). He noticed that some people could start out with attachment disruption and then experience corrective relationships, in therapy or in mindfulness practices, that heal the neurobiology of disrupted attachment. Being able to reflect in an organized way on traumatic experiences, otherwise known as the capacity to 'mentalize', is a crucial skill that leads to healing. Theoretically, the healed therapist can then pass on the healing to the client by providing a secure base for the client to whom they can attach.

Practically speaking, that is not what happens. Clients often help therapists to heal in the course of therapy by stimulating unhealed material in the therapist. We therapists might start the download of secure attachment sooner, but we are still downloading our own health as we help others heal. Wise therapists will tell you that they attract clients who mirror the therapist's own healing needs.

Let's look at the impact of attachment styles in the therapist and how that might affect the therapy of traumatized folks with a range of attachment abilities. Since attachment styles are part of the personality, there is no one right way to be. When we know where we fall on the attachment spectrum, we can know our strengths and weaknesses when paired with other, different styles. I do not know of any research, as of yet, into this topic, but we could make some hypotheses about how different attachment styles of the therapist affect the client. Join me in this thought experiment and by all means add your own ideas to the mix.

Let's start with the securely attached therapist. This therapist does not know what shaky attachment feels like at a deep level and grew up in a loving nonabusive household. They may tend to underestimate the suffering of their clients, since it is not an experience they themselves have had. They may not understand the length of time needed to repair relational suffering nor how their clients scrutinize them for signs of rejection. The downside of this type of therapist might be pleasant cluelessness. On the other hand, they are not shaken easily. They have a steadfast ability in themselves to be kind and supportive under many different circumstances and may not be beholden to emotional manipulation on the part of their clients. They may be able to hold a containing space in the face of client rejection. Toxic transference, however, may be mystifying to them until they have enough supervision to understand the basis of rejection by the client. They might be the least likely of all the types to have an anxious presentation as a therapist (except maybe those with an earned secure attachment), although if there is repeated empathic failure with their clients, performance anxiety as a therapist could develop.

Because the therapist has the upper hand that comes with status in all the interactions in the therapy attachment, attachment issues in the therapist may be less stimulated than in personal relationships, but they are not eliminated. A therapist with a 'preoccupied', or low avoidance, high anxiety style of attachment will be probably be fairly comfortable with conflict and confrontation in the therapy. They might be great at broaching topics that other therapists might hesitate voicing. Because this type of therapist's unconscious underlying anxiety of being abandoned by the client is mitigated by the obvious need that the client has for the therapist, they may be more comfortable with the 'needy' client. The more needy the client, the safer and more competent this type of therapist may feel in the relationship. In that safety, attachment issues stabilize, and they can be great therapists who are comfortable with a wide range of issues in therapy. These therapists intuitively know how to pursue and create attachment with their clients. The downsides of this style may be a tendency to overwork, overschedule, and overrespond to their clients' needs. In an extreme case, they might welcome phone calls (texts, etc.) at all hours of the day or night. They might become more panicky at the thought of high-risk behaviors such as drug use, promiscuity, or self-harm. This type of therapist might also be in denial about when their clients feel abandoned by them. The thought of abandoning a client as a therapist pains the preoccupied type so much that they might minimize the effect of their vacations, illnesses, or other potential attachment ruptures in the treatment on the client. They also might be hypersensitive to signs that the client is critical of them or pulling away in the therapy. (Let me state here that any of the 'weaknesses' of the types can become strengths with good training and supervision. 'Hypersensitivity', for example, is a highly sought-after skill if it is not made into a personal issue. Can there really be such a thing as 'too sensitive' if it is not a narcissistic issue?) Negative countertransference can be a need to be reassured that they are doing a good job and that the client is getting better, which both allays and stimulates the unconscious fear that the client may abandon them—allays in that they believe the client will stay in therapy out of feeling attached to the therapist, and stimulated by the fact that when clients get better they leave therapy. They may unwittingly reward a client for regression or stepping back into therapy. When the client leans out, they lean in.

What about the therapist who has a dismissive-avoidant style? At first glance it might seem that this person is not a good candidate to self-select for being a psychotherapist. When I reflect on over 40 years in the field, I can recollect several of these types of therapists (often psychiatrists) that fall into this category. And it does make sense. The quest to be a great therapist is, for many of us, a quest for healing—whether we are conscious or unconscious of this fact. Dismissive-avoidant types can be very good at the clinical/analytic distance required for therapeutic observation and analysis. They do not tend to be sucked into drama and can easily engage their rational mind for the purposes of treatment. Their low anxiety can make them wonderful to sit with as clients. They can be drawn to academia. Yet, there may be a tendency for disdain towards their needier clients. They may feel easily overwhelmed by clients that pursue them and set very rigid boundaries with clients that leave their clients wondering who they really are and if the therapist can understand their traumas.

At an extreme end, therapists with a dismissive-avoidant style may be perceived as 'cold fish' or even have a shut-down perpetrator-like affect that is off-putting to highly relationally disrupted individuals. It is possible that people with these attachment types may self-select for providing some of the briefer, more mechanistic types of treatment and may be more rewarded by the short-term forms of mental health that insurance companies currently support. Countertransference for these therapists may take the form of blaming the client for difficulties in the therapy and becoming more remote as the patient becomes more needy. Also, because of the low anxiety in this attachment pattern, the therapist may not even be aware that they have attachment issues at all, unless they have done a great deal of work on themselves. Unlike the preoccupied type that is all too keenly aware of their issues and their anxiety, it is easy for this group to maintain a high status and invulnerable feeling about themselves that can be wrongly labeled as 'self-esteem' or 'achievement'. In a dance opposite that of the preoccupied therapist, when the client leans in, this type of therapist leans out.

At first glance it seems unlikely that a person with an actively 'disorganized' attachment type would succeed in becoming a therapist. This highly anxious style coupled with the highly avoidant style would not seem to make for a pleasant training experience and could make the process of becoming a clinician feel intolerable. Over the course of my career, I have seen some of these folks in lower-level human service positions. They usually struggle greatly and can have disruptive effects on the people around them, clients and staff alike, depending on their temperament and other factors. Often they are remanded to therapy by wise supervisors. On the other hand, a person who begins life with this type of attachment style, does a great deal of work on themselves, and 'graduates' to earned secure attachment might make the best clinician of all. She might be able to understand great depths of human suffering and be especially mindful of how attachment proceeds in the therapy. This type of therapist may be especially adept at working with folks who are psychotic, extremely vulnerable, incarcerated, or prone to substance abuse. They may persevere when other therapists would give up and/or refer out because they know the terrain of the journey and can see hope where others get overwhelmed.

Ideally, any therapist with an early disrupted attachment pattern would be working towards and eventually achieve an earned secure attachment. I suspect that many of us are drawn towards counseling as a career because of the safety of the practice of therapy itself as a relationship container. And this is as it should be. To use an analogy of physical trainers, would you rather see a perfectly buff '10' personal trainer who came by their athletic body naturally and without injury, or the trainer who has had numerous injuries and issues they've had to work through? Who is more relatable? Who will be more sympathetic to and knowledgeable about your more average or injured body?

There is a place for all of the different attachment styles in therapists. Historically we have been so focused on our clients' issues that we forget about our own. In treating relationally disrupted people with traumas, we cannot afford this level of ignorance. Areas of relational disruption in therapists will definitely be noticed, probed, and possibly exploited by clients who test us to see if we can bear the burden of their suffering. We need to be able to respond in ways that benefit both them and us.

Attunement

Attunement may be the most important skill for a trauma therapist. Richard Erskine, PhD, defines attunement as a two-part process. He says, "It involves both being fully aware of another person's sensations, needs, or feelings and communicating that awareness to the other" (Erskine, 1993). How we develop that awareness depends on our personality, temperament, and training. As with any skill, some therapists come to attunement more naturally than others. As a supervisor, I find that there are many different paths to attunement for clinicians. Knowing the paramount importance of attunement in the therapy hour is the first step. The second is knowing that no matter how attuned you think you are, you can always be attuned more consistently and in deeper ways.

All failures in parenting, child abuse, neglect, interpersonal violence, and other interpersonal traumas occur in a state of non-attunement to the needs of the other. For many people who have grown up with high ACEs scores, lack of attunement characterized their daily experience. Children cannot adapt well to an environment that is not attuned to them. Primates require the longest care in upbringing of all animals, and humans require the most emotional care of any of the primates. Our brain simply cannot develop well in all of its social-emotional-intellectual complexity without well-attuned parenting. Severe lack of attunement results in catastrophic social and emotional failure for the human being; in extreme cases it can result in physical failure to thrive, psychosis, or even death.

Attunement styles come in all shapes and colors. You can mix and match! As a therapist who started out traditionally and then moved into more shamanic modes of healing, I have found that there really is no end to the depth and breadth of attunement possible. I call this 'running broadband'. As beginning therapists we start out with a very narrow bandwidth of awareness; we move from conventional content-based conversation to process awareness. Depending on our skill sets, we may be more intellectual or more empathic. We may be more or less receptive to visual, auditory, or kinesthetic cues in our clients. We may possess the ability to maintain presence for long periods of time or we may be distractible. As we progress in self-awareness and develop skills, we become able to process large amounts of multidimensional information from our clients and can attune at subtler levels, giving our clients a deep feeling of being understood.

Presence and Mindfulness

Sitting with a client really constitutes a type of single-pointed meditation. Our focus needs to be on them and everything about them with a minimum of distraction in our thoughts. Very few of us have had the opportunity to sit with a quiet-minded, kind person who is focused only on us. It is an extraordinary experience wherever it happens, in an ashram, in a therapist's office, or at a dinner party. We tend to remember those experiences very clearly because they are so rare. Presence nurtures us. It heals us in ineffable ways. Cultivating the ability to have presence is a wisdom practice in and of itself. Being present with a client also means to be present to self. If we are paying attention to the client but neglecting our own feelings and internal stirrings, we are missing half of the equation! If we are putting all of our attention on the client while neglecting our own being, we cannot glean the information to be fully attuned to our client. Many therapists were never really taught to attend to themselves while attending to others. We tend to be talking heads, not only as therapists but also in our culture as a whole. Our entire educational system is geared towards the brain and not the body.

I know of no better way to develop presence in the office than through mindfulness practice. Meditation and mindfulness practices literally grow the parts of the brain responsible for attunement, presence, and awareness. Yogis, monks, and shamans have known this from time out of mind. Neuroscience is just beginning to catch up. Cultivate mindful presence and watch your attunement skills take a huge jump!

Observational Skills

How keen are your powers of observation? How would you know if you are observant or oblivious? Do you challenge yourself to keep growing in your abilities to observe, or do you, like most people, assume that you know what you need to know and see what you need to see? We are conditioned from early childhood not to see too much about other people, both by our culture and by our own aversion to seeing things about people that might make us feel disgusted or unsafe.

The basic training to become a therapist helps us to undo social convention, to inquire into areas that we would not venture in polite company. We learn to violate strongly held social norms that we grew up with, discuss taboo topics, and encourage our clients to do the same. We are encouraged to look closely at our patients' body language and even comment on it. If we are medical social workers, we are trained to look for physical changes and symptoms so that we can help our clients stay up to date on their medical treatment.

As trauma therapists, we need to become intimately familiar with the terrain of trauma in the body and mind and how it manifests in gross to subtle ways in our clients. A too immobile face can be holding back a dam of emotions. Dark circles under the eyes can indicate environmental sensitivities, a lack of sleep, or both. Eyes flicking up and back can indicate a subtle switch in personalities or emotional parts. Our clients may sigh with relief when they feel comfortable with us; their stomach may gurgle when the parasympathetic nervous system achieves 'rest and digest' dominance. We may hear a change in pitch and tone of voice as the client wanders into a childhood memory. Even more subtly, a stereotypical or repetitive motion may give away a traumatic body memory or be an attempt at communication from a hidden small part of the self. The more we attend to these cues, engaging our curiosity and kindness, the greater the potential level of attunement we can achieve with our clients.

Perceptual Modes

We know that people process information in three basic modes: visual, auditory, and kinesthetic. When we meet them in their perceptual processing style they feel deeply engaged and understood. If someone is highly visual we may communicate our understanding as "I see." If they are auditory we may say, "I hear you," or if kinesthetic, "I feel that". When we want to communicate an important concept, we can couch our analogies in the terms that work best for them. "Imagine a picture where . . ." We may ask questions that elicit their preferred mode, "Where in your body do you feel that sadness", for example, if they are kinesthetic. Or give a prompt such as, "what does the voice of your conscience sound like" if they are primarily auditory.

Since traumatic states are so strongly linked to perceptual input, it is vital to know which processing systems we are accessing with them and why. If you are a primarily visual thinker, it can be deeply frustrating to be asked how you feel. This mismatch of styles can be experienced as a lack of attunement of the therapist. In addition, due to the trauma experienced, a client may have a strong aversion to a particular processing area. You can make this awareness part of your assessment and intervention strategy. Over time, as the patient heals they will become more neurologically flexible.

Easily corrected misattunements may arise simply from the fact that the client may not be operating out of the same set of processing preferences that we are. So, physician, know thyself! What are your primary, secondary, and tertiary modes of information processing? Which of these do you find yourself saying more often, "I feel," "I see," or "I hear that . . ."? It can be tricky to perceptually be operating in one mode but verbally be operating in another. This ability requires a great deal of neural flexibility on the part of the therapist that gets better with practice.

Engagement and Communication

Lastly, attunement involves engagement and communication with the client. We can be highly observant, a veritable Sherlock Holmes, but if we cannot reflect back our observations in a way that is helpful to the client, they will not feel engaged to no matter how brilliant we are. And this is where we part way with dear Sherlock, because nobody ever accused him of being highly attuned to his clients. To be a greatly attuned trauma therapist we need to have the observation of the detective, but the empathy of Mother Teresa.

We can come to attunement through many paths: intellectual, emotional, empathic, and spiritual. An intellectual therapist with a narrow emotional range and little to no capacity for psychic empathy can deduce through observation and theoretical thinking what a client is experiencing and reflect that back to them. A skilled emotional observer can understand what clients are feeling through the resonance in their own limbic brains. A highly empathic therapist may not need any thought process at all to know what a client is feeling or even thinking. Some therapists have an almost mystical capacity to know not only what a patient is experiencing, but also what is required for healing in that moment.

It is important that we share our perceptions with our trauma clients, no matter how we arrive at them. Dissociation from traumatic experiences can be so extreme as to make our patients feel like they aren't even 'real'. An attuned, nonjudgmental therapist not only grounds this type of client but makes them feel accepted and understood in their deepest and youngest parts of self. In doing so, we therapists have an opportunity to provide the needed 'corrective emotional experience' that was lacking in their traumatized states, love. Attuned love may be the most organizing and healing force in the universe. Can you think of another?

Notes

1 In *The Trauma Tool Kit*, feeling and releasing is described as the fourth stage of healing from trauma following trauma shock, rebooting, and acceptance.
2 Rogerian person-centered therapy made genuineness, congruence, and transparency a cornerstone of effective treatment, long before the field of trauma emerged.
3 You can find more information about ISSTD's program here: www.isst-d.org/default.asp?contentID=187
4 I've actually heard mental health professionals say this or a variation on it, like "I don't believe that ritual abuse exists." As professionals, we do not get to cherry-pick the disorders that we like or do not like in the *DSM*. If it is in there, and our clients fit the criteria, we must diagnose them or we are committing malpractice. Can you imagine such a thing in the medical field? (e.g., "I don't believe in mitral valve disorders.") We also do not get to arbitrate reality, no matter what you may read in the newspapers. If you cannot accept the reality of ritual abuse, then don't work with these client populations. There are plenty of professionals who excel in these areas.

References

Erskine, R. (1993, October). *Inquiry, Attunement, and Involvement in the Psychotherapy of Dissociation*. Retrieved December 6, 2017, from Institute for Integrative Psychotherapy: www.integrativetherapy.com/en/articles.php?id=28

Fraley, R. C. (2010). *A Brief Overview of Adult Attachment Theory and Research*. Retrieved December 6, 2017, from https://internal.psychology.illinois.edu/~rcfraley/attachment.htm

Geller, L. G. (2001). *Congruence and Therapeutic Presence*. Retrieved September 18, 2017, from www.sharigeller.ca/_images/pdfs/Congruence_proofs.pdf

Hazen, C., & Shaver, P. (1987). Romantic love conceptualized as an attachment process. *Journal of Personality and Social Psychology, 52*(3), 511 524.

Herman, J. (1997). *Traum and Recovery: The Aftermath of Violence—From Domestic Abuse to Political Terror*. New York, NY: Basic Books.

Pease Banitt, S. (2012). *The Trauma Tool Kit: Healing PTSD From the Inside Out*. Wheaton, IL: Quest Books.

Siegel, D. (2010). *The Mindful Therapist: A Clinician's Guide to Mindsight and Neural Integration*. New York, NY: W.W. Norton.

5 Preventing Relationship Rupture
Countertransference and Thresholds

The most functional way to regulate difficult emotions in love relationships is to share them.

—Dr. Sue Johnson, Love Sense (2013)

Attachment can fail or not even take hold in therapy with highly traumatized and relationally disrupted people. Despite well-meaning therapists' best efforts, many trauma clients have had the unfortunate experience of feeling misunderstood, unhelped, and even demeaned in their treatments. In my practice, the average trauma client has been through two or three therapists before seeking out a trauma expert. Because all traumatic experience includes profound attachment ruptures in myriad relationships such as to self, other, nature, government, society, and/or spirituality, it is inevitable that therapy for the traumatized client will undergo the parallel process of relationship rupture. How this rupture is handled is crucial to the full recovery of the client. Many ruptures, however, are unnecessary and due to a lack of experience or preparation on the part of the therapist. Therapists may be unaware that they have thresholds of affect tolerance and belief that affect their ability to stay present to their clients' experiences. This chapter will explore the concept of thresholds and categories of thresholds in the therapist that can cause problems with secure attachment for the client: horror, paranormal, indigenous reality, religious, government/military practices, cults, organized crime, and abuse belief thresholds.

Relational Capacity

Every person has a different natural ability to create and maintain relationships with others. Therapists come to the mental health profession with their own strengths and deficit areas in relationship building. Ideally, therapist education and training would bolster interpersonal strengths and (gently) expose deficits, but relational skill building is often no longer a focus of modern training programs. Many clinical programs assume relational skills and focus on diagnosis, assessment, and 'evidence-based' techniques.

The movement from long-term therapy to short-term therapy attracts a different type of person to be a clinician. In short-term, task-focused therapy work, the ability to create and maintain long-term connection is just not necessary. This type of therapeutic work might, in fact, be attracting a different kind of personality as a therapist than the clinicians of past decades who would see patients for 4–6 years rather than 4–6 weeks.

The needs of folks suffering from complex trauma, dissociative disorders, and PTSD cannot be satisfied in short-term treatment. They demand highly skilled therapists who exhibit relational capacity and who are committed to the therapy for the duration. *Relational capacity in psychotherapy is the therapist's ability to help people form and maintain safe, attached relationships in therapy over a long period of time.* Sounds easy. In practice, it is very difficult to maintain, especially with a population that is inherently attachment impaired, is injured, or might seek to sabotage the attachment consciously or unconsciously.

What is difficult about developing relational capacity is that it is a very personal process, totally different for each person. Techniques are so much easier to look at than interpersonal dynamics. We all take our relationships personally; our ego is entwined with our personality, and we have a great deal of difficulty being asked to grow our relationship skills, especially if we consider ourselves to be a more 'advanced' clinician. Relational capacity does not automatically increase with time and experience in the saddle. It may or may not. *Relational capacity increases with awareness of self and other.* Ironically, one of the best ways to increase awareness is through mistakes, failures of empathy and connection that the therapist actively and consciously repairs in the course of therapy. When mistakes are handled with humility and empathy, both parties get a chance to evolve and the relationship evolves with them.

In the recent TV drama, *Westworld*, robots become sentient through trauma and mistakes on the part of their programmers. Dr. Robert Ford, their creator, discusses this process with his protégé, Bernard:

> "Mistakes" is the word you're too embarrassed to use. You ought not to be. You're a product of a trillion of them. Evolution forged the entirety of sentient life on this planet using only one tool: the mistake.
>
> (Joy & Nolan, 2016)

Who loves a good mistake? Nobody. (Ok, maybe a well-trained improvisational comedian or an exceptionally bold therapist.) Of course, the existential fear underlying mistakes is fear of death—death of one's self-concept, death of the relationship, death of one's business, or just plain old death. And there is a real risk of death during the course of therapy for some highly traumatized folks. Many of the clients we treat become seriously suicidal at a certain point in their healing, and, in some cases, remain suicidal throughout much of their healing. Others of these clients fantasize about homicide or get very close to killing or seriously endangering people in their lives. Or we may work in settings where people have already killed or threatened to harm themselves or others. Some of the people we work with have trauma from life-threatening illnesses. Whenever we work with people who live with the specter of death on a daily basis, mistakes assume a ghastly dimension that can cast an anxious pall over our work. What if we end up making a mistake that hurts or kills someone?

For traumatized clients, fear of mistakes is profound. Often abuse is blamed on mistakes by themselves or by their abusers (e.g., "If you had just done what I said, I wouldn't have to . . ."). Children completely accept blame because they cannot cognitively conceive of a world where everything isn't about them. Even for adults, it is sometimes easier to blame a trauma on a mistake than face the unpredictability and seeming randomness of the universe (e.g., "If I had left earlier I would not have been in this terrible car accident"). Clients may have little tolerance for their own or others' mistakes. Errors by either party can create shame spirals that send them down the drain of dysfunction for days to weeks, torpedoing the therapeutic alliance in their wake.

By definition, our traumatized clients have been the victims of some serious and life-threatening 'mistakes'. If we do not completely cognize this fact as therapists, we do unconsciously sense it, which can create a feeling of anxiety in the treatment on the part of both treater and client. The stakes are higher when mistakes can be seen as relationally threatening. Add to this heightened sense a client who is actively self-harming and suicidal and we can have a toxic brew stewing in the therapy, where the therapist either feels like they need to be perfect or needs to care less by denigrating the relationship with the client or even the client themselves. None of these, of course, are helpful options, but they are common dynamics that surface in trauma therapies.

Relational capacity in a therapist grows by owning and navigating the inevitable misattunements, subtle acting out, and plain old misunderstandings that are a part of any relationship. Trauma treatment that includes and acknowledges mistakes that are repaired in the course of treatment has stronger healing potential than therapies where mistakes are ignored or where the therapist feels they have to be so perfect that mistakes are never made. (No rational therapist would assert that such a thing is possible, and yet so many behave as if it is.)

Equally important to relational repair is the ability of the therapist to maintain connection and attunement throughout disclosures of difficult material. This area separates the ordinary therapists from trauma therapists. Being a big enough pain container to hear and work with any type of disclosure is not for the faint of heart or the least trained among us. Most of my client referrals result from the failure of a therapist to hear, respond, believe, and contain hugely disturbing stories from their clients. Nothing shuts down attunement and connection faster than not being believed or noticing that your therapist is 'checking out' (dissociating) when sharing one's most pivotal trauma story. Wise therapists know how to respond to disclosures in an attuned and empathic way.

Hearing Disclosures

Our clients' assessment of a therapist's ability to hear and respond appropriately to disclosures occurs early, often in the initial contact. How the therapist responds can either help or injure the client and can foster or destroy an emerging alliance. Two recent new therapy contacts come to mind.

The first was a mother who strongly suspected her young child had been recently molested. She had called me to inquire about openings and insurance. When she told me her suspicion, I immediately responded with the statement that I was very sorry that this had happened to their family and wanted to know exactly what services she would find helpful. The woman burst into tears and expressed gratitude that I believed her. I asked her why she thought that my response was extraordinary, and she replied that the previous therapist contacted had become suspicious of her and her story on the very first call. This client did not end up working with me because I do not take insurance, but she still left the phone call in extreme gratitude that I took her story at face value and was not looking to find fault with her. Hopefully she left with a bit of a corrective emotional experience as well. I would like to think that the experience of this client not being believed and treated with suspicion is an anomaly, but I have to say I hear stories like this on a regular basis from clients seeking services.

Why is a suspicious or even a 'neutral' response so problematic? Let's go back to thinking about attachment. When a human being, or any mammal, is in pain, the first need is for connection with aid. The members of the tribe or herd usually move towards the being in need and offer what help they can— emotional and/or physical. The more a client experiences distress, the more urgent is the need for connection and the possibility for healing through that connection. *Our response to a client in need is never neutral to the client.* From the client's perspective, a neutral response to a trauma disclosure can be abandoning. You are either on their team or against them. This is normal. Let me repeat that again. It is completely normal for a person in traumatic crisis to perceive a therapist's response as binary: joining or abandoning. This is the nature of crisis. If it were not a crisis, an immediate response would not be necessary, by definition.

Therapists who have been trained in crisis intervention work understand this dynamic need for joining immediately. Many do not have this training. These therapists may resist believing client's stories and feel that they need to take a neutral stance. Some have even been trained this way. But neutrality is not trauma-informed. At its worst neutrality can even look like perpetration. Sociopaths do not respond with empathy; if we, as therapists, do not respond with empathy in a crisis disclosure, we risk triggering the client with our 'sociopathic' response.

Let me unpack what I mean when I say, "believe your client", by saying what I do not mean. I do not mean that we should think that the client is 100% correct or that they remember everything that happened or that their story will never change. What I mean is that we should extend to them the same courtesy and empathy we would for any disclosure. If, for example, you have dinner with a friend and they are telling you that they ate roast beef for dinner last night, you would believe them, right? If, later, they remembered that they ate chicken and not roast beef, you wouldn't hold it against them or think that they had some kind of agenda to fool you. If they went on to tell you that they got food poisoning and were going to sue the restaurant, you wouldn't ask them for proof or suggest that maybe they were exaggerating (even if you thought they were, because . . . friends). Even if this person were not your friend, but someone you met at a dinner party, a complete stranger, you would not take it upon yourself to question their story or their judgment or pick apart their wording. That would be just, well, rude. So, why do this as a therapist? Responding to disclosures appropriately is very easy and costs you or your client nothing. But an inappropriately unempathic or abandoning response can not only foil attachment with you as a treater but also potentially foil *any relationship with any treater for that client by creating a secondary trauma on top of the original one.*

In this woman's case, not only was she derailed in her attempt to get appropriate help for her child by being confronted with an abandoning response, but it was even worse in that she felt that she, herself, had come under suspicion! Fortunately, her maternal and loving need to get help for her child outweighed the emotional need she had to feel safe and understood. As treaters who first 'do no harm', we really should not be putting people in the position where they might stop seeking help, especially when there are children involved.

Here's another example of unnecessary skepticism. After a colonoscopy, a woman realized that she had all the signs of being raped while she was in recovery from the procedure. She even completed a gynecologic exam within a few days that confirmed her suspicions. The very first therapist she called said, "That is not possible." First of all, let me suggest that the phrase, "that is not possible" should not be a part of any therapist's vocabulary because (a) we cannot really know for sure what is and is not possible in the vast range of human behavior, and (b) if it really is not possible, saying "that's impossible" is an inadequate response to exaggeration, pathological lying, or psychosis. Of course, being raped around a medical procedure is very possible, horrifying to contemplate, but possible. Fact: rapes in medical settings have happened before, and they will happen again.

Telling a patient that what they told you is 'not possible' is tantamount to calling a patient crazy, never a great intervention. The subtext of this phrase informs the patient that they will not get the help they need from you or anyone else and that they are not deserving of any help. For the purposes of therapy, whether what the client tells you is 'possible' or not is potentially none of your business. Therapists are not lawyers. We are not judges. We are not even arbiters of reality; after all, what is our qualification for that job? Our job is not to separate fact from fiction or to define reality in the name of 'reality testing'. *Our job is to discover our patient's reality and to join them there.*

In the great film, *What Dreams May Come* (Bain, Bass, Matheson, & Ward, 1998), a couple loses both their children in an accident. The mother, a sensitive artist, loses her mind to grief; her doctor husband, while sad, keeps on functioning normally. She suffers a complete breakdown at a mental health facility, made worse by the vast gulf she feels between her own and her husband's levels of suffering over the loss of their children. She comes very close to divorcing him, but doesn't when he is able to visit her and rekindle their connection through empathy. She says to him, "Sometimes when you win [keep your head together], you lose [the marriage, the attachment, love]." This scene strikes me as so much of what is at the heart of the therapist's dilemma inherent in working with victims. Treating trauma survivors threatens to engulf us. It is so challenging to stay empathic, to remain connected to such extreme pain. We strive, above all, to remain functional; we need to remain functional. After all, if we jump down the hole with our clients, who will haul us both out? And yet, there is the risk of being too aloof, too remote, too inhumanly together. Sometimes when we win, our clients lose.

So, what stops us from keeping our hearts open, from believing disclosures? And, let's be clear, when I say 'believe', I do not mean in an objective sense, like in a court of law. I mean, believe in the sense of how we enter into the story of a play or a movie, suspending our disbelief in favor of joining the flow. For we are capable of holding more than one thought or belief in our heads at once. We can hear a story, think that it doesn't sound quite right but still engage in the conversation. We can wonder at strange details or omissions. *We can entertain the thought we are being lied to, manipulated, deceived, and still enter into the story with our client.* We actually need to wonder about these things for diagnostic purposes and to assess the next steps in treatment. But we need to wonder privately, to process, formulate, consider, and then return to treatment willing to still be engaged, to be open and not punitive, curious and not condemning in order to maintain whatever tenuous attachment our clients have formed with us.

I have found that most therapists (and humans in general) have a big fear of being fooled. There is something in us that fears the great shame of being hoodwinked and flat out wrong in our judge of character or story. Some therapists would almost rather expose their clients to inadvertent injury through ignoring, say, suicidal feelings than 'overreact' to suicidal ideation that could be false. This choice is rarely conscious. When the choice is made conscious, when we can weigh harm versus embarrassment, it seems easy to make the right choice, to risk believing the client and taking right action rather than being 'wrong' or worse yet 'manipulated'. I have thought that perhaps this relates to our need to be 'right' or rather the need of our ego.

Our ego, that part of ourselves responsible for survival in the world, literally stakes its life on being right. Have you ever been in a fight with a loved one? We can go from intimate lovers to mortal enemies in seconds when our 'rightness' is challenged. People live and die by their uninvestigated thoughts. The mind has a thought, and immediately the ego is there to wrap itself around the thought, to identify with it. The identified thought then becomes part of us, and to attack the thought becomes an attack on us, personally. It doesn't matter how wrong or outlandish the thought is. Once identification has set in, that thought becomes the most preciously defended object in our possession. Whole cultures become built around thoughts. Maybe that thought was even a passing one. Who, for example, had the thought, "it is desirable to break girls' feet for sexual fetish and beauty"? Never mind the pain, the trauma, the agony of 1,000 years of literally torturing girls for this single thought. An entire culture built an identity around this thought against all common sense and compassion. And then, just like that, it was over. The thought changed, and with it an entire culture.

So it is in the world of therapy. We have personal, familial, cultural, and professional thoughts that interfere with a naturally graceful and compassionate response to disclosure. We may fear losing status, confronting our lack of knowledge, or becoming aware of our own imperfections if we are 'wrong' about someone. It can be comforting to assume a superior position and choose confidently what to believe and what not to believe in the name of being an 'expert'. Otherwise, we could feel unskilled, confused, or like an imposter. *This shadow side of therapy, the need to know the 'real' story and sit in judgment, must become conscious as we strive to become a compassionate, accepting, and healing presence for our clients, many of whom have suffered traumas that are literally unimaginable to us.* It is a much more difficult practice to rest in the space of unknowing, to give every benefit of every doubt to the client, to make ourselves vulnerable, to possibly be wrong in the service of attachment. Paradoxically, we must be willing to be controlled, to be 'manipulated', to be fooled, vulnerable and imperfect, in order to be truly great at what we do and safe for our traumatized clients!

Perhaps the scariest reason of all not to believe our patients is that their disclosures not only change their own version of history and reality, it changes ours. We all live with a certain amount of denial about evil deeds in our communities, the prevalence of suffering, and the certainty of death. To be a trauma therapist means to descend into the sewers of humanity where rotten stinking refuse clogs the gutters, where light fails and the heart sinks. This is the last place most people want to go. To be a trauma therapist means to allow one's idea of reality to change. We may see horror where we once saw beauty. We may be thrown into an existential crisis or a crisis of faith. The problem of suffering rises before us like a dragon, making us feel small, undefended, and helpless. Like our clients, we may have to go through a 'dark night of the soul', a Phoenix Process where cherished ideas burn to the ground, where we lack familiar guideposts and landmarks. We can feel overrun with suffering, engulfed, our optimism overpowered. The power to believe or disbelieve our clients may feel like the only life raft we have. But there is a better option, the option of etiquette, which renders the question of whether to believe irrelevant.

Disclosure Etiquette

The beautiful thing about etiquette is that it does not require any internal decisions to be made or processed. Etiquette does not require empathy. I have often wondered if etiquette arose out of deeply non-empathic cultures, conquering cultures like the British or French, because it provided enough of an empathic response without actual empathy being needed, a sort of social exoskeleton.

Etiquette assumes that external behavior may be at odds with internal feelings. We may feel like propping our elbows on the table and yet we don't. We can reserve our right to our own thoughts and feelings about clients' disclosures (believe, disbelieve, not care) and still not act them out in the therapy with dismissive comments or incongruent facial expressions. Therapists, like everybody else, need to remind ourselves of this developmental question daily, "What do you call somebody who doesn't express or act out every feeling? An adult." We need to know that we are not immune to countertransference just because we may have been in practice for a long time.

Etiquette is simple, with a prescribed set of words to address nearly any situation. Etiquette raises us from a state of shock or self-absorption when we hear information that we cannot fully digest. Some of us have been trained not to fall back on social convention and etiquette as therapists, so as not to close off possible avenues of feeling expression for our clients. For example, some of us were taught not to offer condolences upon hearing of a death in the client's family because we didn't know how the client really felt about them. After practicing this way for a couple of decades, I realized that good manners never actually stand in the way of disclosure, whereas social rudeness might create a rupture in attachment. After all, therapists are socialized to therapy but clients are not! I encourage the clinicians I supervise to observe culturally competent courtesy and etiquette at all times, while gently encouraging clients to go further in their expressions by being fully prepared to hear whatever the client has to say.

Traumatic disclosures elicit shock, confusion, and anxiety in the listener. We are culturally, and maybe even biologically, wired to collude in the avoidance of difficult topics. Even very experienced therapists can falter and go 'deer in the headlights' after a bizarre or upsetting revelation. But, in the service of etiquette there is a simple, effective response to any traumatic disclosure no matter how horrifying or traumatic it might be. Ready? It is this:

I am really sorry that happened to you.

That's it. There are some variations: *I'm sorry you had to go through that.* And: *I'm sorry you had to see/hear/feel that.* If the victim was not the client, you can say: *I'm so sorry that happened to your (child, spouse, friend, parent).* Then, just sit there for a few moments and let the client tell you the next thing.

Let go of any agenda you had up to that moment. As one client kept telling me, "*Delete your need to know.*" Be spacious. Be present. Make room for details to emerge, *but do not force them.* Why? Because force is forceful. Our traumatized clients are absolutely allergic to force. Pressuring clients for information is a kind of force; even follow-up questions can be perceived this way. We need to carefully monitor our own need for comfort through information and be willing to sit in the anxiety of unknowing with our clients. Some disclosures are so shocking that the clients themselves may not even know what to believe. Rushing or diverting this process is socially impolite and clinically unhelpful.

Good etiquette requires practice. How many times as a young person were we encouraged to "stand up straight," "look people in the eyes when talking to them," "say please and thank you"? If good manners were natural, they wouldn't have to be taught. I encourage clinicians of all levels to actively practice hearing difficult disclosures that push their comfort zones—either real or imagined. You can pair up with another clinician in your agency, or another student and disclose to each other. For the purposes of role play, I suggest *not* using an actual personal trauma. Remember, this is for practice, and the role player needs to be able to get it wrong without shame and blame or damaging their partner. So, write up a few doozies, stories that stretch your abilities to believe and empathize without going into shock. The discloser can disclose with as much or as little drama as they like. The practitioner's job is to answer, with as much sincerity as possible. "I'm very sorry that happened to you." Even very advanced practitioners can benefit from this exercise, especially when we may be exposed to stories that challenge belief thresholds.

Belief Thresholds

We all possess a comfort zone of beliefs about reality. These beliefs change and evolve with culture, education, age, and experience. When we come up against the threshold of the new or bizarre in sessions, we are challenged to stay present and believing. When our clients hit a belief threshold is when we are most likely to pull back, however subtly, in a way that can threaten the therapeutic alliance for our exquisitely sensitive patients. Our thresholds are largely unconscious and unknown. We tend to assume that everyone is on the same page about what reality is, what horrifies us, and what constitutes outrageous belief systems. But humans have incredible diversity in these areas. To know our thresholds before clients hit them gives us control over our reactions and our clients a larger measure of safety.

Horror Thresholds

I first started teaching about this topic in relation to what I called 'horror thresholds'. In supervising students and social workers for state licensure, I noticed that there was quite a wide variety in what type of patient material therapists could tolerate. When the therapists' horror threshold was exceeded they would either 'freeze' (dissociate) and let the material slip by as if the client had said nothing out of the ordinary, 'fight' by arguing with or resisting the patient's story, or 'flee' by becoming judgmental and abandoning to the client.

When I began supervising trauma therapists, the *DSM* did not yet acknowledge that PTSD could occur through observation rather than direct experience. Clinicians were sometimes criticized as overly sympathetic or having 'permeable boundaries' if they were distressed by their patient's horrific material. Now we have the *DSM 5*, which includes in Criterion A for PTSD two relevant modes for treaters to come by PTSD: (1) "Learning that a relative or close friend was exposed to a trauma." Obviously, we are not treating our relatives or bff's, but in the course of a treatment we do come to care about our clients a great deal. Sometimes extremely distressing disclosures happen after we have been seeing a particular client for weeks to months and there is a powerful caring bond. We may even know more about this person than our actual friends or family members, and their distress can affect us greatly.

(2) "Indirect exposure to aversive details of the trauma, usually in the course of professional duties (e.g., first responders, medics)." The key words here are 'aversive details'. Details vivify horror. It is one thing to hear that someone was raped, and it is quite another to sit through telling after telling with all the gory details of what the rape was like physically, mentally, and emotionally. The more details we hear (and we want our clients to feel safe enough to tell us all the details because that is how they heal), the more we enter into that shared imaginal realm where we can start to relive the experience with them. Not only do we want our patients to tell details, but we also want them to be emotionally connected and not dissociated as they tell. We are asked to sit through a tsunami of technicolor horror so that our clients may finally experience compassion (the word itself means to 'suffer with') for themselves from the external world, a compassion that has likely been denied them up until now (American Psychiatric Association, 2013).

In listening to traumatic material, it is natural to want to avoid being traumatized, and it is deeply ingrained in the body/mind to act in accordance with this avoidance. So the more horror that our clients embody, the more we have to fight to stay present, attached, and engaged. What are some of the horror thresholds for people seeing traumatized clients? They are as varied as the clinicians are. Fortunately, we can all enlarge our capacity to be with and contain horror, but it does require some effort on our part. *We have to prepare ourselves to be ready to hear, believe, and be present with whatever our clients have to tell us.*

One year I supervised a young student from a lovely family. She was not naïve, but she had just not been exposed to much in the way of traumatic suffering. Her clients were not opening up very quickly. I have noticed that people often do not want to 'injure' their therapists with their information. They also do not want to be judged or doubted, so they will wait until they have a mature clinician or they have 'prepared' the therapist that they have before they disclose horrifying information. My prescription for this student was to go out and watch some horror movies and/or read some horror novels. I suggested she start with works such as *Nightmare on Elm Street*, the *Halloween* movies or anything by Stephen King. I wanted her to scare herself just enough so that she had a point of reference for the fear that her clients were sitting with and so that she wouldn't be too thrown when she heard her first truly horrifying story. In other words, we have to practice managing fear. If you think about it, many of us do this already. Have you watched *Game of Thrones*? Did you read ahead in the books? I did. The red wedding was not quite so shocking when you knew it was coming. We can think of this preparation as an 'exposure vaccination'.

Horror is very personal. That is why there are so many different kinds of horror movies. Some people fear the paranormal; some people fear fog. For me, a girl crawling out of a TV does not really activate my fear instinct, but a shark or a bear does! We need to know what scares us, and what strains our incredulity.

After hearing 15,000 stories on the Child-at-Risk Hotline in Massachusetts, there wasn't much that was new for me to hear in the realm of child abuse, or so I thought. I was wrong. There are very common stories one hears on hotlines that one rarely hears in therapy (sock burns, infants falling out of windows, beatings with wet leather straps), and there are many stories I have heard in therapy that I never or very rarely heard on the hotline (child pornography, ritual cult abuse, any perversion that doesn't leave a mark or a bruise or doesn't get reported).

If you are a certain kind of therapist, a story of incest in your practice may be shocking and push your horror threshold. If you are a trauma therapist, a story of incest may not be unusual, but a story about military torture may be shocking. If you are in the military, a story about intelligence community abuses and mind control may put you over your threshold. And so on. Most of us travel in fairly small circles in our lives and have very limited exposure to the sufferings of others by design and by chance. Whatever else we may learn about psychological trauma and horror generally comes through the media. But the media has many constraints, the main constraint being that it is there to entertain and not horrify (unless you are specifically watching the horror genre, but even that is based in fantasy and not necessarily reality). The information we get about the world and its abuses is actually quite limited, although we may feel as if it is not, due to the plethora of stations, internet access, and modalities of entertainment.

So what happens when we hit our horror threshold? If we encounter something truly horrible, something that we have never thought about and never wanted to think about, we can go into shock or denial. We can abandon our client with our own dissociation, judgmentalism, or outright disbelief. We can be made to feel very vulnerable. Maybe you have young children at home who ride the bus to school, and your client discloses horrific abuse by a school bus driver. This is not information you will want to hear or know about. Maybe your client's church engaged in ritual sacrifice 'after hours', and maybe that church is connected to your church in some way; maybe it IS your church. How will you handle this information? Maybe the information is just too horrifying in general to process: babies who are raped, beheadings in homes, cannibalism (all true disclosures I have heard either on the hotline or in private practice).

In order to be a therapeutic agent for your client, you have to be the person in the room who can stay grounded and present during disclosure. Know your horror threshold. If you have a client who seems to be heading into deeper and more horrifying disclosures, rally your support system. Supervisors, peers, helpful reading material, or getting a few therapy sessions for yourself can all help you maintain your 'even hovering attention' for your client. It is also OK to take a time out during a patient disclosure. I've had moments where I have said, "Please give me a moment. I want to process what you are telling me." If I have an overwhelming emotion, I've also said something to acknowledge it, and come into congruence like, "that makes me really angry to think that you were treated like that." I have never had a problem with clients in making statements like these that own my own reactions and needs in the moment. Our clients have finely honed perceptual abilities due to hypervigilance and survival skills. They know exactly when we lose the thread or have a reaction. If we do not own it, we become incongruous—our affect does not match our internal state.

Think about how dangerous it is for a client to have an incongruous therapist. Incongruity equals danger for the vast majority of trauma survivors. Perpetrators can be viciously congruent or irrationally incongruent. A smiling sadist is a terrifyingly incongruous apparition. If we smile when we are horrified, maintain a neutral face when we are furious, or get angry when we are scared, we are very likely to trigger an unpleasant reaction in our clients that can threaten the efficacy of that session and the entire relationship as a whole. We may inadvertently leave our clients to fend for themselves as they leave our office, wondering if they can trust us and return, or manage what the incongruity has triggered in them, perhaps for hours or even days afterward.

Reality Thresholds

Newsflash! We do not all live in the same reality. 'Reality', whatever that is, has to filter through perceptual layers in our nervous system, brain, genetics, and epigenetics. Many factors shape people's individual realities or, some might say, perception of reality. But I would argue that perception of reality = reality. How can we really know anyone else's reality? We cannot assume that their perception is the same as ours.

'Reality' comes to us first through our parents. Let's say your parents are red/green colorblind, how do we learn to identify red and green? We have to wait until someone else points those colors out to us. What if no one else saw red and green in our community, but we somehow did? Would we be accepted for our perception or called 'crazy'? Perhaps we would be accused of making things up or seeing things that are not there. Cultural concepts dictate what we see and what we don't, what we take for 'real' and what we do not. Cultural values shape our perception as well. As do many, many other factors, as therapists well know.

Consensual reality is strongly based in the dominant culture's reality. Every so often White people get a whiff of how different White cultural reality is from people of color's reality. The O.J. Simpson trial exemplified this dynamic. White folks were aghast when so many Black folks celebrated the verdict of acquittal when in White groupthink, the Black man was 'obviously' guilty. To people of color this trial was oppressive 'business as usual', another Black man accused of hurting a White woman, being brought down from high standing by corrupt White people who were obviously conspiring against him for their own reasons—a story they have heard many, many times before, based out of real experiences in their communities.

Many of us take our reality through the media that we consume—which is run by the dominant culture. If the nightly news says it is real, it is. If the nightly news ignores it or denies it, it's not real. If an alternative news site says it's real but the mainstream media does not, it's fake news. And so on. This is called 'consensual reality', the reality that most human beings subscribe to at any given time. Consensual reality changes with new scientific discoveries and cultural evolution. It also changes with geography . . . and profession. Psychiatry, Psychology, Counseling, and Social Work all have slightly different takes on reality, different borders of disbelief and different tolerances for transgressions based on where they put their perceptual emphasis.

Our filters matter—especially our cultural filters. The National Association of Social Workers has written *Standards and Indicators for Cultural Competence in Social Work Practice*, an extremely thorough document outlining the impact of cultural competence in social work, including psychotherapy. These filters are explicitly addressed in Standard 3. Cross Cultural Knowledge:

> Social workers shall possess and continue to develop specialized knowledge and understanding that is inclusive of, but not limited to, the history, traditions, values, family systems, and artistic expressions such as race and ethnicity; immigration and refugee status; tribal groups; religion and spirituality; sexual orientation; gender identity or expression; social class; and mental or physical abilities of various cultural groups.
>
> (2015 NASW National Committee on
> Racial and Ethnic Diversity, 2015)

A common example of a cultural reality disconnect between therapist and client could be between a client of indigenous heritage who can see or sense bioenergy fields (auras) and a therapist who cannot. For some therapists this ability would be a reality threshold, hard to tolerate and understand. For many of us (especially here in the Pacific Northwest), it would not. But what if the client started talking about energies and entities (demonic, angelic, fairy, etc.) that they were perceiving in someone's auric field? Many more Western-educated and -trained therapists might have a hard time staying present with this conversational topic.

Another type of reality threshold has to do with hidden information. According to the *Washington Post*, 1.5 million Americans have security clearances, which, as it points out, is more than the entire population of Norway (Fung, 2014). Our history, like our reality, is consensual, but not necessarily accurate. What happens when we are confronted with information that challenges our sense of the integrity of our nation, our military, or our leaders? How do we deal with previously unknown traumatic realities that might be introduced to us by clients, like the prevalence of government-sponsored mind control around the world? Are we ready to hear about real-life Manchurian candidates, sex slaves, supersoldiers, and their creation through unfathomable abuse and trauma? Are we ready to know the history of MKUltra, both overt and covert? Or do we fear that if we believe our clients we might start to fall under the category of 'conspiracy theorist' or 'fake news' believer?

Yet, for people with these perceptions, such events are real, if not normal in the culture they live in. The exclusion of their reality can contribute to more trauma, depersonalization, and derealization than they are already feeling. The skeptical stance of the therapist, while understandable, creates a field of disbelief where the secure attachment of client to therapist, necessary for the successful treatment of traumatic disorders, becomes difficult or impossible to achieve.

Spiritual Thresholds

Therapist training is supposed to alleviate spiritual and religious clashes with clients. In practice, I find that our religious and spiritual beliefs can still interfere in insidious ways with clients forming trusting alliances with us as providers. If we are honest with ourselves, we will find that we do have our own thresholds of tolerance, no matter how much we have brought awareness to this issue.

The Trauma Tool Kit (Pease Banitt, 2012) discusses the various spiritual paradigms people can find themselves in. They break down into the Abrahamic faiths: Jewish, Islam, Christianity; Eastern traditions: Hindu, Buddhist, Taoist; Nontheistic: Humanist, Rational, Philosophy, and Indigenous (worldwide Earth-based). Even when we examine our beliefs in therapy and supervision, there remain epigenetic and cultural components that can unconsciously drive us or create thresholds of belief to our clients. Practicing in certain regions of the country can create cultural fears in us and in our clients. Sometimes, as therapists, we may have to answer to the 'powers that be' in our institutions if there are affiliations spoken or unspoken. For example, I was offered a job inside of a Catholic hospital system some years ago. The job seemed great, except that the medical social workers were not allowed to speak of abortion or even contraception as a matter of hospital (Church) policy. Many of us find ourselves in similar dilemmas with clients over the years. Understanding the alliance ruptures that occur when religious forces interfere with treatment can help alleviate if not eliminate them. In this case, I had the luxury to not take the job. But how would it have affected my clinical relationships if I had taken the position and agreed to that censorship? How would it have affected my own sense of integrity, and how would that have been communicated to my clients?

Even in a restrictive setting, we can follow our conscience to maintain an alliance with our clients without torpedoing our jobs. One way to do that is to be transparent. Sure, one cannot discuss those forbidden options with a client, but one can (and I feel is obliged to) discuss the parameters on your practice within a religious institution and provide referrals to parties that can accomplish those tasks without such inhibitions. Prescribing search terms on Google or recommending books may be examples of bending the rules without breaking them. To be effective means to confront our own fears and boundaries. We all need to decide how much risk we can take on behalf of our clients. This is a matter of temperament and working through our own traumas and fears. Normally these fears would be a topic for supervision, but agency supervisors may not be able to help you. In this case, paying for outside consultation could reap many benefits for you and your clients.

Our own spiritual/religious beliefs are often the biggest hindrance to believing clients because they inform our beliefs about reality. Strong atheistic and scientific paradigms may not at all mesh well with a client, say, with a psychic or indigenous experience of reality. *Everyone has a belief system.* Atheism is no more neutral than Christianity or a yogic perspective. There is no neutral position. Our beliefs arise in certain cultural conditions, as do our clients'. Our job is to figure out how we can interface with our clients' version of reality and *enter into it.* At the very least, we need to be open to it. If we are dismissive of their beliefs, even subtly, we risk ruptured or incomplete attachment. The client may not ever fully trust us and not even know why.

Sometimes, therapists are themselves afraid of being judged for their openness or 'alternative' belief structures (and that 'alternative' moniker is decided, of course, by what culture we are living in). Just as a Jewish therapist needs to be open to a Christian client about talking about their relationship to Jesus as the Savior, a Christian therapist needs to be open to discussing past lives and crystal healing with their client. Sometimes we have hidden prejudices within prejudices. We may think it is OK for an Indian Hindu to believe in past lives but not a White Californian, and we may, either consciously or unconsciously, make judgments about the Californian that involve the words 'new age'. Cultural competence is not limited to skin color or geography but to embedded personal and cultural belief systems.

Mystical experiences can challenge therapists' belief systems. Yet, so many trauma survivors report having deeply meaningful spiritual experiences during and after their traumas.

A client is recounting a particularly scary incident of torture from childhood. He is very young, maybe 3 or 4 years old. Someone or something is smothering him, and he cannot breathe. It is possible he has been put in a box and buried in the woods for some sort of 'initiation'. At some point he becomes aware of a spiritual being with him. He is not afraid of this being, who tells him in a very calm way, "If you do not breathe soon, you will die." Shortly after this vision he was able to take a breath. It was very comforting for him to feel that he was not alone and had assistance during this bad experience.

It is not uncommon for victims to recall a presence, say, an angel, an ancestor, or a guide that appears at their side during particularly traumatizing experiences, visually or aurally guiding them and providing comfort. Some of these events are culturally congruent to the victim and some are not. These stories can challenge deeply held Western scientific beliefs about reality. If we wrinkle our nose in disbelief, stifle a chuckle, or dissociate we can lose that client forever with an irreparable rupture. Just as we need to be prepared to hear the range of horrifying events that humans encounter, so do we need to be ready to hear spiritual stories beyond our ken.

In the end, threshold work is countertransference work. We need to examine our own reactions to our clients' stories and processes to create a container where we can hold and enter into the various realities that our client shares, no matter how horrifying, surprising, or extraordinary. We can do this through educating ourselves, refraining from judgment, suspending our disbelief, resisting acting out, and utilizing services such as supervision that help us with all of these complex tasks. By doing so we prevent a myriad of problems for them and for us and preserve the sacred space of healing from trauma.

References

2015 NASW National Committee on Racial and Ethnic Diversity. (2015). *Standards and Indicators for Cultural Competence in Social Work Practice*. Retrieved December 8, 2017, from www.socialworkers.org/LinkClick.aspx?fileticket=7dVckZAYUmk%3D &portalid=0

American Psychiatric Association. (2013). *Diagnostic and Statistical Manual of Mental Disorders* (5th ed., DSM-5). Washington, DC: American Psychiatric Association.

Bain, B. B. (Producer), Bass, R. (Screenwriter), Matheson, R. (Writer), & Ward, V. (Director). (1998). *What Dreams May Come* [Motion Picture]. USA/NEW ZEALAND: Polygram Filmed Entertainment.

Fung, B. (2014, March 24). *5.1 Million Americans Have Security Clearances: That's More Than the Entire Population of Norway*. Retrieved December 8, 2017, from Washington Post: www.washingtonpost.com/news/the-switch/wp/2014/03/24/5-1-million-americans-have-security-clearances-thats-more-than-the-entire-population-of-norway/

Johnson, S. (2013). *Love Sense: The Revolutionary New Science of Romantic Relationships*. New York, NY: Little, Brown and Company.

Joy, L. (Writer), & Nolan, J. (Writer, Director). (2017) The Original. [Television Series Episode] In Abrams, J.J. (Executive Producer), *Westworld*. Los Angeles, CA: Home Box Office.

Pease Banitt, S. (2012). *The Trauma Tool Kit: Healing PTSD From the Inside Out*. Wheaton, IL: Quest Books.

6　Repairing Relationship Ruptures

If I had a prayer, it would be this: God spare me from the desire for love, approval and appreciation. Amen.

　　　　　　　　　　　　　　　　　　　　—Byron Katie, Loving What Is (2002)

Despite our best efforts, ruptures happen. Nobody is perfect. While it is important to minimize attachment rupture in the therapy, repairing ruptures is where the rubber meets the road of relational healing. What is a relationship rupture? Relationship rupture occurs in psychotherapy when the client feels they can no longer trust in the therapist's ability to help them. At its worst, the client may feel that the therapist is actively harming them. As a result, the client pulls back from or ends the therapeutic work. The rupture can be obvious, such as leaving therapy or aggressively confronting the therapist. Ruptures can also manifest in more subtle ways, such as the patient stops moving forward in treatment, sessions become argumentative where previously they were harmonious, or the client can be frequently dissociating (fleeing), stuck (freezing), or attacking (fighting) during sessions.

Relational distress is a dynamic that occurs between two or more people. It needs to be addressed in therapy as an interactive process rather than as a one-sided 'thing'. If we address rupture as a 'thing', it is easy to enter a blame game. "The client is resistant, noncompliant, difficult." Or from the client's view, "the therapist is controlling, doesn't get it, is inexperienced or stupid." All of these descriptors may contain relative truth, but they are simplistic and do not address or solve the problem. It is inevitable that clients will become resistant when they hit a psychological roadblock (fearblock), and that therapists will become clueless or deskilled when they are confounded by their client. In and of itself, these occurrences do not have to create impasses. They can, rather, inform the therapy of where healing needs to occur. Dynamics are fluid and changeable; in the repair model blame becomes irrelevant, and the relationship 'dance' can be corrected through multiple avenues.

Five Steps of Awareness

Early on in my career, I was told that the best supervisors I would ever have would be my patients. How true this is! I wish more therapists knew it. Our clients show us where therapy is helping, where it is stagnating, and when it becomes obstructive. They also mirror our effectiveness or lack of it back to us. It is our job, as professionals holding knowledge and power in the therapy room, to take the lion's share of responsibility for how therapy progresses.

In some agencies, it has become fashionable to engage in patient blaming, which I see as an extension of our culture's current tendency towards victim blaming. Sometimes client blaming comes in the guise of 'patient account-ability' or 'empowerment'. When our patients blame us for not getting better, many therapists' first stance is to pathologize them in some way. Rare is the clinician who remembers in those moments how to 'join' with a client, de-escalate, soothe, and repair. Roadbumps and relational breaks are an inevi-table occurrence in any relationship and especially in therapy. These breaks can be a result of something the therapist said or did, a failure of empathy, a trauma trigger, a conditioned response, or a completely internal process on the part of the patient, unrelated to anything happening in the therapy. It is the therapists' job to:

> **Notice** that something is amiss in the connection,
> **Track** the origin and nature of the problem in the relationship,
> **Self-examine** for activation of our own defensive structures,
> **Respond** appropriately to the rupture, and then
> **Repair** the relationship to the fullest extent possible.

Notice

The first step to relationship repair is to *notice the rupture*. The initial rupture can be tiny (a mini-rupture) and barely noticeable or huge and unpleasant. More often, initial ruptures are like little tears in fabric, hard to spot but easy to repair. Think back for a moment of a case where relations went south for a while. When did you first notice it happening? More important, *how* did you notice?

For many of us, our first sign that something is 'off' is a gut feeling. Our usu-ally enjoyable session leaves us unsatisfied, empty, or feeling a lack of the usual level connection to that client. Maybe the client clues us in through acting out in some way or making a hostile 'joke'. We may attribute our unease to an 'off' day. If we are psychodynamically trained, we may track that dynamic through subsequent sessions. If we are beginners, are trained in other modali-ties, or have an unworked through dismissive-avoidant attachment style, we might not note that anything is amiss or see any reason to continue thinking about it through subsequent sessions.

For a couple of years I saw a high-functioning child with Asperger's Syndrome[1] in weekly therapy. Overall, she responded well to this modality, but after a few weeks became fidgety and reluctant to talk. She had been perseverating on cartoon expressions and how they 'overwhelmed' and 'embarrassed' her. For a while I smoothed this topic over, convinced that it was due to her neuroprocessing difficulties and emotional issues.

We talked about cartoons a lot while I 'sympathized' with her. I already tried to maintain a fairly neutral face and demeanor around her due to my previous work with clients on the autistic spectrum, but I really did like this client a lot. One day, she made a comment about my 'sneaky smile'. I apologized, explored this comment a bit, and realized that I did often greet her with an unconscious smile or smiled when she said something particularly charming (which was often). Of course, being on the spectrum, this child could not distinguish a friendly smile from a sneaky smile. We agreed that I would keep my facial expressions as still as possible. This helped her a great deal, and she began moving forward in resolving some important issues.

Fortunately for me and for the therapy, this child was able to identify the source of her discomfort and name it. I had noticed the presence of an issue in the therapy but had not been able to track it myself, even though the perseverative content in therapy had clearly been around her being overwhelmed by facial expressions (derp). She had been trying to tell me of her discomfort for a while, but I had been oblivious until she blurted out the 'sneaky smile' comment. The rupture in this case was relatively minor and easily repaired. I was willing to let her be 'my supervisor' and advise me on what she needed from my face, which was neutrality so she could process our work together. Once I apologized and changed my behavior, trust was reestablished, the distraction was removed, and we were able to successfully move on together.

Not all cases have resolved themselves this well. Sometimes the alliance disturbance remains 'underground' for a while and then erupts with aggressive confrontation, as happened with this case.

A gentleman with an addiction and an elusive abuse history came to therapy weekly for four years. He had a very imposing presence physically. Early on, I had referred him to a shaman therapist I knew for some work on visions he was having that seemed more shamanic than hallucinatory. After a few sessions, the shaman said my client was not yet ready for shamanic work and sent him back for more work in therapy. The client was mad and couldn't let go of it. Every once in a while this client would bring up this issue with me. I felt really uncomfortable and like there was more to the story, but the patient's reactivity and my own shame at having connected the two of them and 'creating' this problem kept me from exploring the story further. During this time, the client informed me that the shaman had looked physically like several members of his family, and, again, I felt reluctant to explore that issue. I kept refocusing the client back on what I thought of as his more central issues of addiction and a trauma history. Eventually this client started to push office boundaries and responded with explosive rage when I attempted to set limits. He ended the therapy after a particularly scary tantrum, where I actually felt physically endangered by him.

This was a particularly difficult case on many levels, and I will preface it by saying that not all impasses or ruptures are solvable. Because of the physical threat I was feeling from this client, it was probably better that the treatment with me came to an end. He needed to work with someone who was not scared of him. But I am not happy with *how* it ended. It was upsetting and traumatic for both of us. Looking back, I can see how my fear was keeping me in avoidance. I was dissociating from my awareness of what this client was feeling (angry) and what I was feeling (threatened), and I was not aware until later how much I was compartmentalizing my strong feelings of fear, shame, and anger about this scary client. For various reasons, some personal and some professional, I was not able to explore the client's issues of rejection and traumatic triggers. I also became unwittingly a part of the Karpman drama triangle (Karpman, 1967) where I was the savior and the shaman was the persecutor. When I could not rescue my client from his own shame and rage, I went from savior to persecutor. Hindsight is, as they say, 20–20 vision. This relationship was beyond my ability to repair with the consciousness I had at that time. We will all have such cases if we practice long enough. The important thing is to keep learning, to keep self-inquiry alive, and to strive for a healthy, compassionate, and safe connection in all circumstances.

Track

In the cases mentioned above, the therapist did not have to do much tracking, only listen to the discomfort of the clients. Sometimes our clients do not know where the discomfort lies. A relationally attuned therapist will begin to track the origin of relational discomfort as soon as it arises. Tracking requires time and attention, especially in the beginning years of practice. I understand that many clinicians these days have less time than ever to do more work and see more cases that are complicated. Nevertheless, if you want to really excel and become the wise therapist you are capable of becoming, you will have to go deeper into your cases, and that does mean making time for case formulation and review.

Time-honored methods of case review are reviewing patient notes, supervision, and what I call 'sit and stare time'—just thinking about the case. Not only thinking, though, but daydreaming, reverie, and pondering. What is the difference? Case 'thinking' could be imagined as walking down a logical path, straight and well paved, to an answer. This path takes you from A to B. Engaging the cognitive mind to problem solve is, of course, necessary and useful. Decision trees, rule outs, timelines, and planned interventions all belong to this kind of thought. Reverie, or contemplation, is more associative thinking, like going off the path to chase a butterfly and then finding a beautiful pond, which leads to a magic cave with a scroll inside. Sometimes loosening the associative bonds of the mind can lead to leaps of insight. You may not be sure how you got there, but it is always magic when you do.

These two types of case review represent the engagement of the two hemispheres of the brain we discussed in our first chapter. When we can marry the insight from both sides, we obtain a very complete multidimensional picture of the issue. Often there will be an 'aha' moment where we realize exactly where the therapy relationship went off the rails.

A highly self-destructive client with a lifelong history of foster care and residential treatment is court-referred for mandatory treatment. This client misses as many appointments as she keeps. She seems to be engaging with me, but every time I try to address any real-world problem to help the client stabilize her life, the client decompensates and misses sessions. This goes on for weeks, leaving me anxious for the client's safety. The client starts talking about spiritual books she is reading and continues to check out any time I make an attempt to focus on the client's life and problem solving. Finally, a light goes on in my mind: everything in the external world is basically a trauma trigger for the client. At this point, I made an agreement with the client that she will spend as much time talking about spiritual philosophy as she wishes, and I will stop raising everyday issues of functioning. I took this approach after much contemplation and a spontaneous flash of insight. It felt therapeutically counterintuitive, but it worked. After a couple of years of mostly discussing spiritual philosophies, the client announced that she was now strong enough to leave some bad situations and begin work on her traumas. She left an abusive relationship, got sober, and made tremendous headway in her treatment.

This client was a major teacher for me. All of my training at that point said that I should keep her focused on safety and stabilizing her life situation. But the triggers inherent in those discussions plus the stimulation of parental transference made it impossible for my client to hang in there. When I let go of my preconceived idea of what treatment should look like and just went with her flow, the insight arrived that she was being so triggered by the work that she could hardly make it back to sessions. Because of the early stages of her trauma work, she had no language to describe what was happening. Now, when I look back at this case, I see that allowing her to explore spiritual realms with me enhanced her inner ego strength, mobilized hope, and *allowed us to build a genuine attachment that was not based on her traumas*. This safe attachment provided the stabilization that she needed. Most important, she kept coming to therapy for another several years and worked through a great deal of her extensive trauma history.

Self-examine

Intelligence knows a lot of things. Wisdom embodies that knowledge. *There is no way to become a great and wise trauma therapist without doing the difficult work of self-examination.* Remember that saying about medical and psychology students: they know just enough to be dangerous? The average therapist falls into this category when treating people with trauma histories. To become a competent trauma therapist means to know oneself very, very well—the good, the bad, and the ugly (unhealed parts of ourselves). Most of the great trauma therapists I know have blended extensive study with extensive self-exploration, healing, and growth. I can think of several off the bat who not only have years of education and years of their own therapy under their belt, but also years of yoga, meditation, and myriad self-help workshops. *This work never stops!* If you love the idea of endless growth and challenges to live in your wisest self, then carry on. If a lifetime of intense introspection and a path of continuing enlightenment do not thrill you, or if you feel like you have 'arrived', it is probably best to stop treating severely traumatized people. At best, treatment will stagnate; at worst, the 'stuckness' in your personality can create attachment ruptures and compromise the patient's ability to get help in the future.

In Chapter 4 we looked at how to foster attachment in great depth. Knowing your own attachment style as well as your clients' will inform you as to advantages and pitfalls in the treatment of this particular person with you (also a particular person). If you are a person with a preoccupied attachment style that you are still working through, then working with intensely rejecting clients may not be for you. You might even do good work, but the toll it takes on you personally could be intense. It could also be growthful and part of your own healing path if approached with humility and good supervision. If you have a tendency to the dismissive-avoidant style, you may discourage attachment without realizing it by taking too much of an intellectual approach to your client, who may need a lot of reassurance about your caring and connection. Knowing these tendencies in yourself can help you identify weak areas in the attachment that are prone to rupture. You can then work proactively to keep your client feeling safe, connected, and able to do the work.

The same idea is true for ego defensive structures. We all have them. How do they interface with our client? If our client is dissociative, and we are too, how will therapy stay on track? Knowing that you tend to retreat into intellectualism when threatened will help you track both your own and your patients' process. You can catch yourself being 'the professor' and realize you are experiencing some kind of countertransference that can lead you into greater insight about your client. At the same time, you can choose to acknowledge your presentation and shift it if need be; your client will most likely shift with you and be grateful for your careful consideration.

Know your triggers! Many of us therapists have a history of trauma. We are all at various levels of working through. With certain clients, we will have to stay on top of triggering behaviors and comments in and out of session. If we do not, we risk becoming reactive to our clients or dissociating. When we know and are conscious of our triggers, they can inform us about what is going on with our client. If you have abandonment triggers, for example, you may be exquisitely attuned to mini-ruptures in the therapy. As long as you do not overreact, this sensitivity can make for a great advantage in giving your client a chance to experience mini-ruptures and repairs.

Respond

Ruptures require conscious acknowledgment and out loud processing. Sometimes apologies are in order, and sometimes they are unnecessary. Talking about what created a break in trust is always necessary. Otherwise, ruptures are shoved into a compartment where they fester and erupt later, as with the earlier case involving the threatening client.

Once we have noticed and examined the nature of the rupture, we are in a position to decide how and when to respond. If the break is immediate and dramatic, it may require a response from the therapist sooner rather than later—even, perhaps an apology. Good apologies consist of five parts:

1. Say "I'm sorry" or "I need to apologize to you."
2. Acknowledge the specific wrong. For example, "I realize that I did not listen to you when you wanted to talk about what happened in your school rather than your family of origin."
3. State the effect that you observed on the client. "I noticed that when I tried to change the subject you pulled back and didn't feel like talking to me anymore."
4. Empathize. "I imagine you might have felt like I am one more person who just does not get it. If I were in your shoes I might have done the same."
5. State your intentions to fix this problem in the future. "From now on, I'm going to focus on your agenda instead of my own. I'm really sorry." (Repetition can be helpful when apologizing.)

An important part of the apology process is letting the client verbalize all of their feelings around the event. Most of our trauma patients have never received any apologies from their abusers (or anyone for that matter). As a person of power in their life, the therapist can make a big healing impact by owning any hurtful behavior, no matter how small it may seem to us ("I'm sorry my waiting room was a little disorganized; I didn't mean to make you feel like I don't care"). The client may need some time to take this in or be suspicious of our efforts. They may need to repeat several times how we hurt, misunderstood, or offended them. Listening patiently provides a powerful corrective experience. Since apologizing makes us vulnerable, we need to carefully work through any shame in our countertransference, utilizing supervision and/or our own therapy as needed. More than one conversation with the client may be necessary to resolve the issue. If the client is allowed to verbalize all of their feelings without interruption (and this can go on for a while), once they are finished and the apology is accepted, the issue is permanently put to rest. And (bonus!) the client has received a profoundly corrective emotional experience that raises their standards for behavior in relationships.

The client may not be able to tell us right away that something has happened to upset them, and they may hide their pain while withdrawing subtly or overtly from the therapy. You may notice a series of cancellations, a failure to return, or a lame excuse to take a break. In that case, you may need to 'reach into the resistance' as one of my teachers used to say. Here is an example of a rupture that was caused by activity outside of the therapy hour but strongly impacted the therapy:

A client who had been coming fairly regularly took a longer than usual break. I debated calling her for a while and then felt like it was the right thing to do. Usually I only talk for 10 minutes free of charge, but I felt this conversation needed to be longer and that somehow I had offended or scared her, so I went with it. She was extremely grateful I called, admitted that something was bothering her, and agreed to come into session. In the next session, she was able to voice her concern at a tweet of mine that she had seen that had a troubling source and symbol, of which I was ignorant. She was terribly afraid I was aligned with scary people and ideologies to whom I actually feel a great deal of antipathy. I apologized and stated my complete ignorance in the twitterverse. She believed me and felt relieved, as she had started to wonder if I was not the kind person she thought me to be. She had been on the verge of ending our relationship!

Social media is a new factor in therapy these days. Many therapists have Twitter and Facebook accounts. As my client reminded me so strongly, "you have to be mindful of your brand." It was humbling to think that a moment of pure ignorance on my part had cost her weeks of anxiety over whether she could actually trust me anymore when I was the one person on whom she had pinned her hopes of doing her healing work. This case is just one of a myriad of examples of how therapists can inadvertently scare and disillusion clients. In order to restore this relationship, I had to actively reach into the client's withdrawal to reestablish connection. Otherwise, she may have permanently drifted away or fired me over a misunderstanding.

Repair

In order to make a good repair, therapists need to get past their own shame and self-recrimination at making an error. When we stand in judgment of ourselves we cannot apply curiosity to the situation, and we lose capacity for insight. If we are defending ourselves against judgment either consciously or unconsciously, we really cannot be present to repair the relationship with our client. I would even go so far as to say that all relationship ruptures are actually self-ruptures, and so relationship repair begins with self-understanding and forgiveness for our very human mistakes in the role of therapist. For a very experienced clinician, this process can take seconds. For a beginning therapist, it might take a couple of supervision and/or therapy sessions. Powerful results can come when we apply intellectual curiosity instead of shame. Here is an example of how rupture/repair played out in supervision with a dramatic parallel process result in the case being presented.

I was supervising a second-year social work student who had a client with a fairly extreme neglect history. Her therapy was stalling with this client, who was very stuck. My student was frustrated. I was sleepy. Very sleepy. The kind of sleepy where drool could run down your chin and your eyes close against your will. It was embarrassing. I was fighting a losing battle in supervision, and I knew it. But after years of doing this work I understood that this kind of extreme sleepiness only overcame me as a countertransference reaction to deeply suppressed rage. So instead of continuing to judge myself I quickly worked through my shame internally and began to talk about my sleepiness. (Had my supervisee noticed? Um, yes.) I talked about how I could feel her client's suppressed rage through her case description, and I asked her to talk about her own countertransference. She did—and she had a lot of it. The following week she came in and told me that her client had a giant breakthrough, and had literally taken a sledgehammer to the walls of her house for remodeling, simultaneously working out and breaking through her rage.

A beginning therapist or supervisor might get bogged down in self-criticism over 'unprofessional' behaviors like sleepiness. An advanced practitioner turns every event to their advantage through understanding and inquiry instead of lingering in judgment and shame. In this process of repair judo, the mini-rupture in supervision was repaired, yielding very dramatic results in the therapy.

Most solid reparations take time and communication. After the acknowledgment and apology, our clients are going to be watching us closely. Spoken or unspoken there is a kind of 'probationary period' where they are going to be assessing whether we are 'walking our talk' or not. We should not expect them to trust us immediately, nor should we use our position alone to insist on this trust, as trust is something we must earn from our clients over time, especially after a rupture. What we can do is check in frequently. "How am I doing?" is an important question to get used to asking. You can bring up the problem that the client had identified earlier and ask specifically if you have corrected the issue for them. Another question to ask is, "Have you had any other concerns about my work?" to give the client a chance to give honest feedback after a rupture. This checking in should be in addition to general monitoring of the alliance. After a period of time, new feelings might emerge around the rupture; these questions will give your client a chance to explore any new feelings or issues that are attached to the incident.

Sometimes repair requires a monetary response. Nearly all therapists double book at some point; some more than others. Depending on what stage the therapeutic relationship is at, this kind of error can be more or less disruptive to the relationship. For highly traumatized clients, this type of error can feel disastrous, like they can be forgotten easily or like the therapist does not really care about them. In addition to a sincere apology and examination of patient reaction, it can help to offer a compensatory free session. Sometimes we are not sure who made the scheduling mistake, the client or our business. I find that modeling humility and assuming responsibility if there is an iota of a chance that my business was to blame for the error goes a long way to a resilient therapeutic relationship.

In the end, relationship rupture is inevitable, and, some might say, necessary for relational trust and progress in therapy. Conflict and disappointment are inevitable components of relationships. When the client has developmental trauma and/or florid PTSD, the relational ante is upped when there is conflict, sending clients into withdrawal or confrontation. This rupture moment is our golden opportunity to show clients a different way of being in relationship, where the therapist neither abandons nor retaliates but seeks to understand and join with the client's intense feelings. Often this moment is a brand new relational experience for our patients. Trust increases, and the client experiences a healthy hope for relational satisfaction where before there was disappointment, despair, fear, or cynicism. This cycle of rupture and repair is the very heart of healing for traumatized clients. Wise therapists do not try to avoid this cycle but embrace it as the relational engine for change that it is.

Alliance Monitoring for Mini-Ruptures

Therapists are fortunate if they have clients astute enough to know when the relationship is feeling threatened or threatening and can verbalize that awareness. Usually, they cannot do this until later stages of treatment. We need to know when our client is feeling uncertain about us, unsafe in the therapy, or just not comfortable with what is happening. Mini-ruptures and repairs in many ways are the heart and soul of therapy as they are in everyday relationships. Great relationships do not happen without conflict and resolution, rupture and repair. We get to discover over and over again that we are lovable. In therapy, we have even more latitude to reveal our most painful selves, our ugliest parts and have them received by a caring and wise person. Healing trauma can only happen in the dance of rupture and repair. In this model, the therapist remains vigilant from session to session for mini-ruptures. The ability to recognize the ruptures are half the repair. The other half is responding appropriately and therapeutically. What are strategies we can use to monitor the therapeutic alliance for ruptures besides cultivating our own ability to notice client behavioral changes?

Miller and Duncan's Session Rating Scale

Scott Miller and Barry Duncan developed a simple metric to assess therapeutic alliance in an ongoing treatment *as part of the treatment*. They found that clients who were able to report alliance problems were *seven times as likely to stay in therapy* as clients who were not able to give this feedback. Their metric is this: they simply ask four questions. They call it the Session Rating Scale. The questions relate sequentially to these four areas: relationship, goals and topics, approach or method, and overall rating. In between the two statements, they ask their clients to make a mark on a 10-cm line indicating how close to each polarity they feel about the session.

1. I did not feel heard, understood or respected . . . I felt heard understood and respected.
2. We did not work on or talk about what I wanted to work on and talk about . . . We worked on and talked about what I wanted to work on and talk about.
3. The therapist's approach is not a good fit for me . . . The therapist's approach is a good fit for me.
4. There was something missing in the session today . . . Overall, today's session was right for me (Duncan & Miller, 2008).

In using the scale, Duncan and Miller found that high ratings staying high or improvement from poor to fair ratings indicated that the therapy was going in the right direction. They also found that if positive changes were not reported in the first three session that the treatment was at risk. This intervention has been so effective that it has been included in SAMHSA's National Registry of Evidence-Based Programs and Practices (Substance Abuse and Mental Health Services Administration, 2017).

Another scale they developed is the Outcome Rating Scale. They use this scale to have the client assess their previous week before the session in several areas. Like the SRS above, it is quick and easy to use, but yields statistically useful information. The form has the 10-cm line where the client puts a mark to the right if they rate that area at high levels of functioning and to the left if that area feels low functioning to them. The four areas are:

1.   Individually (Personal well-being)
2.   Interpersonally (Family, close relationships)
3.   Socially (Work, school, friendships)
4.   Overall (General sense of well-being)

For children they have a simplified version where the child merely draws a sad or happy face in regards to Me, Family, School, Everything. Using these scales weekly provides a statistically significant picture of whether the therapy is progressing in a helpful way or not.

Therapist Check-Ins

"How am I doing?" I ask this question no later than the second session—sometimes even at the end of the first—because I want to know if we got off on the right foot or if there is an immediate problem in the connection. I also ask, "How is this feeling for you?" "Do you feel comfortable here?" "Is there anything you would like me to do differently?" "Will you tell me if there is a problem?" "How will I know?" Clients, especially trauma clients, need to know it is safe to give feedback right away since most of my clients have had previous unsatisfactory therapy experiences where concerns were dismissed or left unaddressed.

Trauma clients who are prone to dissociation can benefit from these check-in questions, as they ground them in the present moment and elicit a reflection on their experience that may not have been forthcoming otherwise, or, at least, not for a while. Because of the tendency to dissociate under stress, our clients may not even be aware that things are going well unless they hear themselves say it out loud! Ditto if things are not going well, especially if things are not going well! Talking defines experience. Trauma survivors often resist defining their experiences because they have been so overwhelmingly negative. Or they may not even know how to define their feelings and experience if there is early developmental ego damage or neglect. That is a good thing to know at the outset of a treatment. Feedback from clients gives us so much useful information about how to proceed next in treatment or whether we are even the right person to provide the treatment.

Take a lot of time in beginning sessions to link to previous therapies and encourage the client to compare and contrast styles and techniques. This requires a certain amount of openness on the part of the treater. If we are stuck in thinking our way is the best way, we may have trouble hearing their perspective. Of course, a client may have other, more pressing agendas and crises to attend to in early sessions, but don't be carried too far down that path without checking in. Misunderstandings can happen at any point in the therapy experience. If they happen in the beginning, the unresolved feelings linger and interfere with the developing therapy relationship. As time goes on, these unresolved questions or issues can amplify considerably, possibly resulting in an impasse or therapeutic failure. With a nervous system that is geared up towards fight or flight, the wobbles from early disappointments and conflicts in the therapy can quickly become earthquakes. Never be afraid to stop a session to address the 'elephant in the room' at any point in the therapy.

How we check in is as important as *that* we check in. In the analytic and psychodynamic community, there can be a dynamic where these kinds of check-ins feel like they will be turned back on the client. Many of our clients have already had the experience of feeling 'shrunk' and not in a good way. Some therapists trained in these traditions practice opaqueness and 'neutrality'. When a therapist is sitting with a neutral face (reading stony or sociopathic to the trauma client) and ready to psychoanalyze any answer (at least in the clients' perception), a client will be understandably reluctant to give any immediate feedback. With highly traumatized clients a friendly, open demeanor can go a long way to defusing fear and suspicion. By open, I do not mean, "hey, let me tell you about my day" kind of open. I mean open as in, "I am committed to friendliness and transparency of affect in the moment, and I will not hold your words against you" kind of open. Open face, open heart kind of open.

These check-ins can go both ways. I see no reason why we cannot give our clients our honest impressions as well, especially positive ones like "I really enjoyed meeting with you last week" or "I'm feeling like there is a good fit between your needs and what I have to offer you." If our impression is negative or incompatible in some way, there are ways to comfortably articulate that as well. "I'm not sure I am the best person for you to work with. Let me give you a referral for someone who is more specialized than I am in your issues."

A male client presented with a history of trauma. He had been in a severe boating accident that left him with chronic body pain and had self-diagnosed as having PTSD. As the first sessions went on, he became increasingly belligerent and wanted to talk about angry, bitter feelings towards his wife and other people. He was stuck in his career and angry at people there as well. I felt safe with him but I just had a hard time finding something likeable about him. It wasn't even about him or his issues; the necessary chemistry was not there where I felt I could be totally present for him. I realized that his anger issues needed to be addressed before diving into his trauma work. After the first set of sessions, I told him my assessment and that anger management was not an area of expertise for me. He expressed some disappointment but accepted my referrals to other clinicians in the area that could help him more than I felt I could.

I do not like to refer people out. I do not know any clinician who does. But the truth was, chronic male anger is really not my specialty area nor an area I care to work in. We all have those areas. For every specialty we dislike, there is a clinician for whom that is their bread and butter. Even though a referral represents lost income (and maybe lost pride), the benefit we gain is confidence in the practice that we do have. It is stressful to work with people we do not like or want to work with, and I know some of you do not have a choice for one reason or another. I feel that it is better to kindly refer out early in the treatment than to try to work with a relationship that does not feel good from the outset. If we are in a setting where we are forced to work with this type of client, I recommend soliciting support from colleagues and supervision.

I guarantee that if you are feeling reservations, your client is too. It can be helpful to pinpoint the moment things felt 'off' and refer back to that instance with them. "So, when I asked you about your relationship with your parents, you seemed really uncomfortable. Should we wait to talk about them? Is there something you want to say to me about that?" Reaching into the discomfort instead of ignoring it can be key to letting your client know that they are seen, heard, and, most important, that you are not afraid to hear their opinions of you or your techniques.

Mini Mental Status Observations

State changes are signs of rupture in any relationship. If your client usually has a bright affect, is talkative and friendly and comes in morose and full of complaints, something has obviously happened. The client usually wants to attribute this shift in affect to events in the world external to the therapy, but often the cause is a dynamic that is happening inside the therapy. Harvesting these moments can be tricky, especially if the therapist is not trained in transference analysis, psychodynamics, or dissociative disorders. We want to gently inquire about the status of the therapeutic relationship, but we also don't want to assume everything is about us. Most therapists that I have supervised err on the side of thinking that they are not important enough for the client to have strong feelings about them. Nothing could be further from the truth! Contemplate how small your client's world actually is, and how few people they have with whom they can share their true self and its pain, and you will start to realize that we take up a rather large psychic space in their lives.

With traumatized populations, we have to assume that a certain percentage will have profound fracturing resulting in hidden ego states or alternate personalities. If your client exhibits distinct and frequent state shifts, you can wonder if there may be a profound dissociative process at work. The process to discover the structures behind these dynamics can take months to years. Cultivate patience and excellent observation skills as needed! Administer some reliable tests, such as the Dissociative Experiences Scale (TraumaDissociation.com, 2017). Keep good notes and do frequent mini-mental status assessments. With clients like this, I will frequently record at least mood, affect, insight, and judgment in every note.

If a client is very fractured, they may be unaware of their state shifts or attribute them to somatic states or 'moods'. If they have DID, this process gets interesting. Maybe one personality hates the therapist, and it might not be an adult! When working with dissociative clients, always assume there is a child in the room that can be any age. Go slowly and establish your trustworthiness by being patient and non-forceful. The therapist may have to wait quite a while before the client is integrated enough to talk about the alliance rupture, even if it minor. The harsher the abuse history, the more likely that your client was silenced with extremely painful means. Opening up can take years.

It is paramount to have a clear diagnostic picture of our client. Many highly traumatized clients of mine are diagnosed with dissociative identity disorder. Often they were previously diagnosed as having borderline personality disorder. Since many therapists work somewhat confrontationally with borderlines, these clients have often had very poor previous therapeutic experiences. I have not found confrontation to be of much use when people can switch out of the personality being confronted! If the client has complex polyfragmentation with engineered DID (see Chapter 2), they will have internal programs and/or active external conditioning[2] running to thwart the therapeutic relationship. The bad guys who do the conditioning know how good we are at this work, and they will attempt to disrupt the therapy of their asset any way they can.

Repairing Mini-Ruptures

Let's say you have checked in with your client and there is a negative feeling about the therapy or you have done a session rating scale and find your ratings tanking. What next? Take a second and imagine such a scenario. Where do you feel this news in your body? Your gut? Your head or heart? Notice your first impulses. Perhaps you feel like defending yourself, making excuses, or even blaming your patient. Perhaps you feel deskilled, like an imposter or a failure. Maybe you even have a brief moment where you feel like quitting the profession entirely. These would be very normal and human responses, and I assure you I have had all of them. In a real moment of confrontation with a negative response, we will need to tolerate all of these feelings and more without acting them out upon our patient. No matter how angry or wounding our client is to us in the moment, they are still the patient. They are dependent on us, our skill and good will, and they are in a one down position with us on top.

If you are waiting for this moment to occur in therapy before you process your feelings around failure you are already too late. Being human, therapists will inevitably react the way any human does when they are criticized, they will react like themselves. The best way for you to learn to be accepting of patient negative feedback is to examine your own defenses to being criticized by others and work on that in your day-to-day life. Any unresolved ego issues can and will be stimulated within therapy sessions. Guaranteed. In fact, many of us have noticed how frequently our caseload reflects and challenges us with whatever we are working on personally at any given time. The beauty and the challenge of being a great psychotherapist lies in our willingness to address those reactive places inside of ourselves *before* we get into the therapy hour. As Byron Katie, pioneer of The Work puts it, "Until you look forward to criticism your Work's not done" (Byron Katie International, 2017).

In the moment of negative feedback, if we have done our work, we can choose from a range of possible reactions. The first thing we need to do is accept our own reaction. As Carl Rogers famously said, *"The curious paradox is that when I accept myself just as I am, then I can change"* (Rogers, 1989, emphasis added). Ideally, there is a sequence that goes something like this:

> Patient challenge ➜ Observe words and affect ➜ Feel your own reaction ➜ Accept it ➜ Censor any inappropriate reaction ➜ Take a breath ➜ Decide what the client needs ➜ Respond ➜ Evaluate ➜ Revisit.

If we feel we need to respond in a hurry, we are probably in reaction. Take a beat. You do not need to respond immediately. You can even tell your client, "I'm not sure how to respond to that, and I need time to think about what you just said." I call this 'pressing the hold button'.[3] Your pause in response can be days, minutes, or seconds. Somewhere between feeling your own reaction and responding you may want to schedule a supervision or therapy session for yourself. Therapists in earlier stages of competence may take much longer to process through all these steps than advanced practitioners do, who still traverse all these steps but in a very short period of time within a single session. Do not be ashamed if you become dysregulated. We are human beings after all. There can be tremendous benefit in our clients watching us struggle with our own human reactions. We model a restraint and thoughtfulness that was sorely lacking for them at crucial developmental times in their lives. The fact that we are having a dysphoric reaction but not retaliating provides a new template for human interactions.

In talks I like to present a graphic with a seesaw that shows the more our judgment increases, the more our understanding decreases. If we judge ourselves and/or our clients, we lose an opportunity to be curious. And there is so much to be curious about! Why this interaction? Why now? Are there any contributing external factors, like an anniversary of a trauma or a medical issue? Why does this particular client get under our skin? Is this a habitual characterological reaction of our client or did we trigger them (same question goes for us)? The questions can be endless. How can we get creative about solutions? Curiosity and creativity can go hand in hand for great treatment!

After the response, give your client a chance to reflect on and even rate the interaction. Again, this could be within a single session or in later sessions. It is powerful for clients to know that the therapist does not necessarily have the last word and that the door is always open for them to continue to process uncomfortable interactions. The dynamic of letting your client have the last word can be potentially empowering for them. If you have a highly dissociative client they may not even know how they felt for some time after, other parts might want to come forward and have their say about the interaction. We, too, need to give our self time to reflect and process difficult interactions. Sometimes we may feel poorly about how we presented but later figure out that the way we handled the situation was perfect. Likewise we may respond with what we feel is good therapy but later come to realize was not the best response for that client. After our reflections, we have another chance to make it right by revisiting the situation with the client. We can do this as many times as we need to until we restore a feeling of flow and harmony to the relationship.

In the end, rupture repair demonstrates a deep caring and compassion to our client as well as excellence of practice. They know that this work is not easy for us. Indeed the work of healing traumatized clients with disrupted neuroregulation, unstable affect, and dissociative defense can challenge even the most experienced among us. We will need to refine and incorporate many qualities to assist us in our journey towards wisdom. Our next two chapters explore some of these qualities in depth.

Notes

1 Since the whole treatment was conducted under this *DSM IV* diagnosis, I have kept it here. I consider all patients on the autistic spectrum to have trauma histories. They have all had to struggle by definition with overwhelming sensory stimuli to the point of chronic physical pain. In addition, many of them have also been abused, taunted, belittled, and ignored by people in their lives. Even if their families are lovely, they cannot avoid the abuses heaped on them by ignorant people in society and in their schools.
2 Colleagues report that their clients have been drugged and left with an actor that impersonates their therapist! See Alison Miller's book *Healing the Unimaginable* for more cases.
3 This technique comes out of phone crisis work. Learning to say 'hold, please' is a crucial skill that defuses escalation and gives the telephone screener a chance to run clinical situations past a supervisor when in the heat of the moment with a dangerous situation.

References

Barry Duncan, P., & Miller, S. (2008). *"When I'm Good, I'm Very Good, But When I'm Bad I'm Better": A New Mantra for Psychotherapists*. Retrieved August 28, 2017, from Psychotherapy.net: www.psychotherapy.net/article/therapy-effectiveness#section-the-outcome-rating-scale-(ors)

Byron Katie International. (2017). Retrieved December 8, 2017, from The Work of Byron Katie: http://thework.com/en

Karpman, S. B. (1967). *Fairy Tales and Script Drama Analysis*. Retrieved March 19, 2017, from Karpman Drama Triangle: www.karpmandramatriangle.com/pdf/DramaTriangle.pdf

Katie, B., & Miller, S. (2003). *Loving What Is*. New York: NY: Three Rivers Press.

Miller, A. (2011). *Healing the Unimagineable: Treating Ritual Abuse and Mind Control*. London, UK: Karnac Books.

Rogers, C. (1989). *On Becoming a Person*. New York, NY: Houghton Mifflin Harcourt.

Substance Abuse and Mental Health Services Administration. (2017). *National Registry of Evidence-Based Programs and Practices*. (SAMHSA, Producer). Retrieved December 8, 2017, from SAMHSA: www.nrepp.samhsa.gov/faq.aspx

TraumaDissociation.com. (2017). *Dissociative Experiences Scale—II*. Retrieved December 8, 2017, from TraumaDissociation.com: http://traumadissociation.com/des#references

7 Qualities of the Advanced Trauma Therapist

Your vision will become clear only when you can look into your own heart . . . Who looks outside dreams. Who looks inside, awakens.

—Carl Jung

We so want to believe that there is an objective way to 'do' therapy, that if we can only find the best of the evidence-based practices we will achieve success with our clients. Therapists shell out thousands of dollars every year for trainings and workshops to get the latest and the best cutting-edge techniques. We read the best books from the best experts—whoever that is any given year. Our licensure requirements support this outward focus of continuing education; we can only get credit if we learn something 'new' that is outside of us. Every workshop has to have measurable learning objectives in order to be eligible for credit.

At first glance these standards seem reasonable. After all, every state and many countries have them. Continuing education is a concept derived from the medical model of practice. Modern medicine, including psychology and psychiatry, evolves quickly and it makes sense to keep abreast of new information. Yet, as we have discussed, becoming a great psychotherapist involves much more than just swallowing and digesting new information from the outside to regurgitate to our clients inside of a session. We, ourselves, are the healing modality and therapy, the medium in which that healing occurs. Does it not make sense that to evolve our practices we have to heal and evolve ourselves: our own brain, nervous system, mind, and spirit?

Many of my clients only want to work with a therapist who has experienced trauma. While someone who is trauma naïve can do techniques, they cannot act as a guide out of the experience of trauma in the same way someone can who has already made the journey themselves. The wounded healer must have already done some significant self-healing or they will become the 'blind leading the blind'. Our continuing education requirements not only do not require ongoing self-healing and development as part of the licensure process, they discourage it! One cannot get any credit for therapy, experiential workshops, or healing practices that do not involve a mostly didactic element. This approach to the development of great therapists is literally half-brained! Stuffing our heads full of new techniques and facts will bring limited improvement to our therapy practices. They may comfort therapists, reassure us that we know what we are doing. But do they really make us better therapists? Bring us wisdom? Make us more full of the qualities of that master therapist we want to have and become? It is a shame that we do not lend professional support to personal development, an area of training sure to bring results in the therapy hour no matter what the diagnostic profile.

Our culture, Western culture, especially in America, defines intelligence as the highest good. We want more facts, bigger research, the biggest facts! But intelligence will never be wisdom. *Intelligence uninformed by wisdom can bring great harm.* We collectively put a great deal of trust in the power of intelligent people with the implicit assumption that people will use their knowledge for good. But will they, really? Sometimes I like to discuss this intelligence vs. wisdom issue with other scientifically minded people. Many scientists hold a bias that intelligence can solve all problems, but this stance assumes morality and a good motivation for behavior in all scientists.

Example: Earth. Scientists agree that intelligent people will want the Earth to survive and thrive and therefore teaching more science is good. But some science that we teach allows people to destroy the Earth faster and with more efficiency than ever before. Take fracking, for example, or coal burning, or nuclear reactor meltdowns. Highly intelligent people using highly sophisticated equipment design all of these modes of energy production. These 'smart' technologies literally destroy the Earth. Wisdom cultures, like American Indians or First Nations People or the Aborigines (or any indigenous culture ever, really) decry these modes as disrespectful and harmful to our mother, the Earth. They think very little of scientific 'intelligence' that destroys the habitats of animals, pollutes the environment for all, and destabilizes an entire global ecosystem! They want to know, if we are so intelligent, why we are destroying our food and water sources. They have a point. Wisdom always holds the Earth in balance. Wisdom weighs intelligence against the larger picture and includes morality as a balancing point. Wisdom includes morality. Intelligence is amoral.

In the field of psychology, we can see the same dilemma and hubris as around science. We elevate the intellect by funding research that may or may not be informed by wisdom. At a major trauma conference I once heard a group of students present a paper on retraumatization that basically showed that repetition compulsion[1] was 'a thing'. (People with traumatic childhoods were likely to have more traumas in their lifespan than non-traumatized people.) At the end of the workshop, I approached the students and asked them if they had heard of or read any Freud. They had not read any of Freud's writings. They unwittingly took one of the founding concepts of Western psychotherapy and did an exceedingly simple study to prove 'their' hypothesis without any awareness at all of the history of the origins of their own field. Talk about reinventing the wheel! While one could argue that money and time had been wasted, there was nothing malignant going on here, just a lack of therapeutic wisdom and instruction.

Worse examples of intelligence uninformed by wisdom occur in psychology, some of them having to do with a different kind of Intelligence, with a capital 'I'. We now know that psychologists and psychiatrists collaborated to come up with ways to 'interrogate' prisoners of war during the Iraq war that were both illegal and immoral. Against all of their professional Codes of Ethics, these clinicians signed off on waterboarding and other equally inhumane techniques as legitimate methods to get prisoners to divulge information. These techniques were not only inhumane, but they lacked wisdom, as experts widely agree that confessions made under torture and duress are unreliable and cause brain damage, especially in the areas of memory (Stone, 2016). Extreme methods also cause blowback in the form of retaliation from the communities of the people tortured. Few therapists would agree with these psychologists and their techniques, but these corrupt characters did come out of our schools and our professional organizations. They demonstrate the endpoint of intelligence divorced from any semblance of wisdom.

Indian Koshas of Mind

Indian sages described five koshas, or sheaths, that surrounded the essential soul or 'atman' of the human being: the physical, the energetic, two levels of mind: intellect and wisdom, with bliss being the final kosha (Prabhavananda & Isherwood, 1970). They described that inside of these koshas dwells the indestructible atman. In this system, the two levels of mind correspond with intelligence and wisdom. Their system is exceedingly ancient, thousands of years old, and probably passed down by oral tradition for a long period before it showed up in ancient writings.

They distinguished, through intense meditation and introspection, two levels of mind in the human being: the manomayakosha (that is, the kosha appearing in God's creation as intellect) and the vijnanamayakosha (the kosha appearing in God's creation as wisdom). We can call them the thinking mind and the wisdom mind. In our own pre-Descartes Western history, we also once had the distinction of ratio and intellect: the thinking mind and the intuitive or 'angelic' mind, as St. Augustine described it. In both the Indian and Western systems, the thinking mind is more gross, corresponding to the brain; the wisdom, or intuitive mind, is closer to the 'mind of God', more subtle and less obvious. In modern times (in the West), we have tended to emphasize the worth of the thinking mind, which is also equated with logic and masculinity, and to devalue the intuitive/wisdom mind, which is often associated with femininity and regarded with suspicion. The phrase 'women's intuition' is common in our lexicon but not always regarded with kindness and respect.

For Indians, the manomayakosha, or thinking brain, has certain qualities. Because it thinks, it is also afflicted by doubt. Like Freud's pleasure principal, it is attached to well-being. This kosha requires empirical proof through the senses, which is how it gathers information. It bears some similarity to our concept of ego; it mediates between the internal needs of the body and the external world, formulates plans, and executes them. It presides over (or is buffeted by) thoughts, emotions, and beliefs. Cognitive psychology theory pairs well with the functions of this kosha. When things go wrong with or affect the manomayakosha, mental illness and afflictions arise such as anxiety, depression, and trauma. The manomayakosha seems to reflect many of the functions of what we might call left-hemisphere thinking.

The vijnanamayakosha, or wisdom mind, is not subjected to thinking and therefore is not afflicted by doubts. This intuitive or angelic mind senses reality as a gestalt. It knows without thinking. Indian scripture describes this mind as attached to deep knowledge married to action.[2] It acts on the principal that true knowledge brings beneficial actions that benefit all. This mind is not informed by bodily needs for survival, but by higher consciousness, archetypes, and noble truths. Its method consists of inspiration, genius, leaps of imagination, and flights of fancy informed by profound connection. The mood in this state of mind is not doubtful or brooding but joyful and blissful. This bliss is not giddy or silly but a calm abiding state of connection to self, other, and the Divine. The average human does not abide in the wisdom mind. We may have trouble understanding the voice of the vijnanamayakosha, especially if it is outside our cultural reference. Where our thinking minds shout at us continually, this voice merely whispers. In order to tune into the wisdom mind, one needs to engage in wisdom practices such as meditation, selfless service, ceremony, and contemplation. It corresponds to the big picture thinking of the right hemisphere.

In making the leap from competent therapy to the wise therapy of master therapists, I find it useful to contemplate these different but related aspects of mind. To do so requires a suspension of materialistic thinking and an engagement of a holistic view of the human being and mind. When we have engaged both the rational and intuitive minds, certain qualities manifest in the therapist.

Best Qualities

Over decades of work and training other therapists, I have noticed some qualities that make them work well with traumatized people. These qualities integrate the best from our thinking minds and wisdom minds. Our clients with the most trauma challenges are great teachers. They know what works for them and what doesn't because there is nothing subtle about being triggered. They know who they feel safe or unsafe with and why. Some of these clients may not have normal intelligence. They may live in hospitals, prisons, or residential treatment centers. Perhaps lacking language and impulse control, they teach us through extreme acting out behaviors what works for them (and for us!).

Before I was in private practice with a relatively genteel group of patients, I worked on inpatient units and residential treatment centers for almost

15 years. If I messed up and triggered clients in these settings, I could end up being assaulted. I was, at various times, hit, bitten, spit upon, sworn at, scratched, and had feces thrown at me. I learned fast, and loved these clients fiercely, as they were my best supervisors. Feedback was instant and uncompromising. People either loved this work or hightailed it out to a less demanding setting. The workers who stayed developed mastery in several areas of themselves. The qualities of master therapists (and master residential counselors) are fairly universal and are compiled below. These qualities will get refined over time one way or another. We can help that process along by embracing them and developing them consciously.

Intuition

Americans are exceedingly well trained, some might say overtrained, in the thinking mind and are lacking in access to (and value of) their intuition, at least compared to some cultures. Great therapists are intuitive. Intuition is a big word. It covers phenomena that range from gut feelings and hunches to full on ESP or psychic abilities or, as it is called in the yoga world, siddhis. It is widely understood in the East and in indigenous cultures that spiritual practices such as meditation or yoga will naturally increase one's psychic 'powers' or abilities. Well, what is a great therapy session but a single-pointed meditation on another human being? For clinicians who take their craft seriously over a long period of time, it is not unusual to start to develop a sixth sense about their clients or even to uncover some more profound intuitive gifts inside themselves. We do not talk about this very often as professionals, and when we do it is not in public forums. After I give talks on this subject, I always have people who want to pull me aside and talk about the 'unusual' experiences they have had with clients in the treatment room. Most of the time the growth of intuition is incremental and based, in part, on pattern recognition. But sometimes there can be an explosion of consciousness or an intrusion of spiritual consciousness into a session (or series of sessions).

I was sitting with a client whom I had been seeing for a couple of years. Every year this client would have an anniversary reaction to the death of his father, resulting in a several week period of depression. I asked the client what he had done to celebrate the passing of his father that year. He reported that he made himself mashed potatoes, because his father loved mashed potatoes so much he used to order them for dessert at restaurants. As my client was telling me this, I started to smell mashed potatoes in my office. I shook it off and told myself that it was only the pizza party going on downstairs that

I was smelling. As my client continued to talk, I had an overpowering experience of the smell of mashed potatoes, as if they were sitting in a big steaming bowl in my lap! It was weird. I had been experiencing a lot of psychic phenomena that year—seeing lights coming out of clients, feeling spiritual presences in treatment rooms, and processing clients' physical pains through my own body. I knew enough to go inside and ask for more information. When I did so I saw very clearly, in my mind's eye, the picture of a tall Irish looking fellow sitting in the chair between me and my client, and I knew it was his father. I asked my client, "Was your father tall?" "Did he look just like you?" "Were you his favorite?" He answered affirmatively with an enquiring look on his face. I hesitated. Nothing in my Harvard teaching hospital psychotherapy training had prepared me for a moment like this. Since I had good rapport with this client, I leaned forward and asked him if he would mind if I stepped off the formal psychotherapy page for a moment and share something a little unusual with him. He nodded. I shared with him the vision I was having of his father, and communicated the message that his father loved him very much. Tears streamed down my patient's face, and he left without saying another word. It was two years before we revisited that moment. In the meantime, I noticed that his anniversary reaction was completely cured from that moment on. When we finally did talk about that session, I asked him how he felt about me stepping so far away from my usual role as therapist. He shrugged his shoulders and said, "Well, I knew you were intuitive."

This incident happened 15 years ago and set me on a path of much discovery. It is the only time I have had a dead person show up for family therapy.[3] I am not a medium. What I discovered in the course of getting my intuitive 'gifts' under control was that this ability did run in my family, in my Celtic blood down a matrilineal line. Many therapists have natural gifts of intuition that are genetic. I have a theory that Europeans shut down these abilities due to the prolonged 300 years of terrorism known as the Inquisition, but I will save that thesis for another book. Suffice it to say that we all have some level of giftedness with intuition. Like athletes, great intuitives can be shaped by practice and determination, but some start with more aptitude than others.

As with this client, I find that most people benefit from the judicious use of intuition. They feel even more deeply heard and considered when I access my vijnanamayakosha (wisdom mind) in session and share my impressions with them. This process is akin to what psychoanalysts call 'reverie', daydreaming into the life and mind of the patient. Analyst Thomas Ogden, MD, described reverie as "our ruminations, daydreams, bodily sensations, fleeting perceptions, images emerging from states of half-sleep, tunes, and phrases that run through our minds, and so on. I view reverie as a personal/private event and an intersubjective one" (Thomas, 1999).

Where an analyst might use the unconscious material in their reverie to formulate an intervention (or to withhold one), an intuitive or shamanic practitioner might share the undigested material with the client directly, as I did above, without assigning any particular meaning or intervention to it. In this way of working, the client assigns the meaning to the reverie, not the therapist. The intuitive therapist just shares the raw material without saying it is 'real' or 'fantasy'. Usually I say something like, "I'm seeing this image in my head right now that I feel moved to share with you," and then I share the image without censoring or interpretation. This method of working with intuition appears to be particularly powerful in working with traumatized clients. Invariably these images evoke powerful emotional reactions that make the client feel deeply understood and joined with by the clinician.

A Sense of Humor

If you are going to work with traumatized millennials, humor might be one of the most important qualities you can develop in yourself as a therapist. The millennial generation has been raised on a steady diet of *The Daily Show*, *The Simpsons*, *Sponge Bob Square Pants*, *Saturday Night Live*, late night television, and BuzzFeed, with comedy that predigests the horrors of the day for them. Even with other generational groups, humor can be your biggest ally. There is a famous definition of humor in the comedy world: *Comedy = Tragedy + Time.* In order to survive the unsurvivable, many of our clients have already developed several types of humor: absurd, gallows, silly, dry, sarcastic, etc. In order to join with these clients, we should know how to laugh with them, but never, of course, at them.

Over the years I have found, to my great surprise, that there is nothing that cannot be laughed at during the course of therapy. People can sublimate their horror, their rage, and their inexpressible feelings into comic reflection. If you remember from the earlier discussion on ego defenses, humor is a higher-level ego defense. The ability of a client to laugh[4] in the face of unspeakable events shows a very high degree of trust in the therapist and a certain amount of healing that has already occurred. Our ability to reflect on our clients' commentary with a well-placed humorous comment not only can lighten the mood, it can offer a loving perspective on what our client has endured. Humor moves us out of our place of habitual response and offers us another place to stand in regards to suffering and even extreme suffering.

Cultures who have been extremely oppressed already know the power of humor; they have evolved humor to survive and as an act of defiance in the face of oppression. Why do you think so many comedians are Irish, Black, and/or Jewish? Clients can make jokes and laugh at therapist reflections about events like cancer, death, childhood torture, regaining horrendous memories, the experiences of being DID, and other things that most people do not want to hear about, much less joke about. Amazingly, it's OK or even really bonding to find humor in such tragedies when you are attuned to the client, and you do it from the right place.

Besides enhancing the therapeutic alliance, humor has been shown to:

- Promote the relaxation response
- Boost the immune system
- Improve brain function
- Lower blood pressure
- Reduce anxiety and depression
- Be cathartic
- Enhance intimacy in a relationship

The comedian Tig Notaro made comedy history in 2012 by performing stand-up a couple of days after she was diagnosed with breast cancer in both breasts. Other comedians who watched her that night called her performance 'legendary'. Here is a transcript of the opening of the set delivered in her typical deadpan style:

> Hello, I have cancer. How are you? Hi. How are you? Are you having a good time? . . . It's a good time, diagnosed with cancer. It feels good. I was just diagnosed with cancer. Oh. God. Oh my God. It's weird because with humor the equation is tragedy plus time equals comedy. I'm just at tragedy right now. That's where I am in the equation. Here's what happened.
>
> They found a lump. I said, "Oh, no, that's my boob" [Tig is famously small chested]. "Oh, no we found a lump on the other side too." "Yeah, that's my boob too. Those are my boobs."
>
> Somebody over here keeps going, "Ohh! She might really have cancer." It's OK. It's going to be OK . . . It might not be OK. . . *You're* going to be OK. I'm not sure what's going on with me.
>
> (Notaro, 2013)

To use humor well in therapy, comments have to be empathic and well timed. They need to come from an ineffable place inside made of equal parts insight, affection, and good will. Sometimes, I would say much of the time, humor comes from just being completely present to what is happening, as Tig Notaro did. Life can be quite absurd. Therapists can also use some stock jokes; one does not have to be a comedian to use humor effectively. When I started therapy (decades ago), my therapist was trying to address my potential reasons for lack of social supports. She quoted Groucho Marx, "Maybe it's like this: I never would join any club that would have me for a member." It cracked me up, eased tensions, and made it OK to go deeper into my own mind by universalizing my fears. For several years I worked with a survivor of ritual abuse and mind control; then I closed my practice for a period of a year. As we were winding up our termination process, my client volunteered that she would miss the 'entertainment factor' of our work together. I took this as a high compliment.

There are many ways to cultivate your inner comedian. One of the best is to take some classes in improvisational comedy, which is different from stand-up or sketch comedy in that nothing is pre-written, and all the comedy unfolds in the moment. Humor that arises in improvisational comedy comes from purely being in the moment in a real way, not from trying to be funny. Real life is funny all by itself. Improv recognizes it and heightens those moments. When the audience sees themselves and their everyday dynamics up on stage, it tickles their funny bone, especially when the actors are spontaneous and unselfconscious. If comedians become narcissistically injured on stage—not funny; if they do the same scene and fail miserably with joy—funny! There is a parallel here to great therapy. When the therapist is sincere and present without defensiveness, all things become possible in healing, including (and maybe especially) humor!

To develop your sense of humor and timing, take an improv class. Watch comedy shows. Go to live comedy. Read funny books. Sometimes our work gets so heavy we ourselves forget how to be light in the face of so much suffering. A good dose of self-deprecating humor does wonders for the occasional case of inflated self-importance. Remember the saying, "Angels can fly because they take themselves lightly!"

One of my big discoveries was how much improvisational comedy games enhanced my classes on PTSD. Many traumatized folks arrive to class with social anxiety, suspicion, hypervigilance, and all the usual symptoms of trauma. I decided to play a little warm up game called 'Zip, Zap, Zop'. The game is simple. It starts in a circle. Someone begins by pointing and looking at another play saying "zip". The receiving player points at another player and says "zap" and then the third player points at someone else and says "zop," at which point the cycle repeats.[5] The most important part of this game is failing! When someone misses (and they inevitably will as the game speeds up), the whole group steps into the circle with their arms around each other and says "AH-OOH-GAH," just like an old-timey car horn. Alternatively, the player who missed can take a failure bow, saying in an Elvis voice, "Thank you. Thank you very much!" Before long my class is breathing, looking each other in the eyes (because you have to in order to play the game well), and bonding over shared failure. Time and again I see hypervigilance relax, laughter bubble up, and bonding start to occur immediately as we play this and other comedy games.

Curiosity

When I think about curiosity, I think about the Zen concept of 'beginner's mind'. To approach a client in curiosity is to empty oneself of concepts and judgments. Or if we can't empty ourselves, we can at least suspend our tendency to believe what we think. Curiosity is rarely talked about in trainings and psychological circles. I'm not sure why this is, as it is one of the most valuable qualities a great therapist has.

To be truly curious about someone else requires humility. When we are in the middle stages of therapeutic competence we may want to impress our clients with our level of expertise, to show them quickly what we know and how we can help them à la Sherlock Holmes. This tendency to quickly assess and show what we know can arise out of both internal and external pressures. Maybe we only have a few sessions to work with a client and we need to give answers to insurers and administrators quickly. There are also internal pressures we put on ourselves at a certain level of practice, so that we can show our competence to ourselves as well as the client. If we are not careful at this stage we can develop a rigid professional ego—the opposite of 'beginner's mind'.

I have said that part of clinical intuition is pattern recognition. While this is true, we don't want to take a cookie cutter approach to clients. The tricky part of excellent practice is that we need to be able to make quick initial assessments and see patterns while still maintaining the awareness that human beings are infinitely complex and worthy of deep inquiry and study. If we need to 'be right' too much we may miss important clues as to the best way to help the specific person sitting in front of us. Who are they really? How are they the same as and different from other people we have seen with similar issues?

Curiosity requires intellectual honesty and rigor. If we think that all the answers have already been found—from a previous diagnosis or disorder— we have already lost at greatness. We can never assume that we know all there is to know about anything, any diagnosis, or anybody. At some level we know this, but many of us are reluctant to stand out from the crowd and ask questions or put forward different ideas. What is difficult in today's world is the emphasis both academically and professionally on validating our ideas through other people's ideas.[6] In America in particular, we are taught to look outside of ourselves for answers, to look to others' genius and accomplishments and to footnote them. I hear from colleagues that this standard is not so rigid in other training centers in other countries and that at places like Oxford, for example, professors encourage students to come up with their own ideas rather than regurgitate others' ideas.

So we know a lot about what other people say, how other people treat certain disorders. What about our own instincts? How did the so-called geniuses and masters come up with their ideas in the first place? They did it by going inside, being curious, and not stopping at the existing information available to them. It is the only way our field progresses—through curiosity, exploration, and daring to have our own thoughts.

Most of the traumatized patients I have seen have been misdiagnosed, and have been in two, three, or more treatments before they come to see me. I get curious about that. What happened? Where did they feel the previous therapy went wrong for them? What was that therapist's formulation? Do I agree with it? I give myself permission to start over and do not feel like I owe any previous treater allegiance, even if they are well known, even if they are a friend. That is not why my client has come to see me. My client wants something different or they wouldn't be here.

Great therapists empower themselves to be curious and incorporate new pieces of information both at the beginning of treatment and as the therapy goes along. Every new piece of information is another piece of the puzzle. Sometimes the new piece is so big it requires a new perspective on the puzzle, and maybe a new or additional diagnostic profile. I get excited when this happens, and curious all over again. Because trauma work is so complex and still really in its infancy professionally, we all have a chance to contribute much knowledge and understanding. The variables are infinite, and so can be our curiosity. I have seen plenty of clients who were fed up with clinicians that they felt could not hear or incorporate information that was important to them, but I have never had a client complain about their therapist's curiosity and spirit of honest inquiry.

Curiosity can be a great tool to use when you are at an impasse with a client. If you ever watched the TV detective show *Columbo*, you might recall the actor, Peter Falk, squinting and scratching his head while he asked a question 'out of curiosity' just before he nailed the suspect: "There's just one more thing I don't understand. . . ." I find this approach really helpful in gentle confrontations where there is a discrepancy in information or perhaps truthfulness. The curious approach slides past the defensiveness that is aroused when definitive interpretive or even accusatory statements are made. Motivational Interviewing technique calls this 'curious inquiry' and references the 'Columbo Technique' as their example, too.

Awareness

At the beginning of the movie *Contact* (Steven, Hart, & Zemeckis, 1997), there is this amazing shot where the camera pulls back from a girl at a window, and it keeps pulling back while widening its view and ours. As the camera travels further up and out from the girl's eye we see the house she lives in, the farm, the area, and eventually we pull up into Earth's orbit and further out, into the solar system, the galaxy, through nebulae, and then into interstellar space where entire galaxies float, numerous as grains of sands. We realize we are hearing every broadcast that has ever come out of Earth, broadcasts that echo around our universe. As the camera continues to pull us further into space we realize we are also being pulled back in time, eventually to the very beginnings of the universe itself, billions of years ago. It is an astonishing view that makes us realize how little of the universe our consciousness occupies. We all tend to get caught in the weeds of daily life and can drown in the minutiae without ever 'pulling back the camera'.

Accomplished therapists are masters of awareness. They can see the forest, the trees, and the bugs crawling on the trees. This multidimensional focus makes therapy a demanding discipline. As students, we learn to expand our bandwidth from the ordinary content of conversation to the realization that discourse also contains dynamics and process. Clinical work teaches us to push against the previous limits of our awareness. Like all growth, this accommodation can edge us out of our comfort zones. As medical students do, we start to see the world differently and to assume a different role in it—sometimes to a fault, diagnosing everyone around us and ourselves with various maladies. As we mature clinically and integrate our expanded awareness, we settle down and can move back and forth between social and therapeutic interactions with ease and boundaries. We integrate new skills into our clinical conversations.

Eventually we hit a plateau where we feel comfortable with our level of practice and our tools. It is at this point that our practice may stagnate if we are not careful. We may miss things or encounter 'difficult' clients that make us feel deskilled. We may fall into habits and ruts that we are not aware of. Therapists who have broken through the gravity of mundane practice all have this quality in common: they are on fire! Either they are on fire with a passion for the work and/or a passion for personal growth, or they are painfully in the fire of trials and tribulations with clients and/or in their own personal life. Aging helps with this process of awareness, because the longer we spend on this planet, the more adversity we will face personally and professionally. It's simple math, really. To modify our earlier comedic equation, $Time = Tragedy + Comedy$. We are given infinite chances for personal growth and maturity to emerge.

Awareness is not the same as knowledge. Think of the *Contact* camera shot. We know there is a universe out there and we know it is immense, but grasping that immensity, the sense of deep space and time, is a matter of awareness, not cognitive knowledge. It is the difference between knowing water is wet and getting pushed into the pool. Knowledge, for a therapist, can become a barrier to awareness by keeping us in our head and out of our intuition, in the 'safe zone' where we are insulated from awareness. Our clients will sense this about us: either that we are not completely willing to take the journey of healing with them or that we really are. Every single client, no matter how verbal or nonverbal, no matter their IQ, how trusting or untrusting, knows if we are with them or not. They always know.

When we really become aware of the immensity of the human mind, what little we have explored of it, how fragile humans are, the amount of abuse and trauma there is in the world, what greatness and horror human beings are capable of, the amount of time and effort it takes to heal from the 'ocean of suffering' as the Eastern philosophers put it, we are overwhelmed. At this point, we have some choices. We can allow ourselves to be deeply humbled. We can become paralyzed with the immensity of it. Or we can defend against our awareness with any means at our disposal: our reputations, our intellect, our habits of ego, our degrees, our articles and books. In order to become a mature and wise clinician, we must allow our hearts to be broken, to accept the (seemingly) random pain in the universe,[7] and realize the profound limitations of our knowledge to help people move out of suffering. The path of awareness can be painful, but it is also the only sane and mobilized path. Being paralyzed or defended is to engage in freeze, fight, or flight. If our nervous systems are engaged in sympathetic activation, how can we help our patients to heal? How can we grow?

The first time I drove through the Alps I went through a pass at over 10,000 feet, and the bottom dropped out of my world. Tears sprang to my eye. I felt myself but an ant in the immensity of rocky spires, glaciers, and spacious skies on this spinning ball hurtling through the immensity of a solar system I could not grasp. Did my life even matter in such immensity? There is something obliterating to the ego about awareness, and this is a good thing! Underneath a shattered self-importance that I did not even know that I had, I found immense gratitude and the realization that everything I had or would ever experience was a complete gift.

As a trauma therapist, when I allow myself to drop into the immensity of the work between two people, I am simultaneously humbled and uplifted. This person, this client, who has perhaps known only betrayal and trauma is putting their faith in me. Me! I stand between them and utter despair and darkness. I have to trust that what I have to offer is good enough, and that they will continue to keep themselves alive (after all, they have so far) for the work. I know that good technique, awareness, and connection heals in a magical and ineffable way, and I know that it is a privilege to do my job, that I am being given an immense gift—when I am in awareness.

Therapists need to cultivate awareness consciously. We cannot count on a spontaneous or automatic awakening. We need to do the dirt time. It is a full-time job, actually not even a job, it is a way of life to cultivate awareness from moment to moment. There is no wisdom, no great therapeutic moments without awareness chosen daily, month after month, year after year. I have not yet, in 40 years in this field, found the bottom to awareness, no moment where I've thrown up my hands and said, "That's it! I have all the awareness that there is to have!" I hope you do not find the end of awareness either.

Humility

The word humility derives from the Latin word *humilis*, which means grounded, low, or 'from the earth'. Merriam-Webster gives a definition of humility as "the quality or state of not thinking you are better than other people" (Merriam-Webster Dictionary, 2017). Our clients, if they have been betrayed by other humans, have almost always been betrayed by people with more status and power than they have had. They are exquisitely sensitive to the dynamic of arrogance vs. humility. They want us to be good therapists; they want us to be knowledgeable, even at the top of our field, but they do not want us to think we are better than they are. Many of them already feel worse than everybody else due to their trauma or abuse history.

Humble people embrace their mistakes as learning opportunities and do not have trouble admitting when they are wrong. Unfortunately, we live in a culture where many see failure or mistakes as a sign of weakness or incompetence. This conditioning begins in school, where mistakes are punished and 'perfection' is rewarded—with grades, with college admissions, and later with salaries. In order to be able to be really present with our clients and help them, we need to be able to accept our status as 'not better than anyone else' and accept a perception of failure from our clients from time to time.

> *After many years of working with a dual diagnosis client who also had profound medical issues, a client became stuck in his anger towards his providers. He was in pain; nothing helped. His doctors did not understand. His friends did not understand. His partner did not understand, and I did not understand. Week after week he came in rejecting any possible avenue of approach for his medical and psychiatric problems. These sessions were grueling, but I told myself that he needed this time to rant. Sometimes it felt like a much younger self was in charge of his behavior. I worked hard not to defend myself or to try to 'fix' him. Finally, this stage of work burnt itself out. He had a massive shift and started telling me that he knew he was out of line, that he would leave my office wondering why he behaved like that. It was as if he was in the backseat of the car that another part of himself was driving. He discovered that his angry, tearful self was an early teenager, stuck in a time zone of helplessness and abuse. He accepted, embraced, and integrated this part of himself, after which the rants and attacks stopped. It had never been about me, but only this unintegrated part of himself.*

I'm not gonna lie. This was a tough time. I don't think I could have withstood it in an earlier phase of my career. But it was absolutely necessary for me to hear this client out completely and thereby let him hear himself out. If I had made this be about me, or about 'respect' (still me) or about 'acting out' (still me) or about 'being appropriate' (still me), I could have lost him to suicide, or to a drug relapse or to the streets. Part of what helped me get through this time was the thought, "There but for the grace of God go I." That thought can both comfort and terrify us, because it is true. Deep down we know it is. Any of us could have been born into different and more adverse circumstances. When we separate ourselves from our clients, put ourselves above them ("I would never behave that way, no matter what"), we lose the opportunity to join with them, to understand. And they know it! Always, our clients know when we are with them and when we are sitting in judgment (no matter how subtle) of them. Don't you? Don't you know when folks are judging you, thinking they are better than you are? Have you ever had a supervisor or professor like this? We have all been there.

It is never too late in a therapy to be humble, to admit that perhaps we misunderstood, had a bad day, got it wrong. We can take ourselves off our own pedestals before our clients dump us off! Besides, the more work we do, the more we see and are challenged, the harder it gets to stay up there. Eventually you won't be tempted to climb up at all.

Some therapists have the opposite problem and suffer from a lack of confidence or low self-esteem. Or they may have ego involved in being the most humble. Low esteem in your abilities can be as big a problem in the treatment room as overinflated self-esteem. Our clients need to believe that we can help them, and for them to believe us we need to believe in ourselves. Some clients are belligerent and need a therapist who is not easily intimidated and can stand up to them. If knowledge and good supervision are not enough to boost your own sense of status in the clinical hour, therapy may be required. An insecure therapist can easily become an arrogant or ineffective one.

I do not believe that any of us are there yet, including myself. It is a journey, a process like everything else. I only know that if anyone claims they have mastered humility, they probably haven't.

Creativity

Therapists who cannot engage their creative faculties can easily become stuck in power struggles with clients. Without creativity we have to rely on procedures and rote methods. Some of the evidence-based therapies give us such tools. But what happens when they stop working? Do we keep hammering away at the procedure, blaming the client when the method doesn't take, or do we find another way?

In India, the gods and goddesses hold several tools in their many arms. These tools are all for the mind, to help struggling humanity reach enlightenment. Working with the mind is such an incredible challenge; we need as many tools as possible to help people surmount and put to rest their intense suffering, or as Freud put it "to reduce abject misery to ordinary unhappiness."

For difficult cases I like to use what I think of as the 'dartboard approach' to treatment. The dartboard approach requires humility and flexibility on the part of the practitioner, and it's very simple. If one intervention doesn't work, try another one. And keep trying different ones until you find one that hits the bull's-eye. There really are no wrong interventions (as long as they are ethical), just ones that work and ones that do not. We cannot always predict ahead of time which those will be.

The League School group home housed several teenaged male residents who had varying degrees of autism and trauma. Some had speech; some did not. We had an excellent psychiatrist and behavioral consultation team. One boy would have frequent tantrums in the spring and fall. In the summer, this was not an issue as he could always wear shirts and shorts from rotating piles. In the winter, he could do the same with long pants and sweaters. But when the weather was variable he would have fits if a counselor instructed him to wear shorts (because it was 80 plus degrees!) when he had worn pants the day before. He would tantrum, lash out, and hurt people at times. We addressed his behavior with carrots and sticks, rewards if he did not tantrum, privileges withheld if he did. One day his primary counselor proposed an idea at staff meeting. He had figured out that this boy's behavior had something to do with the seasons and the unpredictability of temperature, not about compliance to authority. He thought this boy (who had limited verbal skills) needed a rule that he could understand; in fact he pointed out, this boy already had a rule, "wear the same thing you did yesterday." It was the breaking of the rule that undid him. Like many autistic individuals, rules stabilized him and made his environment predictable. The counselor bought a thermometer and put a red mark on it. He told his charge that there was a new rule. When the silver was above the mark he was to wear shorts and when it was below the mark he was to wear long pants. After years of seasonal struggles, the problem was fixed just like that!

Sometimes it is hard to say who gets more stuck in treatment, the client or the therapist! As the saying goes, "if your only tool is a hammer, the whole world looks like a nail." When we feel we have to stick to certain pre-approved interventions, we cannot respond creatively to our clients. Prolonged exposure therapy works great for some people. Others want to run screaming from the room when it is proposed. We need to have a variety of tools that we can employ creatively, and know how to improvise our own tools if none of the tools in our tool kit is right for the job.

How many of you, for instance, stay in your chair all session, or insist that your clients do? Are all your sessions verbal? Do you ever play games with adult clients or just sit and talk with young children? I have one client who does not want to do any work at all until we have smudged the treatment room space. Many of the younger clinicians I supervise feel that they must do some agency-recommended protocol. They get very anxious when I ask them what they would really like to do in session. With some encouragement, they start engaging their own creativity in sessions. There are ways to satisfy agency requirements while still keeping basic human creativity alive and meeting the needs of both you and your clients.

Here is a great secret from decades of therapy. Ready? There is no right way to do therapy! We will never find the Holy Grail of evidence-based treatment.

Research studies point us in a direction, but it is up to us to determine whether our interventions hit the mark. You are the Holy Grail for your client. Your knowledge plus your intuition coupled with your creativity will give you the genius you need to come up with the right intervention. And if it isn't right, throw another dart!

Receptivity

We all need to be received and accepted in order to heal. If we as therapists are too aggressive, too yang, too much in the mode of doing therapy instead of being therapeutic, we miss a great clinical opportunity. When we come into therapy with an agenda, even if that agenda is a great new technique, we take opportunities for healing away from our client. Our agenda can interfere with a client's sense of agency, a chance to be fully heard out, and an opportunity for them to discover themselves.

The brain is a weird thing. When we have thoughts that remain unspoken, they can bounce around inside of us but never really settle or become integrated. Those thoughts need to come out our mouths, travel around the side of our head, and go into our own ears before we can really process them. If we are sitting with a receptive listener, we can process our thoughts and feelings even more efficiently. This is the magic of the 'talking cure' of psychotherapy. When the listener has an agenda, the ability to be present diminishes, and the magic is lost.

Another important component of receptivity for the trauma patient consists of being believed. Great trauma therapists (and great therapists in general) do not trouble themselves with validating memories. We are not lawyers after all; we are after healing, not convictions. To listen carefully to a trauma disclosure is to suspend disbelief and enter into the world of our client. We understand that the symbolic value of the memories are as important (maybe more important) than what happened. To be a receptive trauma therapist is also to understand that early disclosures are the 'easiest' memories that our clients share. It is best to leave plenty of room for revisions and the unfolding of context and detail over time with those memories. If we try to move in and 'go for' memories, we have to let go of receptivity and can scare our clients into forgetfulness or suspicion. All trauma clients are allergic to force because of what they have endured. We may not feel that a line of questioning is forceful, but *any move we make towards a client can be experienced as force*.

Again, I'd like to highlight that receptivity, like other qualities mentioned in this chapter, can be counterintuitive in such an aggressive, doing culture. The quality of receptivity is sexualized and feminized in a patriarchal culture. We all want to act but not to be acted upon. Yet, for our clients to experience their own empowerment, they need to feel that they can affect us, change our minds or even our hearts with their stories and perspectives. We do not need to be monolithic 'bastions of strength', stoically bearing the banner of healing. We do need to allow ourselves to be fluid, to be moved. To fully embrace another's story is to have one's world changed. Will we allow it? When we do, miraculously, our clients can then shift, too.

Hopefulness

In the face of so much suffering, it takes great courage to keep our hearts open to hope, especially in dark times. I had lunch recently with a colleague who asked me about my hope for the world. She, like so many of us, felt overwhelmed with the piling up of bad news upon bad news. She saw her patients heroically struggling against odds that were not ever in their favor, emotionally or societally. She is not alone. I think all of us will hit that point in our practices sooner or later; some of us do on a regular basis. Just when you think you can't hear anything worse, you do. The sad truth is that sometimes things can and do get worse, much worse.

Spiritual groups talk more about hope than therapists do. It is one of those areas we carefully skirt with each other. Some people don't like the idea of hope. They believe that hope constantly leads people out of mindfulness, out of reality. Maybe it does. But lack of hope can lead people into suicidality and poor choices. Even if we want to be hopeful, how can we do that in a time when it feels like so much is being lost? That the darkness has overtaken the light?

When I think of hope I think of that seminal line in the movie *Apollo 13* where actor Ed Harris as mission control flight director Gene Kranz says, "We've never lost an American in space; we're sure as hell not going to lose one on my watch. Failure is not an option" (Grazer, Lovell & Howard, 1995). Even though this line was written for the film, it represented the real Kranz's philosophy so much that he named his autobiography after it. To be hopeful for our clients is to take the attitude that failure with a client is not an option, meaning, as he did, that of all the possible futures to contemplate we will contemplate the future with the best outcome. It does not mean that bad things can't happen. They can and they do. But to hope in this context means to assume a position of success mentally rather than to anticipate failure, even if the situation feels hopeless.

Hope Is a Choice, Not a Feeling

If we are aware that we can choose hope even when we feel hopeless, we empower ourselves and our patients. Hope mobilizes us. Hope gives us a reason to keep going. Hope may be an act of faith, and it doesn't even have to be a spiritual faith, but a faith in anything: faith in therapy, faith in human resilience, faith in your client or yourself. The opposite of hope is despair, hopelessness, the place where our patients (or we, ourselves) can falter and fail. I would even go as far as to say that hope is a function of the ego. Mature hope grounds people and helps keep their bodies and minds functioning smoothly.

As for any other deficient ego function, the therapist can 'lend' a part of their own ego to help the client traverse difficult terrain. We can hold hope for our clients when they cannot hold hope for themselves. That hope can be for so many things: finding love, a better job, the end to suicidality or self-harm impulses, recovery, rediscovering joy, or even finding it for the first time. If our hope is based in an immature ego, we can come across as fake, Pollyannaish, or 'new age'. We need to have walked through the fire with the client and make sure that we are not engaging in some form of clinical or spiritual escapism with them or for them (which would also be selfish of us, not to mention poor practice).

Empathizing with cynicism and despair can be a necessary component of trauma work, but we should not identify with them. If our client is in the hole, and we jump in the hole with them, now we are both stuck! We need to be able to see into the (w)hole while holding the rope and anchoring ourselves in a solid place while visualizing pulling them out, not falling in. Failure is not an option!

Joyfulness

To be honest, I'm feeling a little bit like a happy tyrant right now. Be hopeful! Be joyful! Don't be mad, get glad! Always look on the bright side of life! OK, OK. It's not so easy. Don't I know it. Remember, I did hear 15,000 stories of child abuse in four years and work routinely with clients who were tortured in childhood. And yet . . .

Joy is necessary to be great. To be the truly great, inspiring, awesome therapist of your dreams, you need to cultivate joy as part of your being. To pull your clients from the depths of despair to the shallow waters of mere passing sadness, you need to add joy. Or you, at least, need to uncover it. In the beliefs of Hinduism joy is always there, part of the substrate of the human being, not something we have to earn or create. That is my experience too, but I realize that for many it is not their belief or experience. Whether you believe joy is part of humanity's true nature, or something you achieve, you and your clients can always become more joyful.

It is not intellectually sophisticated to be morose, cynical, glum. It may be fashionable (have you seen fashion models lately?), but it is not helpful. Any old confidant can provide cynicism. Joy is contagious. Not happiness, not pleasure, but deep abiding joy. Joy is related to the word ecstasy, the word of Greek origin that means to 'stand outside oneself'. It transcends a limited personal experience.

My model for joy is the Dalai Lama. He has been through so many losses and heard so many thousands of stories of trauma from his people. Still, when he walks into a room you feel it, this immense bubbling fountain of joy. Where does he get all of that? From inside himself. He has figured out how to unlock joy in amounts that defy comprehension. His joy is grounded in compassion, in empathy, so it never feels callow or self-absorbed. If we can embody even a little bit of that joy, our clients benefit in ways that we don't often acknowledge. It can be such a challenge for us to maintain a joyful center; we hear so much pain and trauma. That makes it even more necessary to pursue.

Being joyful as a therapist doesn't mean you have to be all 'love and light'. It may involve holding the doors open to profound sorrow and rage. Supporting joy means we see that light shines even more brightly in the darkness. Why should we ask our clients to do the hard work of exposing themselves to painful memories if we have only lumps of coal to offer them in the end? They (and we) need to know what they are working towards. Joy is a worthy goal. You can even put it in your treatment plan!

Notes

1 Repetition compulsion is a mechanism that Sigmund Freud described in which a person will unconsciously repeat undigested (usually traumatic) events in various forms throughout the lifespan until the original events are emotionally processed and understood. Retraumatization is one form through which repetition compulsion can manifest as a drive towards mastery of the event.
2 For you yogis out there, the wisdom mind acts in the world as karma yoga or seva: work without egoic agency or selfless service for the good of others. There is no meaningful distinction between awareness and action in this level of the being.
3 Honestly, I do not know if this was an actual being or a psychic representation I was picking up from my client. It does not matter, and it did not need to be stated for the client. Sharing the image and impression for the client was powerfully healing without a definitive interpretation of the event.
4 I do not necessarily mean to laugh, literally. We can smile, chuckle, or deadpan our way through humor as can our clients.
5 For a bigger challenge, players can repeat "zip" any number of times in the circle and then have to repeat "zap" and "zop" the same number of times.
6 We footnote or, in my case, endnote the heck out of documents. Some articles have a citation at the end of nearly every sentence. This renders them unreadable. It also comes across as insecure, as if writers cannot come to conclusions on their own and need to justify every thought.
7 It bears mentioning here that several billion people believe in karma and that nothing that happens in life is random. That is a Western idea, and we, in the West, are in a minority.

References

Brian Grazer, T. H. (Producer), Jim Lovell, J. K. (Writer), & Howard, R. (Director). (1995). *Apollo 13* [Motion Picture]. Universal Pictures.

Falk, P. (Producer, Actor). (1971–2003). *Colombo.* [Television Series]. New York, NY: National Broadcasting Company Universal

Merriam-Webster Dictionary. (2017). *Humility.* Retrieved August 17, 2017, from www.merriam-webster.com/dictionary/humility

Notaro, T. (2013). Tig Notaro LIVE. *Hello, I Have Cancer.* Bloomington, IN: Secretly Canadian.

Steven, J. B. (Producer), Hart, J. V. (Writer), & Zemeckis, R. (Director). (1997). *Contact* [Motion Picture]. USA: Warner Bros.

Stone, R. (2016, May 8). Science Shows that Torture Doesn't Work and Is Counterproductive. *Newsweek.*

Swami Prabhavananda & Isherwood, C. (1970). *Shankara's Crest-Jewel of Discrimination: Timeless Teachings on Non-Duality.* Calcutta, India: Vedanta Press & Bookshop.

Thomas, O. H. (1999). *Reverie and Interpretation: Sensing Something Human.* London, UK: Karnac Books.

Part III

Love

8 Superhuman Empathy and Trauma Work

To my mind, empathy is in itself a healing agent. It is one of the most potent aspects of therapy, because it releases, it confirms, it brings even the most frightened client into the human race. If a person is understood, he or she belongs.

—Carl Rogers

Empathy and compassion. Compassion and empathy. These two qualities are the essential qualities of master therapists. Without these qualities, therapists could be computers spitting out procedures for healing. Of course, one does not have to be a therapist to embody these qualities. Many other people of compassion walk among us unnoticed. They leave people feeling good in their wake like a good fragrance blowing through a garden. They can be grandmothers, teachers, bus drivers, comedians, actors, artists, spiritual practitioners, atheists, holy people, and ordinary people. We know immediately when we are in the presence of a human with these qualities. We use words like 'warm', 'held', 'contained', 'understood', and 'loved' to describe the experience of empathy in the room. If we are honest with ourselves, the threat of judgment, criticism, or harm hovers around all relationships. People with abundant empathy and compassion are so remarkable because they tend to be low in these negative traits. But they do not consider themselves remarkable; they consider themselves pragmatic. People with naturally abundant empathy have a very hard time hurting other people simply because they feel it in their own body and mind if they do.

Most therapists have a modicum of empathy, or they probably would not be drawn to such a difficult profession. If you have been fortunate enough to sit with a master therapist as a student, client, or colleague, you may have seen what I call 'superhuman empathy' at work. I was inspired by the phrase 'superhuman sympathy' that was used to describe the speech therapist Lionel Logue, whose work was portrayed in the movie *The King's Speech* (Bowen, 2011). Therapists with superhuman empathy can engage all three aspects of empathy: cognitive, somatic, and intuitive. Watching such a person at work is like watching a maestro conduct a symphony. A therapist who can engage all these levels of empathy has much to offer people with trauma.

Our highly traumatized clients need therapists who can operate with this degree of empathy and attunement. Traumatized people feel everything keenly. They often describe feeling as if there is no barrier between themselves and the world. Their nervous systems rev to highs and lows without warning. A person with a trauma history often feels the feelings of others around them more intensely than does a person without trauma.[1] Or maybe it is the other way around, and the people who are naturally sensitive can be traumatized more easily. Or there may be some mysterious interaction between nature and nurture. The emerging field of epigenetics hints that these experiences entwine and influence each other, sometimes over generations.

There are so many avenues to explore around trauma and empathy. It seems that neurological functions get heightened post trauma, including mirror neurons and other mechanisms that can produce empathy. We know that the amygdala can become sensitized to react ever more vigorously with more incidents of traumatic experiences (Rabinak, Angstadt, Welsh, & Kennedy, 2011). Of course, the opposite can be true, and victims can dissociate away from their feelings or go into a full lockdown mode on any of their feelings. If they stay open to their experiences and feelings, they will tend to emerge with more empathy and compassion in the healing of their traumas. This mechanism explains why so many folks flock to become healers after their own traumatic experiences.

Empathy is not one mechanism. To really dig into empathy we need to look at its different manifestations. Chapter 7 described the Indian system of the koshas, or sheaths, that correspond to the physical body, energetic body, cognitive mind, intuitive or wisdom mind, and bliss body. The quality of empathy can arise in and through any of these koshas, and there is a direct correspondence between types of empathy understood in the West and their kosha counterparts. This is good news, as therapists come in all kinds of packages and temperaments. If one style of empathy doesn't fit, we can always cultivate another.

In the talk that inspired this book, I have a slide that talks about two different types of therapist. We could understand these types of therapists as generally corresponding to a more intellectual (cool) approach to empathy or to a more intuitive or warm approach.[2]

The cool approach is a primarily cognitive approach. This type of therapist may not have many intuitive or somatic empathic abilities, but they can deduce much about their cases utilizing curiosity and a logical approach to the treatment. They often tend to be solution focused and have a steady, if maybe slightly flattened, affect that can be reassuring to their clients. Intellectual therapists can be rocks for their clients and withstand high-demand caseloads because they are not tired out by what I shall call 'empathy circuits'. Extremely emotional clients do not overwhelm 'cool' therapists, and their clients often feel confident that they can say anything to these therapists without injuring them. Drawbacks to this temperamental style can be a dismissive or minimizing attitude towards suffering and an overfocus on evidence that results in the client not feeling believed and heard. Engaging visualization and imagination for this type of therapist can be more challenging than for other types as they tend to be more concrete, but they can also tolerate a high degree of difficulty in the violent imagery of a traumatic history.

Highly empathic or 'warm' therapists rely on how they feel about their clients to inform decisions and diagnostic work. They rely on interoceptive input and let their bodies inform them about their work. In other words, they have a highly developed 'gut feeling'. When these therapists speak, it is often in a feeling language, and they encourage their clients to do the same. Their face tends to be very active and expressive, which can be reassuring to some clients and overwhelming to others. Their clients invariably feel cared about, but some clients may wonder whether this type of therapist can handle the amount of horror they have to process in recovering from trauma. Disadvantages for these therapists include the fact that they can easily be drained by their work, they can be prone to reactions or even overreactions, and they can become overwhelmed by their clients' experiences. Highly empathic therapists usually have a wonderful ability to stand with their clients in their imagination, but can be overcome with suffering as they do so.

Carl Rogers developed a therapy style that is famous for being client-centered, rather than procedure- or theory-centered. He refined empathy to a high art as a valued tool in his work with clients. In his eloquent writings, quoted here from the *Stanford Encyclopedia of Philosophy*, he describes empathy as the ability to enter:

> the private perceptual world of the other and becoming thoroughly at home in it . . . It means temporarily living in the other's life, moving about in it delicately without making judgments; it means sensing meanings of which he or she is scarcely aware . . . It includes communicating your sensings of the person's world . . . It means frequently checking with the person as to the accuracy of your sensings, and being guided by the responses you receive . . . To be with another in this way means that for the time being you lay aside your own views and values in order to enter another's world without prejudice.
>
> (Stueber, 2013)

Cognitive Empathy

The human being has to have achieved a certain level of developmental cognitive maturity in order to be capable of the mental act of empathy. Piaget's theory of the four stages of cognitive development give us a good framework to understand cognitive empathy. To review, Piaget asserted that our brains do not merely take in new information as we age throughout childhood but actually change its functions as we age. How we learn changes as does what we learn, and how we can learn is based upon what level of development has been achieved through maturity. A young child, for example, does not have the cognitive ability to take another's perspective. This is not egocentricity; it is how the brain functions at that age. Let's review the stages as regards empathy:

1. **Sensorimotor Stage**: lasts from birth to around 2 years of age. As discussed in Horner's theoretical model, the baby is fairly undifferentiated, but the tasks of infancy and early toddlerhood are to see oneself as separate and distinct from Mother and other people. There is no cognitive ability at this age to take another's perspective.

2. **Preoperational Stage**: occurs from 2 years to 7 years old. The child continues to mature. She learns to play and to think about things, but that thinking is still very literal and concrete. The child can notice what another child is feeling but cannot accurately attribute causality because they still lack the ability to move their point of reference into another's body/mind. Because of this they appear egocentric, but, again, this is a cognitive process, not a characterological one. At this age, the child still very much struggles with language and vocabulary to express themselves and understand the world around them.

3. **Concrete Operational Stage**: lasts from 7 years to 11 years or so. Sometime during these years, kids start to develop the ability to have cognitive empathy, that is, to be able to imagine themselves in another's shoes. They also develop logical thinking but are still quite concrete. They make discoveries about some of the 'laws' they have developed in their own mind. For example, they may start out by thinking that everybody hates licorice because they do but then discover and incorporate the idea that some kids love licorice (and that they can trade their licorice jelly beans for just about any other favorite flavor!). But because they really cannot yet master abstract thought, more subtle aspects of empathy are lost to this age.

4. **Formal Operational Stage**: 12 years to adulthood. Here's a little-known fact: only 35% of youth in industrialized nations achieve the stage of formal operations by the end of high school (Moursund, 2007). Many adults never achieve formal operations! This stage is the only stage where people have the full ability to cognitively empathize with another person. This stage is characterized by abstract thought and hypothetical situations. Thought experiments become effective at this age, as do critical abilities. We may all evolve this stage as we age. To have a deep understanding of another human, the therapist needs to construct a model of their mind, which can be informed in therapy by trial and error. For example, we may hypothesize that they need us to be gentle and receptive when they may, in fact, need us to be active and encouraging (thus the need for feedback mechanisms and check-ins described in Chapter 6). Therapists need to be able to take in and synthesize new information and come up with new hypotheses on a regular basis, which makes cognitive empathy a highly engaged and active process.

Piaget said, "I believe that knowing an object means acting upon it, constructing systems of transformations that can be carried out on or with this object. Knowing reality means constructing systems of transformations that correspond, more or less adequately, to reality" (Cherry, 2017). Is that not what we do with our clients, construct systems of transformations for our clients that act on them for the better and that correspond to reality, and, especially, their reality? But to know their reality, we need to understand how they are thinking, and that means knowing which stage of development they are operating at. With this awareness we can communicate in ways they can process. For example, if there is little to no ability for abstract thought, then the therapist needs to address the patient with concrete examples or step-by-step instructions. Otherwise the client will come away feeling like therapy is a waste of time, and, for them, it will have been. Some of the most common mistakes I see in beginning clinicians is the lack of awareness of cognitive stages and functions in their clients, concomitant with an overestimation of their clients' ability to integrate new concepts and behaviors.

Cognitive empathy requires imagination. We have to be willing to imagine ourselves standing alongside of a client in whatever situation caused them to have trauma or dissociate. This is unpleasant work! Normally a mind avoids troubling topics as self-defense. Not only do we want to avoid thinking about horrible things, we may lack the personal and cultural references to really understand the experience. Like a lifeguard, we have to do what is counter-intuitive for survival, jump into the churning waters and hope that our skills carry us both to safer shores. Only for a more full analogy, imagine that the water is potentially toxic and full of hazards that can sink both swimmers!

In movies and TV, we have been exposed to a certain number of traumas that can augment our imagination. Car and plane crashes, natural disasters (earthquakes, tsunamis, fires), wars, and other general trauma are well represented, and most of us probably can pull up immediate visuals from shows like *Castaway* or *The Day After Tomorrow* or *Lost*. But unless you are into horror as a genre, you probably have not seen a rape, or a session of torture on a young child, or a ritual abuse ceremony. Nor have you spent much of your precious time imagining such scenarios until you have a client that comes from such a background. Entry into these worlds, even by imagination, is horrifying.

There are other groups that deserve our contemplation as well. Some groups reflect back to us that we don't tend to contemplate their suffering much if we are members of the dominant culture; that phenomenon is called privilege. If we are White we may have a difficult time imagining the pervasiveness of macro and micro aggressions against people of color, what it is like to be hated and possibly hunted just for being you. If we are straight, we cannot imagine the various traumas and uphill battle for self-integrity that the LGBT community endures on a daily basis. If we are able-bodied, we may minimize the experience of accessibility issues as well as the chronic pain common to abuse survivors.

To be a great trauma therapist means to willingly enter into these worlds in our imagination. Graduate schools educate therapists to become self-learners and help us network in order to understand the different perspectives of our client populations; this is a big part of our training. But there's another level we need to reach emotionally to be fully present to the experiences of our clients. We can only fully engage our cognitive empathy by educating our emotional selves, not just our intellect. Reading novels may be more help-ful to understand the emotional impact of traumas than reading textbooks or policy statements. When I worked on the Child-at-Risk Hotline in Massachu-setts, Stephen King was a favorite author of telephone screeners, as was Dean Koontz. I think we were all looking for mirrors to our horrifying phone call experiences as well as a way to be empathic with the folks who were calling. I remember one shift where I was reading a particularly grisly scene in a King novel when the phone rang, and the exact same scenario was being reported.

Memoirs can be a helpful genre for developing cognitive empathy, espe-cially with topics that can be hard to find on bookshelves, such as ritual abuse and mind control. These books give context, personal history, and detailed descriptions of actions taken. A first person account pulls the reader into the immediate experience of the author/survivor. True stories help us overcome our natural disbelief in extreme abuse scenarios before we are confronted with them in session. They push us past belief thresholds about the horrors humans can perpetrate on each other. In the extreme read category I would recom-mend such books as *When Rabbit Howls* (Chase, 1987), *The Enslaved Queen: A Memoir About Electricity and Mind Control* (Hoffman, 2014), and *Unshack-led: A Survivor's Story of Mind Control* (Sullivan, 2003). Women therapists who survived horrendous abuse and mind control programming wrote the last two.

Somatic Empathy

There is a cartoon by Peter Steiner that shows two people at a party. One says, "I'm sorry I didn't hear what you said, I was paying attention to my body." We all do this. We are hardwired for somatic empathy. As a therapist we can hone and harness this ability to profoundly attune to our clients. We can also get lost in our own sensations and lose focus if we are not mindful.

All mammals have some sort of somatic empathy. In fact, the mediator of much somatic empathy, mirror neurons, were discovered first in monkeys in the 1990s. Italian neuroscientists Giacomo Rizzolatti, Vittorio Gallese, and their colleagues discovered that some motor neurons that control movement in the body also fired in the same part of the brain when monkeys watched other monkeys perform an action that they, themselves, were not doing. Just observing another monkey's movement was enough to activate the passive monkeys' brains! The researchers called this subsection of motor neurons, mir-ror neurons, because they fired as a mirror to another's actions. Humans also have these neurons, and soon scientists were hypothesizing that mirror neu-rons could be the foundation of human empathy (Winerman, 2005).

V. S. Ramachandran, an Indian neuroscientist, gave a popular TED talk in which he revealed some telling research (Ramachandran, 2009). Not only do we have mirror neurons that enable us to sense what others are feeling, we also have inhibitors that let us know that what we are feeling is not our own body but someone else's body. This feedback signal vetoes sensation in the location of the body being observed. In other words, if we are watching a human touch another human's arm, our own arm gives us a feedback signal to let us know we are watching someone else's arm. But here's where it gets weird. If our arm is anaesthetized, according to Ramachandran, the feedback signal is inhibited and we might experience someone else's arm being touched as being touched ourselves. Whoa! For this reason, Ramachandran calls mirror neurons 'empathy neurons' or 'Gandhi neurons'.

A similar area of research has been done in the area of phantom limb pain. When a portion of a limb is amputated, the brain can still register pain in the missing limb, because, although the limb is gone, the circuits in the brain that monitored the limb are still there. Ramachandran helped phantom limb pain disappear by using actual mirrors to engage mirror neuron circuits. He demonstrated how a person with phantom limb pain could watch someone with that intact limb be massaged, with the result that their pain disappears as if it was their own limb being worked on. Ramachandran maintains that mirror neurons lie at the interface of science and the humanities. Their actions reinforce the traditional Indian idea that we are all profoundly connected, some would say one, and that it is only through a series of filters mediated biochemically that we can distinguish ourselves as individual beings from each other.

All of us have mirror neurons. Some of us have more refined sensations that we can decode from these circuits than others have, and we call this 'sensitivity'. There are some sensations that are very contagious, like gagging or yawning. But other sensations can be communicated as well, depending on our level of observation and our ability to decode our own mirror neuron sensations. It is likely that the more time we sit in a therapist's chair wanting to know what is going on inside of somebody in a focused state of mind, the more likely it is that we will begin to feel our clients' feelings, subtly at first, and then with increasing strength. Practice makes perfect.

For a long time it was not unusual for me to experience somatic sensations in my body that my client was repressing. It took a while to figure out that the mysterious sensations of my throat closing up, a spinning dizzy sensation, or lower back pain were actually not my own! In working with a mental health supervisor who was also a shamanic healer, I learned to distinguish between my body's own sensations and that of my clients'. It was easy to assess whose was whose. All I had to do was ask my clients if they were feeling anything in the part of the body I was experiencing discomfort. An extremely high percentage of the time they would own the sensation as theirs. What was interesting was that as soon as the client admitted to the sensation in their own body, the sensation would release the grip on my body. For instance, if

I felt a very tight throat I asked my patient, "What is going on in your throat right now?" They would stop for a moment, think (feel), and then respond something like, "Wow, my throat *is* really tight right now! How did you know?" At that moment, my own throat would release and would resume its naturally pain-free and open position. Naturally, that meant that my throat was not actually a problem in the moment, only my mirror neurons, and their mysterious activation by my client's dissociated sensations. Many of my colleagues have reported such phenomena. I even have met some highly sensitive therapists who do all their therapy long-distance because they cannot manage the overwhelming somatic stimuli when they are in the room with a client!

Even when therapists believe they do not or cannot experience these things, I am not so sure that it is true, but maybe a matter of selective attention. I am a trained dancer. I spent years in front of a mirror training myself to move selective muscle groups, feeling for the minutiae in sensation that would make all the difference in a double pirouette or difficult set of steps. I had to cultivate intense somatic awareness as part of this training. Most therapists have no such somatic training. Some therapists hardly stop to get grounded in their body, functioning basically as talking heads, a stance that is reinforced in our education and supervision. I asked one couples therapist how her body felt when her clients yelled at each other; she responded she never thinks of her body at all. This is not uncommon in our culture and for therapists, but it may be problematic because blocking off these sensations blocks off avenues of empathy. One can cultivate a more somatic sense by consciously intending to pay attention to bodily sensations during therapy sessions. This attention may feel forced, unfamiliar, or distracting at first. Persist, and you may find a world of information opening up to you with your clients.

You may, like myself, fall on the other end of the spectrum where your body is constantly lighting up to other people's sensations, both gross and subtle. When they cry, you want to cry; when they are angry, you feel angry; if their gut is paining them, yours may as well. You may have had these tendencies your whole life and identify as a lightworker, highly sensitive person, and/ or empath. It is likely that other members of your family do as well. In that case, you will want to work on dampening and containing these sensations while maintaining empathic connection with your client. Sometimes getting overwhelmed by stimuli is a simple case of a conditioned response that we can work with in supervision or on a yoga mat.

Over a period of decades, I started to realize that my most sensitive clients and therapists all came from the same groups of peoples. If they had any Irish blood, Eastern European ancestry, or indigenous ancestry they were prone to empathic sensitivities and anxiety. If they had two of these or all three, their anxiety was usually off the charts, as was their ability to intuit client issues, even before the clients knew themselves! Sensitivity and anxiety go together like peas in a pod.

Western society is not set up for those of us with sensitivity to function well. We start trying to shut humans down at birth by having babies sleep away from their parents and ignoring their crying in favor of a 'sleep schedule'. In indigenous cultures, the values could not be more different. Many tribes value functioning as a unit and being able to sense wildlife and natural phenomenon that would be too subtle for the coarsened 'civilized' mind. Historically their survival depended on this type of awareness. Heightened sensitivity mixed with hypervigilance from a previous trauma history can make for one heck of a sensitive therapist, but also a therapist that may need a lot of support to do their work without becoming burnt out. We will address those needs in the next chapter.

Despite the drawbacks of sensitive mirror neurons, I would not trade my gift of somatic empathy and would encourage other therapists to develop theirs to the highest degree. The more we work to heal ourselves, the fewer problems this sensitivity will awaken in us. Like a mother who is exquisitely sensitive to her baby's needs, a somatically sensitive therapist can attune to a client's needs like no other. To sit with such a therapist is a profound and rare gift for the client. To be that therapist is a great gift to ourselves.

Intuitive Empathy

If cognitive empathy corresponds to the kosha of the thinking mind (manomayakosha) and somatic empathy corresponds to the body (annamayakosha), to what kosha does intuitive empathy correspond? In the Indian model of the koshas, there is an energy or 'prana' body (pranamayakosha) and also an intuitive mind (vijnanamayakosha). Intuitive empathy interacts with both of these koshas of the human being in a mysterious and sometimes ineffable way that I will attempt to elucidate here. If you are a very concrete, nonintuitive, 'rational' type of person you may find this material challenging. I encourage you to read it anyway and suspend your disbelief. Even if intuitive empathy will never be your 'thing', I guarantee that you will have clients for whom it is definitely a part of their human experience.

In 2015, the National Association of Social Workers published *Standards and Indicators for Cultural Competence in Social Work Practice*, a comprehensive, thoughtful document that all mental health professionals should read. They stated, "cultural competence requires self-awareness, cultural humility, and the commitment to understanding and embracing culture as central to effective practice" (National Association of Social Workers, 2015).

Cultural humility—what a term! What a concept! What does it mean to be culturally humble? It means that we have to accept people's experiences on their own terms and not define them in the terms of our own cultural and belief systems. It means that other cultures have a different relationship to reality than we do, and that we are no longer colonial arbiters of reality for our clients or our colleagues as we once were in the field of psychology. Clinicians need to generate a sincere spirit of inquiry into others' experience without judgment.

The document goes on to say:

> Cultural competence is dynamic and requires frequent learning, unlearning, and relearning about diversity. Social workers need to expand their cultural religious traditions, spiritual belief systems, knowledge, and expertise by expanding their understanding of the following areas: "the impact of culture on behavior, attitudes, and values; the help-seeking behaviors of diverse client groups; the role of language, speech patterns, religious traditions, spiritual belief systems, and communication styles of various client groups in the communities served.
>
> (National Association of Social Workers, 2015)

Some of my readers have already had intuitive experiences with their clients and have never breathed a word about them in supervision to anybody for fear of being labeled 'crazy' or 'new age'. That's a shame. In other times and places, the people with the gifts of intuitive empathy were the most highly revered healers of the tribe, and sometimes the only people allowed to even call themselves healers. Western colonialism has not been kind to these types of awarenesses and has sought to stamp them out.[3] Occasionally, I have presented posters or talks that incorporate some of this more esoteric knowledge. It is common for young practitioners of all disciplines to approach me in hushed tones, wanting to talk but very afraid of professional repercussions for admitting to their psychic sensitivities and perceptions.

Below is a case example of intuitive empathy and vision that some of you will be able to relate to and others of you really will not. Even if you are not an intuitive type of person, I would recommend keeping an open mind because some, maybe many, of your patients fall into the category of psychically sensitive. Severe trauma can open up intuitive faculties. In the interest of cultural competence, we need to keep our minds and hearts open to different ways of perceiving reality.

At my patient's request, I am giving her a session of Reiki, a hands-on healing on a massage table where my client is fully clothed and deeply relaxed. In my mind's eye, I see a 4- to 5-year-old child rise out of her body who runs up to my face and says, "She's not ready to integrate me yet!" I am very surprised, as I have never seen anything like this before. Although I know that shamans talk about soul retrieval as an important phenomenon in healing, it has not occurred to me that the 'parts' or 'alters' we talk about in psychology might also be soul parts that have an ethereal existence that is tied to, yet independent of, the physical body and mind.

Later, in another session, I 'see'[4] this same 4- to 5-year-old sitting and quietly playing around a very, very old wizened woman from the spirit world. The child seems very composed, very content. At my client's request, I tell her what I have seen in the session. My client nods and says, "Yes, I'm not like that now, but I was very much like that at that age, quiet and focused." She goes home and reports deeper sleep, better digestion, and a sense of hope she has not felt for a long time.

A week later she returns. She asks me many questions about the old woman. "Was she very small?" "Yes." "Was she so old with so many wrinkles you could not even really tell what race and gender she is?" "Yes." "Did she seem to know the child?" "Yes." The questions went on and on. Finally, my client looked at me with a funny look on her face. "I want to tell you something but it's going to sound weird." I replied that we were already in the weird zone and that I wanted to hear whatever she had to tell me. She said, "When I was around that age, 4 or 5, I had a pond behind my house. I went out there one day, and I saw a woman spirit exactly like the one you described. I haven't thought of her in forever. But I am convinced that the woman you saw in your vision with my inner child is that same person. When I met her at the pond she asked me a question." I asked her what the question was. She visibly struggled with telling me. Finally, she said, "This is strange but the woman asked me what I wanted to get out of this life. It's weird because I was so young, but I answered her that I wanted to seek wisdom."

This client was subjected to a very severe trauma at that age; we do not know if it was before or after her vision by the pond. Being able to tune into her at that age and seeing the wizened woman was deeply comforting and awe inspiring for her. It helped her feel that I was really with her, and also that her mysterious experiences as a child had validity. It is strange to think that I somehow saw the same spirit person she had seen by the pond so many decades earlier. But, hey, 'there are more things in heaven and earth, Horatio than are dreamt of in your philosophy.'[5] As this client and I continue to work together, many more interesting visions, coincidences, and general unexplained phenomena have arisen. She gets better and better and ranks our intuitive discussions highly in terms of what she finds helpful in her healing process.

Sympathy vs. Empathy

Being extremely sensitive has its disadvantages. Those of us in touch with these layers of reality are prone to becoming depleted, burnt out, or even ill.

Indigenous healers acknowledge the reality of a kind of energy signature of trauma that comes out of the energy bodies of those who have been traumatized. Different sources call it 'heavy energy', 'goo', 'the trauma vortex', and 'darkness'. One of my daughters refers to it as 'squid ink' because she can feel it squirt out when someone goes into fear. I'm sure there are many other ways to describe it. For me, this energy is not subtle. It is completely palpable, as palpable as touching a hot stove. Perceiving this energy is not dependent on distance; I can feel it as easily over the phone or in the waiting room from inside my office as I can if the person is sitting right in front of me. I am not alone. I know many practitioners who have the same ability. Those who can feel it feel it strongly; those who cannot do not know what the heck I am talking about. To me, it is like seeing color. Some of us can see all the colors; some of us can see all but red and green, and some cannot see color at all. It is as strange to those of us who perceive these biofield energies that people cannot perceive them as it is to the muggle therapists that we can.

For some reason, people with this type of perception also seem more prone to taking on the energies *and maladies* that we perceive. Before I received shamanic training, I was constantly bringing home the complaints of clients and friends: a bad headache from a dinner party, a feeling of the worthlessness of life from my depressed patients, very intense intestinal cramping from a patient with a colostomy bag.[6] These incidents could not be explained by mirror neurons alone or a vivid imagination. They were bringing me down and making me feel completely burnt out. In working with the Celtic-Russian shaman and psychotherapist Shannon Kelly, I realized that I was inviting these energies into my energy field and body through sympathy. Shannon is no longer on this side of the veil, but his teachings remain an important part of my life. He gave me the boundary of sympathy versus empathy.

He defined sympathy as having an element of pity, a thought that the person should not be going through what they were going through and an underlying desire to carry their burden. For whatever reason, genetics, spiritual practices, I don't really know, I have the ability to attract suffering into my own body and carry it for people. Whenever this happened, the patients (or friends) in all cases would report a dramatic remission or elimination of their symptoms, and I would be terribly sick or uncomfortable. It is a type of shamanic healing 'gift'. The problem was I didn't know why it was happening or how to turn it off. Many highly sensitive therapists report similar burdens on their work. Some may be unwittingly carrying these physical and psychic burdens, but they may not know that they are and what it is that is making them feel so bad.

Empathy can allow us to connect with the person's pain without taking it on. Sympathy opens the door to taking on people's suffering without permission or guidance—not cool spiritually or physically. Key thoughts can violate the internal energetic boundary such as "you shouldn't have to go through that" or "let me take that from you." If you feel like you carry others' sadness, trauma, or anger, if you collect physical symptoms like the crazy cat lady collects cats, then you, too, may have to set some pristine internal boundaries.

Use empathy, not sympathy![7] It may not be so easy to accomplish separating these phenomena on your own. It can be very helpful to seek out shamanic training or supervision with a highly sensitive therapist. There are reputable shamanic healer training programs all over the world and in the United States.

Developing Intuitive Empathy

Perhaps you fall on the other side of the spectrum. You wish to develop your capacity for intuitive empathy but you come from a long line of muggles— folks who have shut down their capacity for intuitive perception. You want to believe that there is more capacity available for you and wish to develop those skills. Or you have some rudimentary intuition and want to refine it. The good news is: you can!

It is known among practitioners of Eastern religions that yoga and meditation naturally expand the intuitive faculties of human beings. Expanded psychic perception is such a common side effect of these practices that scriptures warn about them being a distraction from the spiritual path. We constantly engage our senses when moving through the world. In order to perceive our intuitive faculties we need to quiet the external noise from said senses. One of the best techniques to do this is meditation. Right now, like many others, you may be lamenting the monkey mind and thinking that you cannot possibly still your mind. Yes, meditation leads to a slowing and stilling of the mind's activities, but not right away! It takes years of practice to meditate effectively. You don't take your first hike on Mt. Everest, right? Take baby steps. Learning to still and focus the mind is a skill that we therapists practice as we sit with patients hour after hour, year after year. Good therapy practice spontaneously becomes a single pointed meditation on the client if we learn to calm the body/mind. Focused awareness is both the path and the goal.

Trust what your body has to tell you. Intuition can enter through many gates: the body, the imagination, any of the internal senses (internal sight, hearing, smell, taste, etc.), through a kind of direct knowing, or with the help of spirit guides.[8] Intuition arises out of the layers of the unconscious mind all the way to the depths of the collective unconscious of humanity, as Jung so famously described. Through the realm of the collective unconscious mind and the realm of archetypes, our minds connect to every other mind on the planet and to every mind that has ever lived. This realm comprises a vast storehouse of knowledge if only we know how to access it and believe that we can.

If only we knew how to access the unconscious mind . . . hmmm. Wait, we are therapists! Ha! Review your tools to access the depths of our unconscious material from Freud's royal roads to the unconscious:

- Dreams
- Slips of the tongue
- Free association

In my experience, the more we practice consciously dipping the wick of our awareness into the unconscious part of our minds, the easier it is to recognize and receive messages from it. Start keeping a dream journal; it doesn't have to be about your patients, but about practicing making your unconscious mind conscious. Of course, you may have a dream about a patient that is revelatory and a valid use of intuition.[9] More likely, you will notice a pattern to your dreams that can point you in a helpful direction both personally and professionally. If you are very sensitive, you may end up dreaming about your patients' repressed material. This can be very disturbing, but also instructive. If it happens a lot, you may need help resetting your internal boundaries.

Notice if you make a 'Freudian slip' during a session. It may be about you or about your client. Maybe you accidentally call your patient by another patient's name. Sure it could be a 'middle-aged moment'. It could also be that some pattern or feature of that client reminds you of the other. If you have not consciously linked the two people before, this tip from your unconscious can help you put two and two together. If you consistently mis-schedule the same patient, perhaps you have an underlying feeling of dread or hostility towards that person. Instead of judging yourself, ask why? Note that this work is a lot like working with countertransference. In fact, working with intuition *is* working with countertransference. What is countertransference but the movement of strong unconscious impulses making their way to consciousness? These moments can just as easily inform you about the patient as yourself. Some of you may be thinking, "this is just pattern recognition!" Perhaps it is, in the beginning. As you flex intuitive muscles, you will find yourself with more information that is less easily explained.

Lastly, we have the royal road of free association, the cornerstone of Freudian psychoanalysis and the origin of 'the talking cure'. Freud observed that when people were left to talk about whatever they wanted to, free of social inhibitions or conventions, their talk would lead them to the source of internal neuroses, traumas, and conflict. Like a whale, issues can only stay submerged so long before they surface, at which point they become available for psychological awareness and healing.

Free association is not only for our clients. We can use this tool to gain access to our deeper mind for ourselves and for our work. One method to free associate is through journaling or free writing. Want to know what's in your unconscious mind? Put pen to paper (or fingers to keyboard) for 30 minutes every day and just write what comes into your head. You can also draw or paint without agenda. Paint whatever you feel like painting and see what emerges.

In session, free association is one of my major tools for accessing intuition. If a client has a dream, I ask them to free associate to it, and then I also free associate to their dreams and their associations. For me a somatic state of awareness accompanies these associations. Ever play the game 'hot and cold'? Someone hides and as the seeker gets closer the other players say, 'warmer, warmer', or 'colder, colder' if they get further away. My body tenses up if my associations are not in the direction of healing, and become relaxed if my free associations are hot on the trail of important clues. Intuition is a whole-body process; many streams of information can interweave and overlap giving a rich texture and depth of awareness to our intuitive experience.

Pay attention to the most minute sensations in your body as you enter, conduct, and exit a session. Our body is the interface for all knowledge. Get to know it. Can you feel your solar plexus tighten up when you say something that is off the mark, and open wide when you speak truth? Do you get 'truthbumps'—goosebumps that prickle when you say what is real, or a spiritual truth? Can you feel a surging sensation in your chest or throat when you are urged by some mysterious force to speak, not from a place of urgency or defensiveness but because it is the right moment? In improvisational comedy, we have a saying, "Follow your feet." It means that your body knows when you are supposed to enter a scene while your mind may still be hesitating (and letting the scene lag). Intuition moves us, even speaks through us. The more you play with your intuition, the more it can guide you.

Superhuman empathy is a blessing and a curse. If a therapist is one of those highly sensitive souls, they feel everything along with their client, and it can become debilitating after a while. Yet, without profound empathy, our clients will be reluctant to open up to us. They constantly test the waters, sending up trial balloons of experiences while they scrutinize our body language for signs of disgust or judgment. When they find a therapist willing to journey with them into the depths of suffering they experience relief and gratitude. Without this company, our patients cannot fully heal. Superhuman empathy gives us tools for profound relational healing. When we train ourselves to engage an optimal level of empathy and increase our own window of tolerance to be fully present to our clients' experiences, we really can be the wise agents of healing we want to be. Even if the work is tiring and painful at times, the rewards are bountiful.

Notes

1 For centuries, indigenous cultures have induced controlled traumas to induce states of high awareness and enlarge consciousness. Every medicine person has to come through some sort of traumatic initiation in order to be recognized as the tribe's healer.

2 These correspond to personality types and one could even place them on the Myers-Briggs spectrum in the feeling–thinking category of decision-making.

3 If you are an intuitive type, no explanation may be necessary. If not, answers to honest questions on this topic must be found in a deep open-minded journey to awareness and by studying the practices of colonialism. For example, one of the first thing that British soldiers did in India was to hunt out the advanced Marma practitioners and cut off their fingers—not because they did not believe in their powers, but because they did!

4 This type of seeing is in my mind's eye, using imaginal faculties but not making anything up. Some clairvoyants actually see these images in the room with them as if they were seeing with their physical eyes. Both types of seeing are valid and common.

5 Famous quote from Act 1, Scene V of *Hamlet* by Shakespeare and one of my personal faves.

6　In each of these cases, I was able to verify that the person received a remission of the symptom after it was transferred to my body.

7　The exception would be that you are called to this kind of healing at a soul level. There are those healers who, for whatever reason, volunteer to make their body the place where others' issues are worked out. Before you volunteer for this heavy duty, make sure you are not coming from a place of masochism or unresolved issues.

8　People with indigenous bloodlines and/or who have studied shamanic practices may be working with spirit helpers at any point in their lives: before, during, or after they become therapists. In certain areas of the United States, such as the Pacific Northwest, these topics are commonly discussed.

9　Be aware that helpful dream interpretation, especially of an intuitive nature, takes practice and skill. I would recommend working with an intuitive to refine any of these skills. Do not take any of your dreams for truth without doing your internal homework of separating your own working through of psychological material from information about a patient.

References

Bowen, C. (2011). *Lionel Logue: Pioneer Speech Therapist 1880–1953*. Retrieved August 30, 2017, from Speech-Language-Therapy: www.speech-language-therapy.com/index.php?option=com_content&view=article&id=53:lionel&catid=11:admin&Itemid=108

Chase, T. (1987). *When Rabbit Howls*. New York, NY: E.P. Dutton.

Cherry, K. (2017, May 14). *Piaget's Theory: The 4 Stages of Cognitive Development Background and Key Concepts of Piaget's Theory*. Retrieved August 30, 2017, from Very Well: www.verywell.com/piagets-stages-of-cognitive- development-2795457

Hoffman, W. (2014). *The Enslaved Queen: A Memoir About Electricity and Mind Control*. London, UK: Karnac Books.

Moursund, D. (2007, November 11). *Improving Mathematics Education*. Retrieved August 30, 2017, from Developmental Theory: http://pages.uoregon.edu/moursund/Math/developmental_theory.htm

National Association of Social Workers. (2015). *Standards and Indicators for Cultural Competence in Social Work Practice*. Retrieved September 8, 2017, from Socialworkers.org: www.socialworkers.org/practice/standards/NASWCulturalStandards.pdf

Rabinak, C. A., Angstadt, M., Welsh, R. C. & Kennedy, A. E. (2011, November 14). *Altered Amygdala Resting-State Functional Connectivity in Post-Traumatic Stress Disorder*. Retrieved October 25, 2017, from National Institues of Health: www.ncbi.nlm.nih.gov/pmc/articles/PMC3214721/

Ramachandran, V. (2009). The Neurons That Shaped Civilization. *TEDIndia*. Retrieved September 4, 2017, from YouTube.com: www.ted.com/talks/vs_ramachandran_the_neurons_that_shaped_ civilization#t-7293

Rogers, C. (1986). Carl Rogers on the development of the person-centered approach. *Person-Centered Review, 1*(3), 257–259.

Stueber, K. (2013). *The Study of Cognitive Empathy and Empathic Accuracy*. Stanford Center for the Study of Language and Information. Retrieved August 31, 2017, from Stanford Encyclopedia of Philosophy: https://plato.stanford.edu/entries/empathy/cognitive.html

Sullivan, K. (2003). *Unshackled: A Survivor's Story of Mind Control*. Tempe, AZ: Dandelion Books.

Winerman, L. (2005, October). *The Mind's Mirror*. Retrieved September 4, 2017, from American Psychological Association: www.apa.org/monitor/oct05/mirror.aspx

9 Self-Care for the Trauma Therapist

If Mama ain't happy ain't nobody happy.

—*Folk Saying*

The importance of our work as trauma therapists can hardly be overstated. Our clients come to us clinging to hope, and sometimes to life, by a thin thread. Those of us who claim this field as our own open our arms and hearts to the most needy, wounded, vulnerable people, and we do it with joy. Yet, so many of us underestimate our value. I used to really bristle when people said, "you must be a saint to do that work." Now I smile and nod and think maybe we all are a bit saintly to be doing this work. Few humans want to sit and listen to such intensity of pain and suffering in anyone, much less for a living. That willingness does not make therapists intrinsically better than anyone else, but it does make us a very special group of humans, indispensable to society. I once heard Harville Hendrix call therapists, "the white blood cells of society"! How long can humanity last without its helper cells before it devolves into darkness and failed states? In the stress of the work, it is easy to forget that we are somebody's lifeline. We really are, for that time when a person is in crisis, the lifeguard with the rope, hauling folks out of enormous waves of grief and trauma.

When we do the heavy lifting of trauma therapy over a long period of time, it can take a toll on our body, mind, and spirit. Vicarious traumatization, burnout, compassion fatigue—these conditions plague trauma therapists. Therapists can also be vulnerable to short-term threats such as violent clients and difficult settings where we can get hurt. We cannot afford to be unconscious about how we do this work. We need to have strategies for surviving and thriving in this most difficult of specialties. Since we are in a time of low funding and high expectations, we might have more difficulty with self-care now than did any previous generation of therapists. It is not uncommon for me to supervise social workers who have 30–60 high-need/high-risk clients on their caseload. They are being asked to do more with less, and the impossibility of the work can be disheartening at best and harmful at worst.

Risk Reduction

As trauma therapists, we work with some of the most stressed and distressed members of society. Our clients can have large ACEs scores and be prone to intense states of dysregulation. Sometimes this dysregulation leads to acting out in the treatment with aggressive behavior towards self or others. A large portion of self-care lies in mitigating risk through prevention and taking self-protective measures, whether we work in a private office, a residential treatment center, or a community agency.

Extreme Pain and Suicidality

Some of our clients don't make it. The great tension of this work lies in the reality that the higher the ACEs score of our clients, the heavier their trauma load, the greater likelihood that they could suicide, die of drug overdoses, develop life-threatening illnesses or extreme psychiatric conditions, and/or be prone to violence, either against self or others, even against us. The great stress of this work isn't just in listening to horrible stories and sitting with brutal pain, it is also in witnessing the technicolor sequelae of trauma in real time, such as self-mutilation, shattered hearts, flashbacks, and self-hatred.

Many therapists lose people to suicides and parasuicides gone wrong (car accidents, drug overdoses, etc.) At one trauma conference, about one-third of the therapists in the room raised their hand to indicate that they'd had a patient complete suicide. According to one article from the American Psychological Association, one out of four psychologists can expect to lose a patient to suicide over the course of their career (DeAngelis, 2017).

I have had a few clients so self-injurious and suicidal that I wondered from week to week if they would be alive for their next appointment. These clients forced me to dive deeply into strategies for work, which helped me tolerate the anxiety of the uncertainty of their safety. Since I previously worked in oncology as a medical social worker with patients who had terminal illnesses, I applied a thought experiment to my clients with severe traumas and mental disorders. Could it be that some conditions could be seen as terminal? Are some of our patients' early deaths as likely as for those with Stage 4 cancer? As with cancer, perhaps death can be delayed and pain alleviated, but should we really consider death a treatment failure any more than an oncologist does? In oncology, I observed that doctors did the best with what they had while also maintaining an acceptance of outcomes. They did not blame themselves for their patient's inevitable passing. They were glad that they could bring their patients some peace, give them more time with loved ones, and allow them to die with as much comfort as possible, knowing that even that is not always possible. When I started to think this way, when I accepted death as a possible (or even inevitable) outcome for some clients, I noticed that I was a lot less afraid of my patients dying. I started to feel admiration and gratitude for my clients who were slugging it out heroically, staying alive against all odds. I was able to see my clients' suicidality as a process I could help with but ultimately not have any control over, just as with my medical clients.

To take care of ourselves with these high-risk clients we need to walk a fine line in our own psyches. If we loosen our boundaries to the point where we feel that we alone are responsible for keeping our clients alive or worry about our clients day and night, we injure ourselves. That kind of stress does not make for sustainable practice. We can lose our objectivity that makes us valuable to our patients to begin with. Our stress levels will rise as our capacity to make good judgment calls decline. We may need to develop discipline in holding our minds focused on what is helpful and modulating our own empathy responses and psychological filters. Thinking back on our discussion of attachment styles of therapists, we can see that perhaps therapists with preoccupied attachment styles could be vulnerable to looser boundaries and an overdeveloped sense of responsibility for the client.

On the other hand, if therapists avoid or dismiss clients' suffering as merely manipulation or drama, clients could get hurt. As a supervisor, I have heard clinicians complain about 'manipulation' all too often. The truth is, when human beings suffer in the extreme, they do anything to get themselves out of that suffering. I'm not sure we should call that 'manipulation' or 'drama'. When we call our clients names (which is what this labeling is, thinly disguised as clinical work), we dehumanize them and by extension ourselves. When we close our hearts to our patients' suffering, we close our hearts to our own suffering. In failing to respond appropriately to client suffering, we put ourselves and our agencies at risk through poor practice that opens us to malpractice lawsuits.

When clients are in extreme pain and/or suicidal, a middle path is best for them and for ourselves. We need to notice if we are calm or anxious, over- or underreacting. We need to stay in our 'window of tolerance', as Pat Ogden, PhD, puts it, neither activated to fight/flight nor deactivated to the 'freeze' state (Ogden & Minton, 2000). Good supervision can help us take care of our practices, ourselves, and our clients all at once.

Supervision Mitigates Risk

Clients with a high trauma load can challenge even very advanced clinicians. When our clients' trauma is activated, they can make us feel deskilled, angry, fearful, or even despondent. Clients with the most extreme developmental traumas evoke the most extreme reactions in their therapists. In order for clinicians to stay within our window of tolerance, we need to have a mentor who has our back emotionally and practically. This is where great trauma supervision becomes indispensable as part of self-care for the trauma therapist. Supervision may be the single biggest help for us in this work.

Modern education for therapists often assumes that therapists already possess advanced people skills such as attunement, empathy, and self-regulation. Before managed care, internship and post-graduate weekly supervision provided opportunities for the therapist to learn about herself. Many of us who began our careers in the 1980s or before had supervisors who were heavily influenced by psychoanalysts or who actually were analysts.

Analysts are required to have several days a week of psychoanalysis for several years, geared towards becoming a practitioner; this is called a training analysis. In the world of psychoanalysis, one is not considered competent to analyze others until one knows oneself thoroughly and has worked through a series of intrapsychic conflicts and issues in addition to mastering the concepts of the therapeutic work. Otherwise, these conflicts will play out in the therapy unconsciously, and the patient will not get the full benefit of the therapy or might even be harmed by the well-meaning but ignorant therapist.

Although modern clinical supervision derives from psychoanalytic training analysis, it has undergone some significant changes. Psychodynamic supervision, for example, meets only once per week. The focus is on transference and countertransference in therapy sessions, with an eye towards eliminating unhelpful therapist behaviors while kindly illuminating areas of repair needed in the psychotherapist. In this model, supervisors are given leeway to point out unconscious conflicts for the beginning therapist, but they do not enter into those issues with the supervisee. Supervisors may identify lingering issues that need resolution in an outside therapy setting or through intense introspection. It is understood that the therapist should periodically undertake a course of therapy to resolve issues that surface in the treatment of their patients. Unfortunately, psychodynamic supervision is a rare commodity in 2017, often found by paying privately. Effective psychodynamic supervision requires discussion of long-term therapy cases (months to years) that are in short supply in modern training centers.

I would like to note one traditional tool from the world of psychodynamic supervision as being of great help in learning to treat trauma patients—the process recording. It is, essentially, a mindfulness exercise. Process recordings are written by the therapist in training and consist of three parts:

1. the dialog of a session
2. the therapist's observation of the patient's nonverbals
3. the therapist's internal conversation and feelings about what is happening

Recordings can be laid out in three columns or written as a narrative. Here is an example:

Table 9.1 Process Recording Example

Dialog	Nonverbals	Therapist reactions
Client (Ct): I had an anxiety attack last night. It lasted 4 hours.	Ct looks tired. She is breathing heavily and looks unsure of herself. Her eyes are teary.	I'm breathing heavily too. I'm worried she's going to have one here. I want to help her.
Therapist (Tx): I'm really sorry to hear that. Four hours is a long time. Let's check in with your body. How is your anxiety right now on a scale of 1–10?	Ct looks at me. She puts her feet on the floor like we've practiced. Her breathing slows down, but she still looks pale.	I'm grounding myself to be with her. I am relieved to see her become more focused and grounded. I think meds might help but she really doesn't want them. I'm OK with this.
Ct: It's about a 6 but I feel better now that I'm here.	Ct is still engaged visually. She seems more present.	I am glad she is here. My breathing is back to normal.

Usually the supervisor takes the recording, reads it, and comments on aspects of the therapy including important interactions that the therapist may have missed. The recording is then discussed in supervision. Some people do recordings as audio or video transcripts; some do not. Both have merit. The recording illuminates many different processes, especially the attunement between therapist and client. When a therapist is writing a recording from memory, it is interesting to note where she remembers easily and where she does not. Memory blocks can be points of therapist dissociation or inattention. Both are important to understand. Lapses in attunement can be subtle and difficult to call out in a process recording but even more so in self-reporting supervisory sessions. 'Checking out' can be the therapist dissociating to the patient's material or the result of a parallel process triggered by the client's dissociation. These moments often do not make it into supervision because . . . dissociation! The therapist can't see what she doesn't see and so does not talk about it in session. With a third party observer via process recordings, these moments are more likely to be noticed and worked through in a trauma supervision.

We are in danger of losing the hard-won clinical wisdom of depth-oriented supervision. In many agencies, clinical supervision has largely become an administrative endeavor, focused on procedures that adhere to insurance regulations and evidence-based protocols. Since the length of time spent in 'therapy' has shrunk to a few weeks, the emphasis in training is on quick diagnosis and punched out treatments that give the most bang for the buck. If one is in an institution doing research, clinical focus may be on research protocols as well. An in-depth look at clients, the therapist, and the interplay between the two has become almost outdated. Yet, traumatized people with relational damage need more than just a few weeks to develop a working rapport with the therapist and even more to unwind years of trauma. The current climate in mental health is such that many internships no longer provide an in-depth therapy option for training. Practitioners may have to wait until they graduate to pursue training as a trauma therapist or even as a psychotherapist who does long-term work. Since many agencies do not provide this level of training, many folks pay for these services out of pocket as an additional educational or professional expense. If you are going to be a wise and helpful trauma therapist, you may want to write the expense of outside supervision into your personal budget. Nobody likes to spend extra money, but the gains you will receive for you and your patients are many. Not only will you gain extra expertise and the right to label yourself a 'trauma-trained therapist', but you will also save yourself many headaches and dangerous situations as these tricky treatments unfold.

Safety in the Workplace

When I began my internship as a social worker in Boston, the clinical community was recovering from an incident in which a social worker had been shot at her workplace. As I began writing this section, I googled 'social worker shot' and received over 32 million responses to this query! The problem of workplace violence against clinicians is still a big problem, and it informed much of my early training. What I have found in my work in Oregon is that most clinicians are not educated around physical safety and violence. I suspect this is true in other states as well. Many therapists do not even know if their agency has a procedure for dealing with violent patients. The problem can be worse for private practitioners, many of whom have not considered that their clients or clients' families could initiate violence in their office.

Self-care as a trauma therapist includes acknowledging the fact that many of the traumas our patients have endured have given them the potential for violent behavior, against either themselves or others. I know it is not popular to say this. In an effort to destigmatize people suffering from mental health issues, many people downplay this reality. I'm not convinced that it is helpful to ignore the potential for violence in clients or anyone suffering from a great deal of trauma, including ourselves. In my state, we had a terrible tragedy at a local social work school when two beloved professors who were married to each other perished in a murder-suicide. One of them taught a course on trauma. To this day, people in my community rarely talk about this event and only in hushed tones. Anybody is capable of violence under the right circumstances.

We know from neuroscience that trauma, especially developmental trauma and high ACEs, results in emotional dysregulation and overreactivity in the amygdala. Dysregulation can lead to violence. Attempts to squash violent impulses can result in self-harm or suicidality. It can also lead to drug abuse, or, as I like to call it, artificial dissociation. Coming off drugs with intact trauma circuits can also put clients at risk for acting out violent behavior secondary to traumatic dysregulation. *We need to acknowledge that our traumatized patients' brains contain neurological landmines that render them capable of violence under certain circumstances in the course of healing.* Understanding this does not make us less compassionate; it makes us more aware and ultimately more helpful to our patients and ourselves.

As the PSA[1] goes, "safety is no accident." Mindfully anticipating safety issues in our practice is the best way to avoid or de-escalate potentially violent situations. Areas that we need to address in our practice include:

- office equipment
- safety procedures
- de-escalation techniques

Office Equipment

Most mental health agencies and hospitals have equipment in place to call for help, such as phones, intercoms, and safety alarms. Most private practices do not. If you see clients in private practice, have you thought through the possibility of an attack? Who is around to help you? How would you call for help?

Perhaps you rely on your cell phone for emergencies. That reliance is reasonable if not optimal. Do you have the capacity to speed dial or hands-free call 911 or your local county crisis team? If you have an Apple iPhone, you can yell, "Siri, I'm having an emergency" and Siri will automatically call 911. But if you yell, "Siri, emergency," Siri will not dial anyone. You have to include the correct phrases and have 'Hey Siri' activated on your phone. They are:

- "Hey Siri! Call emergency services"
- "Siri! Dial 911"
- "Siri! Phone 911"
- "Siri! I'm having an emergency!" (Horowitz, 2015)

Siri does not automatically activate speakerphone when you do this, so you can activate the call from a distance but you cannot speak to dispatch unless you can reach your phone or have Siri activate your speakerphone. If you have another brand of cell phone, explore what the capacity of your phone is to get help in an emergency. When you activate the call by voice, there is a five-second countdown window in which the call can be terminated. Be aware that some 911 services do not answer immediately but require you to enter a command on your phone or stay on the line so they can weed out accidental or prank calls.

Safety Procedures

Most of us work in a building with other tenants. Make an effort to get to know your office neighbors and arrange a code word to which they can immediately respond in case you need help. Clinicians are conditioned to be private about therapy, and we should be, except in case of emergency. Never put your life or safety below the need for confidentiality.

Arrange your furniture so that you sit between your client and the exit. Two years in a row I supervised students that became trapped in their offices at an agency after people had already left. In both cases, the client made a casual show of force by deliberately blocking their exit from the room. Both students were badly shaken and had not been oriented to safety procedures,[2] which brings me to . . .

Make sure you are oriented to safety procedures, that you orient your supervisees and students, and that you document this training for liability reasons! What is the protocol for a therapist in trouble? Do you have a safety alarm in the room? Who does it notify and what happens after notification? Are people expected to use the office phone or their own phone to call for police, for a supervisor, for a security guard? Is there a supervisor on site who can help with difficult or dangerous clients? We do best when we know exactly what protocol to follow: if A, then B. In a crisis, the amygdala will shut down the ability to slowly think through a problem, so we need to have a well thought out plan ahead of time. In the case of my students, neither one had the idea to use the desk phone to call for help. It's not that they had the idea and discarded it; it never occurred to them because their brain was on amygdala hijack, and nobody had previously suggested it!

Make sure that your safety procedures are sound. When I worked at a runaway youth shelter in Charlestown, Boston, we were located in a notoriously racist area. One night a Black girl had a psychotically murderous break from reality. A 45-minute struggle ensued before I could get to the White male security guard. When he saw the girl, he turned away in disgust and refused to call the police or help me, even though she was still trying to kill another resident with a weapon, and I had blood smeared on my blouse.[3] Fortunately, we were able to access police help on our own, but it could have gone very differently and with tragic results. Our director thought he had an agreement with security, but it was not solid.

De-escalation Techniques

Simple de-escalation techniques can be life-saving in a threatening situation. Unless you worked on an in-patient unit, in prisons, or in the field of residential care, you may not have any experience with violent behavior as a professional. Even if you have, you may or may not be formally trained in de-escalating behavior. I highly recommend that at least once in your career you get this training. I have used these techniques often across a variety of settings: medical hospitals, psychiatric units, residential programs, phone crisis work, and in private practice. Below are some techniques that I have used multiple times.

When a client's behavior escalates towards fear or aggression due to triggers, we will notice a few things about their behavior:

- Their eyes will engage in a hard stare at the target of their aggression. We are predators and our eyes are on the front of our heads, unlike prey animals whose eyes are on the sides of their heads (horses, mice, deer). Predatory behavior involves stalking and challenging with the eyes. This behavior can occur in close proximity or far across the room.
- They will literally 'square off' their body towards the object, locking in shoulders and hipbones in an aggressive stance squared to their target's hips and shoulders. Notice that if you assume this position in a threatening way with someone it becomes hard for them to disengage or flee. That is because fleeing signals a predator to attack. We instinctively know we cannot do this when somebody squares us up in this way.
- They will either become menacingly silent or loud and threatening with their voice. The timbre will drop into growling, or raise into hysterical tones. Speech becomes choppy, loud, and full of expletives or threats.
- Their 'bubble' becomes really big! When we are angry or fearful our threat perimeter increases and we need space. It makes sense. If there is a threat in the environment, we want to respond to it at the earliest opportunity, so what we can tolerate in our bubble decreases and we increase the space around our body to deal with the threat. Next time you become angry, notice if you, too, need more space around you to feel safe.
- They will become oppositional. Sometimes this is the first sign that someone is escalating. A neurological system at ease is fluid and responsive. When someone is escalated, they become more rigid and resistant. If pushed, they could explode.

If escalation is an arousal of the sympathetic system due to threat, real or perceived, then de-escalation means we need to return the client to a state of parasympathetic calmness. In other words, *we need to make them feel safe.* This behavior is counter-intuitive for humans. Humans are biologically programmed to respond to threats with shows of dominance and escalations. But neurobiology tells us that we need to do the opposite! A safe brain is a calm brain. Unless you are working with a truly predatory client,[4] returning them to a state of safety should de-escalate them and calm their nervous system, bringing them down out of amygdala activation. As they escalate with their body, their voice, their nervous system, and their behavior, so can we de-escalate them with how we use our body, our voice, our nervous system, and our behavior. Here's what you can do:

- Be conscious of how you use your gaze. Do not return their hard stare but keep your eyes soft. Break your gaze briefly and periodically to indicate that you feel safe and are not about to fight with them. Be aware of their position, of course. Do not look completely away or avoid looking at them.

- Do not engage in 'squaring off'. I like to keep my torso slightly angled so that I am neither in a fight or flight position, but can do either if needed. Many martial arts start with this stance for de-escalation or quick response. Notice if you are tempted to puff up your chest. Relax your shoulders and take some deep breaths to maintain a neutral and nonthreatening posture. If you are higher than your client, maybe come down to their level if it is safe to do so. Also do not turn your back to the client as this total disengagement can trigger abandonment rage or a predatory chase.

- Remember in Chapter 2 how we talked about prosody and the timbre of voice that is soothing rather than agitating, indicating the state of polyvagal activation? Engage your smoothest, softest, and calming tones. Avoid harsh, choppy, and low tones when you are talking to the client. Think of yourself as a mother soothing her agitated infant and adopt the idea of a lullaby as you speak to the client. Be careful not to be incongruous or come across as patronizing. This caring voice has to be backed up by genuine caring. Your client will know the difference.

- Do not get inside your patient's bubble if you can help it! And if you do, prepare for the violent escalation that will likely follow. Notice how big their bubble is. The body bubble of an agitated person can extend all the way across the room. If you must approach the client, approach slowly and carefully without staring and without squaring. As the client calms down, their bubble will shrink down again to the point where you may even be able to touch them in a nonthreatening manner.

- If your client becomes oppositional, give in any way that you can. They don't want to sit down? No problem. They don't want to talk? Not an issue. They don't like what you are wearing? That's fine; they are allowed to have an opinion. If my client is so raw that anything I say or do could become an issue, I might say something like, "Do you mind if I just sit here with you?" If they say no, I might move three feet away and ask again. Do not engage in a power struggle with your client at this time. You will lose. The ability to say "no" is sometimes the last vestige of power our client has. When we take that away, we can incur a state of total helplessness in our patient where violence becomes a possibility.

In order to calm our patients we need to calm ourselves. Incongruity is always escalating to people who are upset. Do you remember ever being told to "calm down" by someone who was pretending to be calm but was as or more agitated than you were? Nobody responds well to this kind of intervention. We model what we want our patients to achieve and activate their mirror neurons positively in the process. We need to become experts at calming ourselves.

Self-Care and the Koshas

The yogic model of the human being says that there are five sheaths or koshas that surround and embody the human soul. In *The Trauma Tool Kit* (Pease

Banitt, 2012), I use this model to sort interventions for dealing with traumatic stress. Trauma pierces through all the layers of our being, like a sword through a Russian doll. In order to become whole again, we need to heal all of the layers. In order to keep ourselves whole and well while working in such a stressful area as therapists, I recommend that we attend to the wellness of all of the koshas: the physical body, the energy body, the cognitive mind, the wisdom mind, and the bliss (or love) body. Strenuous demands require strenuous self-care.

The Physical Body

If I had realized how much time I would spend sitting in a chair as a therapist, I might have chosen another profession! It's not something I considered when I was young. Maybe you haven't either. We now know that sitting for several hours a day can result in ill health for the body. Sitting plus listening to stressful material can add up to a lot of stress on the body over time. How is your chair? Is your spine aligned and comfortable? Do you take standing breaks between clients? Can you get a ball for sitting part of the day that will help you use more of your muscles? It is definitely worth investing in a comfortable and healthy chair to preserve your health. Now that I am doing Reiki part of the time, it is a relief to be standing for some of my hours rather than sitting.

The rest you probably know. But here is a reminder to eat well, get moderate exercise, and move your body as much as you can when you are working. Drink lots of water! Massage can be expensive for a therapist, but over the long term you may find it a helpful investment to loosen up tight muscles and connective tissue. Some therapists have begun taking walks with clients as part of their sessions. An advantage of this practice is that the bilateral stimulation that walking provides can help in the processing of traumatic material.

The Energy Body

I have seen the same tic in several female therapists. A client says something disturbing or troubling, and the therapist clenches their legs together, pulling them slightly upwards towards their body, as if the therapist wants to go into the fetal position. They never seem to be aware that their body visibly tenses. Every time I've seen this I've wondered what was happening to the therapist's energy. It looks like they are sucking in and binding emotions through muscular tension in the lower legs, pelvic floor, and hips. After these observations and because I am a yoga practitioner, I have made an effort to make sure that my own energy flow is smooth and unclenched during and after therapy sessions.

Here is a technique you can use before, during, and after a session to make sure you are unblocked in your energy flow:

> *Sit with two feet flat on the floor with an upright relaxed spine—neither slouched nor too rigid. Feel the floor under your feet and the stability of the building you are in, the foundation going deep into the earth. Imagine there is an opening in*

the middle of each foot and allow it to dilate, sending roots deep into the earth like a plant. Allow any negative energy to flow out with the breath down the body, down the legs and through the opening in the feet. At the inhale draw up beneficial healing earth energy into the body. If you like, you can imagine there is a beautiful white light coming down into the crown of your head. This is a healing, cleansing light that fills your body with good energy. See the light circulating through every part of your body, releasing toxins and negative energies. Let those flow out through your feet and into the earth, inhaling again the sweet loving earth energies. Sit like this for a few minutes inhaling and exhaling.

At first you may have trouble sensing energy movement—that's OK! When you become adept at this exercise you will be able to notice when you are clenching and can instantly pass negativity out through your feet, even in the middle of a session. You can do this exercise for any length of time—2 minutes to 2 hours! Your clients may also find this exercise beneficial. You could do it together!

If you are into yoga or tai chi, you have heard much about the prana body, energy body, or the importance of the flow of chi (or qi) through the body. Clairvoyants, empaths, and others can sense the flow of energy through the body. Disrupted or stagnant flow can lead to illness if unremedied over time. Chinese medicine and yogic therapies aim to balance and reestablish flow in the body. They make excellent self-care practices for therapists. One does not need to do vigorous lengthy practices to gain the benefit of energy movement.

As a Kriplu-trained yoga teacher myself, I recommend several postures for establishing flow and releasing workday stress. These can all be done in your office or at home. If you do not know them already, you can easily look them up online, or go take a local yoga class! Tadasana, or mountain posture, grounds us and helps us restore the good posture of our spine. Also good for spinal health are stretches in the six directions of the spine: Cat Cow moves the spine from curved to flexed, front and back; lateral stretching can be achieved with the Crescent Moon pose; the final stretches are twisting, such as in the Seated Spinal Twist pose, or you can do gentle standing twists. You do not have to lie on the ground for any of these postures, and they can be accomplished in a few short minutes. Be sure to breathe deeply during them. Speaking of breath there are several breathing exercises that you can use. As a trauma therapist you probably teach some! Now be sure that you practice them, too.

If you are struggling with deep fatigue or sleepiness during sessions, energy stagnation may be the issue, and you may want to seek deeper healing modalities. Shiatsu massage is a clothes-on modality that helps regulate the flow of qi in the body with acupressure technique. You could seek out a local acupuncturist for help with opening up energy pathways. Reiki deeply nourishes, restores, and clears your energy body.

Clear your office of negative energies on the regular with smudge sticks, aerosolized smudge, or essential oils. Smudging is an ancient indigenous practice found on every continent to clear the atmosphere of a room or the aura of a person from negative energies.[5] I prefer to burn white sage to cut through the thickest atmosphere, but there are many smudge materials you can burn: cedar, sweet woodruff, desert sage, sweetgrass, etc. Of course, make sure your office allows you to burn something; if not, there are many wonderful aerosolized smudges on the market. I have one client that is so sensitive she will not even let me work if I have not smudged her and the office at the top of the session. I encourage you to also smudge yourself! Traditionally the sage is burnt in an abalone bowl with a feather that fans the smoke around the person or room. Some therapists and clients are so sensitive that they can feel the difference before and after smudging. You can assess effectiveness yourself by rating your own distress before and after the smudging.

Without these energy clearing and grounding modalities, there is zero chance that I would still be a trauma therapist after all these years. I highly recommend them, especially for highly sensitive or highly empathic therapists. If you find them beneficial, find a way to work them into your routine weekly, if not daily.

Cognitive Mind

We all know that time management is a part of our business, but so few therapists are great at it! We need to give ourselves permission to think and plan. I call this 'CEO time'. Whether you are self-employed or work for an agency, we all need time to plan our schedules and our lives. *Build time into your work life to actually think about self-care.* During this time do nothing but think about you. Decide if your schedule is working for you, if you have enough time between clients, and if your caseload is balanced with the type of clients you want to see. Think about start and end times. Do you like to do 50-minute sessions or 75-minute sessions? Check in with yourself. Maybe you were happy seeing 20 depressed people last year, but this year you need a break. How many severely traumatized clients can you serve without becoming secondarily traumatized yourself? Are you still interested in your work? Can you mix up your days with other billable tasks, such as supervision, or lighter caseloads? Are you getting enough physical and energy care? Make some appointments with yourself. I would suggest an absolute minimum amount of time for CEO time would be 2 hours/month. CEO time does not include administrative tasks like billing, financial planning, maintaining files, or cleaning, but also plan time for those tasks.

Supervision is a cognitive task we covered earlier. You need time to integrate what you are learning in supervision and augment that professional development with reading. Make sure you leave some time every month for your cognitive learning needs and to keep abreast of changes in the field. If the DSM 5 has come out and you are still in DSM III, you are going to feel stressed (and for good reason!). Review diagnostic procedures, look up medications, read helpful articles. The more confident you feel in providing great care, the less stress will come knocking. Trauma work challenges us deeply at every level, including cognitively.

Take a look at your thoughts around being a therapist and check your perfectionism. Remember to be the 'good enough' therapist and that batters only need to hit the ball one-third of the time to be considered outstanding. What we do is incredibly difficult, analogous to playing Bach on the piano, remember? Examine your self-talk and decide if you are being honoring or critical of yourself. Do you give yourself pats on the back after a hard day or do you harangue yourself with what you could have done better?

If you work at an agency, remember to take time to evaluate them, just as they evaluate you. Really think through what you need to be happy and then take steps to make that happen. When the fun-to-crud ratio gets out of whack for a prolonged period, it may mean that you need to change jobs. Just as we talked about having our patients rate us, we also need to rate the aspects of our work that impact our lives.

Wisdom Mind

What inspires you to go beyond your workaday mind and into your deep knowing? Keeping up on peer-reviewed research, perusing the latest *Psychology Today*, or reading your favorite therapist blog all stimulate our cognitive minds and keep us informed about cutting-edge clinical practice. They can also feel like chores that drain us. Wisdom readings, on the other hand, inspire and nurture us. They make us feel like we can tackle another difficult day while eliciting our best clinical selves.

Wisdom readings don't just grow our knowledge, they grow us as people. Writers like Brené Brown, Maya Angelou, Carl Rogers, or Mr. Rogers, for that matter, allow us to expand our horizons and encourage us to expand into our own knowingness, our own intuition. Or you may feel drawn to reading world scriptures and wisdom teachings such as the *Tao Te Ching*, the Bible, the Upanishads, *The Four Agreements*, or *Black Elk Speaks*. I have yet to meet a therapist I admired who was not well read in wisdom teachings. When what you read feeds your soul, you create fertile ground to be the wise therapist you want to be. Take a refreshing dip in jnana[6] once in a while. The journals will always be there.

Wisdom elevates and integrates intellectual knowledge, making it one's own. It takes time and effort to abide in the wisdom mind. Swami Vivekananda[7] is said to have remarked, "A yogi should neither work too much, nor too little," meaning that there is an optimum amount of time to spend working on oneself. In India this practice is called sadhana. With our highly paced lives, it can be nearly impossible to develop wisdom without taking breaks to go on retreats or personal growth workshops. We need to interrupt our normal flow of activities and thoughts to make room for inspiration and elevation. Intention hastens the formation of wise thought. Without intention we may or may not learn from painful errors; we may just keep repeating them. When we set ourselves the goal of wisdom, not mere knowledge, a magical thing happens. The path opens to reveal itself in stages. We get a flash of insight. Like lightning on a dark night, our next step is illumined. We need time to both harvest our insights and act on them.

What is your method for harvesting wisdom? Do you need a weekend at the beach? Maybe a trip to holistic growth center such as Omega in Rhinebeck, New York, or Kripalu in the Berkshires could help facilitate your growth. One social worker in licensure supervision with me writes to harvest and integrate her thoughts about her busy complicated job at a local hospital.

I want to stress that I do not consider these suggestions as optional to become a wise trauma therapist. If wisdom were so easy to develop, everyone would have it! If trauma therapy were so easy, everyone would do it! When you develop a deep comfort in tuning into your intuition and engaging your wisdom self, there is a feeling of flow in treatment that is deeply healing to both you and your client. Ideas and images flow smoothly from your inner being into your treatment, facilitating a deep rapport with your clients' mind and experiences, a communal space of connection where relational attunement is effortlessly achieved. You have almost certainly had those moments already. Like raindrops, over time those moments coalesce into a vivifying stream where deep pain dissolves. In a wisdom-based clinical practice, the therapist can help clients draw on self-love from even the darkest experiences. With practice, these healing moments become more frequent until, finally, they pervade the entire therapy experience.

Bliss Body

In the teaching of the koshas, the most subtle of all the bodies or sheaths is considered to be the anandamayakosha, translated as 'the body appearing in the world as bliss'. Bliss is a resource in the treatment of trauma, both for practitioners and for clients. In our culture, bliss is overhyped and underdelivered in the media and is used to sell us things. So many therapists feel burdened and stressed that bliss seems irrelevant when doing trauma work. Yet blissful experiences have been a powerful antidote to trauma from time out of mind.

In many indigenous cultures, song and dance are considered cures for trauma, deep grief, and depression as they induce blissful states. In an interview with the magazine *Anchor*, Dr. Bessel Van Der Kolk talks about his work with Archbishop Desmond Tutu in South Africa, where so many people were traumatized and the nation was at risk for further bloodshed:

> Tutu was a master trauma therapist . . . He would come into a room with 40, 50, 60 people, and we would pray together, and we would sing together, and we would dance together. We got this sense of communal rhythm and pleasure and belonging and being in sync, and then somebody would start talking about their trauma. To talk about your trauma sometimes separates people because you are into your own misery and your overwhelming feeling of terror and rage. Tutu would just get people to that certain point, and he'd say, "Let's get up. Let's sing and dance."
>
> (Melaragno, 2015)

Bliss takes us out of our small self and connects us with a larger reality. It lifts us above our suffering without dissociating us from it. Bliss is an experience of extreme connectedness, to self, to community, and/or to the God of our understanding.

Bliss arises out of the experience of flow. If we are awake to it, there can be a kind of bliss present in the therapy hour when we are totally and completely present to another human being. We sit rapt and are lifted out of the mundane concerns of ordinary life. The experience of flow does not depend on the happiness of the experience; it transforms the experience. Flow is the experience of complete here and now, in a no-time space. In flow our own thoughts slow down or cease completely. Obviously in session flow our thoughts do not cease completely, but they do become single-pointedly focused on our client. In that complete presence, bliss arises naturally and transforms horror into sadness, sadness into poignancy, grief into gratitude. Bliss does not erase our client's experience but it imbues the experience with grace and meaning. It is not silly or giddy. Bliss lends depth and solemnity to therapy without negativity.

Like other skills, some people have more of an aptitude to naturally abide in bliss than others do, and, like other skills, bliss can be cultivated. Many of us trauma therapists are naturally drawn to blissful activities as a counterpart to the heaviness of our work. Anything that puts us in the present moment of flow can cause bliss to arise: knitting, horseback riding, hiking, dancing, making art. Bliss also naturally arises in response to the mind settling down in meditation. That is why all swamis in India have the word 'ananda', meaning bliss, as part of their name: Yogananda being the bliss of yoga, Vivekananda, the bliss of wise discrimination, and so on. There are spiritual practices that are said to enhance and bring on bliss, such as meditation or chanting the names of God (japa).

In *The Trauma Tool Kit* (Pease Banitt, 2012), Chapter 9 lays out the five steps for entering into a blissful state at will. They are:

1. Engage in a healthy ecstatic activity
2. Pay full attention to your senses
3. Surrender the illusion of control
4. Engage your inner child
5. Cultivate the attitude of gratitude

Nature assists the development of bliss consciousness greatly. In Japan, 'forest bathing' or 'shinrin yoku' is encouraged as a regular activity due to the many healing and calming benefits of being in wilderness. But any wholesome activity entered into with these five steps can yield blissful states of consciousness over time.

Mindful regular self-care yields beautiful results for a therapist. When we know our needs are being met we can soften into our difficult work. We become resilient and develop endurance. We increase our health of both mind and body, and we model these results for our patients, lending our counsel integrity and power.

Notes

1 Public Safety Announcement.
2 They actually had no idea what to do or how to behave in that situation. Crisis responses are learned, not innate.
3 I am fine and was not hurt in that struggle, although I did seek another job due to the lax security.
4 I do not work with predators in my practice, but my colleagues who do need to take certain precautions in their work that are unnecessary with the average traumatized client.
5 In some belief systems, these negative energies can attract negative entities that 'feed' off the energies. Lore states that uncleared energies can bring disease and/or misfortune.
6 *Jnana* is the Sanskrit word for wisdom (ghee-ah-nah).
7 Swami Vivekananda was one of the first swamis that brought the wisdom of yoga to America. He spoke in Chicago at the World Parliament of Religions in 1893 at the behest of his guru, Sri Ramakrishna, making headlines in papers all across the US.

References

DeAngelis, T. (2017). *Coping with a Client's Suicide*. Retrieved September 29, 2017, from American Psychological Association: www.apa.org/gradpsych/2008/11/suicide. aspx

Elk, B,. & Neihardt, J. (1988). *Black Elk Speaks: Being the Life Story of a Holy Man of the Oglala Sioux*. Lincoln, NB: University of Nebraska Press.

Horowitz, P. (2015, July 17). *Siri Can Call Emergency Services for You With iPhone If Need Be*. Retrieved September 30, 2017, from OSX Daily: http://osxdaily.com/2015/07/17/siri-call-emergency-services-iphone/

Melaragno, E. (2015, November 18). *Trauma in the Body: Interview with Dr. Bessel van der Kolk*. (S. Harbor, Ed.). Retrieved October 23, 2017, from Still Harbor: http://stillharbor.org/anchormagazine/2015/11/18/trauma-in-the-body

Ogden, P., & Minton, K. (2000, October). *Sensorimotor Psychotherapy: One Method for Processing Traumatic Memory*. Retrieved October 1, 2017, from Sensorimotor Psychotherapy Training Institute: www.sensorimotorpsychotherapy.org/articles.html

Pease Banitt, S. (2012). *The Trauma Tool Kit: Healing PTSD From the Inside Out*. Wheaton, IL: Quest Books.

Ruiz, D. M. (1997). *The Four Agreements: A Practical Guide to Personal Freedom (A Toltec Wisdom Book)*. San Rafael, CA: Amber-Allen Publishing.

10 Awakening to Wisdom, Love, and Compassion

Love is the real power. It's the energy that cherishes. The more you work with that energy, the more you will see how people respond naturally to it, and the more you will want to use it. It brings out your creativity, and helps everyone around you flower. Your children, the people you work with—everyone blooms.

—Marion Woodman, PhD

Our modern language around love tends to be somewhat limited. Attachment, selfless love, personal love, compassion, sexual attraction, and lust lump together under the single word 'love'. For this reason, many people do not really like the word love at all and find it meaningless. Others assume that we all mean the same thing when we say "I love you" or feel love in our hearts. But we don't. Not remotely. I believe this is a reason why therapists have been so loathe to talk about feelings of love towards their clients, and clients' love towards their therapists. It is a sticky wicket fraught with potential misunderstandings, this territory of love.

In my years of training and practice as a therapist, I can count on one hand the number of times I have had an honest discussion about love in the therapy hour. Early on, many therapists considered love only as a manifestation of transference (on the part of the client) and countertransference (on the part of the therapist). I recall endless discussions about whether the therapy relationship was a 'real' relationship, with very impassioned points of view on both sides of the argument. I wondered with my peers whether every relationship is merely a manifestation of transference and countertransference, and whether 'real' love even exists in relationships as we know them. All of us shied away from using terms like 'love' in session regarding our relationship with clients, and our own therapists avoided the subject with us as well. Even as sex therapy was on the rise and becoming a booming business, love had become taboo in the therapy hour (Baur, 1997).

Erotic Transference

Freud talked about the successful resolution of 'erotic transference', in other words the patient falling in love with the therapist, as an essential element of healing in analysis. A classic erotic transference is exemplified by the case below.

A man arrives at therapy deeply angry with women and completely stuck in his life. People at work are afraid of him. He is frustrated and angry with women; he has violent fantasies about them. This client unsettles me so much that I do not want to see him at the end of the evening, feeling that he might stalk me as I leave the office. I worry that he could be a potential sex offender, although I am fairly sure he has not acted on any of these fantasies yet. After seeking supervision around my fears, I switch his time to mid-evening and start to feel safer. At one point he shares a rather kinky and violent fantasy about a sexual act with me that I find distasteful in the extreme. I hold a space of 'even-hovering attention' and 'unconditional positive regard' for him through this difficult session and do not show my feelings of disgust or make it about me in any way. Afterwards it is clear that the client is becoming more attached to me and starting to develop feelings of affection and love that we keep contained to sessions. We keep working through those feelings in therapy, along with other feelings they evoke from his history: abandonment, an atmosphere of potential violence, abuse, and neglect. After several months he softens and appears more regulated and connected in sessions. Threatening and inappropriate behaviors decrease to zero, both in and out of session. As his feelings about his therapist resolve, he realizes he wants to start a relationship with a woman in his life. There are many complications to work through as he moves into a stable relationship with this woman. Sexual issues are addressed and worked through successfully. Our work together comes to an end. Eventually the client marries and invites me to the wedding. I decline attendance but send a card wishing them both well.

Although the working through of this type of classic erotic transference may not be as common as Freudian therapists would have us believe, this case was a clear example of the necessity for this work. I do not believe this client could have resolved such deep-seated issues around women without it. Initially, as his therapist, I experienced a great deal of revulsion and fear, but in the end grew to like him very much. I was thrilled when I received the wedding invitation. Yet, for all my feelings of connection, I did not feel like it was right for me to go to his wedding. One could argue that going constituted a dual relationship, but I did not feel that way. In theory, I think it would have been fine to go. I cared deeply and in a real way about this client and had no worries about keeping personal boundaries intact. I was neither attracted to him nor in love with him at any time in our work together. Nevertheless, it felt important to be proud of him from a distance and not to let our previous therapeutic (but real) relationship intrude on his wedding day. Our relationship had come to an end.

Agape vs. Eros

In the early 1600s, Christians began to use the Greek word *agape* to distinguish a humanitarian love that was distinctively different from sexual love, eros. Dictionary.com defines agape as "unselfish love of one person for another without sexual implications; brotherly love." *Eros*, by contrast, derives from the Greek word meaning desire. Agape describes very accurately the potential type of love that can emerge within a therapeutic relationship and is appropriate to the therapeutic relationship. Some definitions even describe agape as a type of motherly or godly love. The key word in the definition of agape is *unselfish*. Since the word love, itself, does not distinguish between selfish and unselfish forms, agape becomes a useful concept to describe the type of deep, yet unselfish, caring that many therapists strive for. It also hearkens back to the concepts of the therapeutic relationship related to mother/infant holding, discussed in the first chapter relating what master therapists had to say about the ideal therapeutic relationship (unconditional positive regard, holding environment, attuned, etc.).

Many of us are drawn to be therapists as an expression of the love we feel for humanity. We long to be part of the solution of the pain and sorrow we see around us. We feel we have something to offer and long to bring our loving hearts into the equation of healing on a broader scale. As we get into the work of being a good therapist, we realize that we have blocks to our ability to be effective and so we work these blocks out through our own therapies, supervision, and self-monitoring. As we become better therapists, some of us realize we have been given a rare and special gift to develop true wisdom and compassion.

Some therapists hail from a religious background that encourages selfless service to the world as a spiritual path. Christians call this charity. Jews call it tikkun olam, which means repair of the world. Hindus and Buddhists describe selfless service as seva or karma yoga, meaning we are entitled to the work but must surrender the results to God (Brahman). In yoga, karma yoga is considered one of the great paths to enlightenment or 'self-realization', meaning that to know who one is at the deepest level is to know God (Spirit, Allah, or whatever name for the great Divine one uses). Humanistic atheists call it making the world a better place or living a moral life. Agape encompasses all these ideas and more. It is a heart-to-heart love that desires nothing for itself but only to serve, gaining delight from that service.

Eros, on the other hand, is a passionate love that encompasses healthy desire. When we come from the place of eros, we want the person to be ours in every way. We desire to be with them, to make them happy, to make love to them, to possess their heart and affection. We do not mind it if they obsess over us as well (at least in the beginning). Eros is that kind of in love feeling that is called madness by the poets and artists. We cannot stop thinking about our object of affection and think we want only to make them happy. We want to make ourselves happy by basking not only in the glow of our beloved, but also in the glow of eros, itself. Eros makes the world a happier place for a while. Colors are brighter, people are more kind, and the world is an optimistic place when we are possessed by eros.

Eros has a dark side that can flip into obsession and the need to own as the initial glow of eros fades. Where agape lives to serve others, eros seeks to possess and be possessed. In the mutual embrace of eros lies a kind of bliss for two people, but it is not a stable bliss. Eros is conditional. Eros is fickle. It is a wild joyride that can be both beautiful and deadly as it is tangled up in unfulfilled desires of the ego. In neuroscience, we could describe eros as a dopamine high. Once the levels of dopamine start to return to normal, as they will over time, the desire *for* eros starts to supplant the desire *of* eros. At this point there is a choice, to continue to chase after eros, which can escalate the highs and lows of the relationship, or to settle down into the work of a relationship filled with agape, accepting eros as the temporary condition that it is.

In the work of psychotherapy, there is no room for eros. Eros is no respecter of boundaries, but we can work with it as a phenomenon of countertransference just as we would any other strong feeling that arises in our work as therapists.

Erotic Countertransference

When therapists become confused about agape and eros, a dangerous erotic countertransference can develop, whether or not the client feels any love for the therapist. I want to be clear that not all sexual transgressions by therapists fall into this category. Some therapists are predatory. Some are not at all confused, and set out to have sex with patients as a matter of course. They carefully groom and manipulate their clients to the point of sexual interaction. I think most of us are clear that this is wrong, evil even, and has nothing whatsoever to do with love, only with power. What is more difficult to parse lies in the confusion that can arise in the therapist when they genuinely feel attracted to their clients for reasons real or imagined.

Simple lust or erotic attraction can be contained relatively easily. We need to heed Freud's words, "whatever is not acknowledged or remembered is destined to be acted out." If we allow ourselves to have the full range of feelings (anger, sympathy, sexual attraction, and so on) towards our clients, we are less likely to act out those feelings. To whatever degree we dissociate away from those feelings, we start creating risk in the safety of the therapeutic container. Susan Baur makes the argument in her book *The Intimate Hour: Love and Sex in Psychotherapy* (Baur, 1997) that this most recent generation of therapists has become so frightened by lawsuits and license revocations that to even contemplate one's attraction to a client is taboo. Paradoxically, this reaction can sow the seeds for more acting out down the line.

In order to remove the threat of inappropriate behavior, therapists need to take these feelings to their own therapies and supervisions and work through them. By keeping these feelings conscious, they can avoid acting them out. Often a feeling of sexual attraction can be a manifestation of projective identification or a response to the client's transference.[1] Many clients who are sexually traumatized in childhood by a caregiver feel that they cannot be cared about if there is not a sexual component to love and will (unconsciously or consciously) go out of their way to realize that sexual component in therapy.

If a therapist cannot shake strong feelings of sexual attraction through their own therapy or supervision, then perhaps it is time to refer the client out to a colleague who will be immune to this dynamic.

A full-blown erotic transference, however, goes beyond simple attraction. The therapist can feel like they are falling in love with the client in a very profound way. The sexual attraction may even be secondary to what feels like a heart connection. Feelings of tenderness, caretaking, and attraction merge into a feeling of closeness that feels physical as well as emotional. Baur points out that this pattern has been present since the earliest days of psychotherapy when Jung fell in love with his patient, Sabrina Spielrein, who went on to become a great analyst in her own right. She points out that these types of relationships are less clear because they are an expression of the humanity of both parties, and historically there have been different understandings around the boundaries of psychotherapy and love relationships that corresponded to different understandings of abuse. Not that long ago it was considered OK for a therapist falling in mutual love with a client to terminate that therapeutic relationship in favor of a love relationship. Now, licensing boards and professional organizations frown on a sexual relationship with a client for any reason and after any amount of time has passed due to the power dynamic and powerful transference relationship that is created in therapy.

And yet, it happens. Eros is a powerful force in the human psyche. Under the influence of eros, it is easy to start rationalizing reasons to become involved with a client, especially if that client is encouraging such a relationship. But the toll on the patient is enormous. Baur interviewed Nancy Avery, codirector of BASTA, the Boston Association to Stop Therapist Abuse. Avery identified five stages that clients move through when their therapists cross the line into personal relationships with them. At the end of this process they tend to move away from the feeling that they fell in love and can recognize that they have been manipulated by the therapist, who had both more status and more power than they did and therefore more responsibility to prevent such a relationship from forming to begin with.

1. Self-blame—they feel that their behaviors caused the therapist to cross the line, such as how they dressed or their fantasies about the therapist.
2. Feeling stupid—clients feel they should have 'known better' and are stuck in feelings of shame and despair over the affair.
3. Rage—Avery describes this stage as the most dangerous of all, as the rage can turn inwards leading to suicidal ideation.
4. Looking at causes—clients are able to develop insight into the behaviors and thoughts that made them vulnerable to exploitation.
5. Prevention—clients can see patterns of abuse and avoid abusive situations in the future.

When trauma therapists are not able to hold a safe container for their clients due to the intensity of the material being processed, they cause harm. Period. There are no conditions under which it is acceptable for therapists to act on eros with a client, even though it is understandable. The greatest prevention is the understanding and self-analysis of the therapist. When we understand our own attachment style, our sexuality, and our relational needs, we can act to protect both ourselves and our clients. When we act out, we not only cause harm to our clients in the betrayal of our role, thus recapitulating for them the previous betrayals of their lives, but we lose the opportunity to help them work through their erotic transference to a joyous and healing conclusion.

Real Love in Therapy

Few of our traumatized clients arrive at therapy having experienced real love, agape. Many do not know that such a love even exists. We can describe it to them, but it falls on deaf ears. There is no point of reference for this concept. The only way our clients, or any humans for that matter, learn to love is by being loved. Therapy that stays in the intellectual realms without moving into the body and heart fails miserably at love. Intellectualization is an ego defense, a poor substitute for true connection. True love comes from the heart and either is the product of coming through a loving family upbringing or is earned through years of hard emotional and spiritual work. To be a true master, a truly great therapist, we need to awaken that kind of love inside of ourselves. When we do, our patients can feel it. Without it, our clients will feel an essential element of healing is missing from the therapy. Even if they stay in such a therapy for years, and many do, they will ultimately need to find resolution and healing elsewhere.

Alison Miller is a psychologist who has made a career out of working with victims of ritual abuse, mind control, and organized crime. She has written books for both therapists and victims about working with this highly trauma-tized population. One of her clients, Wendy Hoffman, who healed fully from a lifetime of such abuse and became a therapist herself, has written two memoirs inspired by her therapy with Dr. Miller. The amount of abuse Wendy suffered borders on the unimaginable. Her books are tremendously difficult to read for the average therapist. So, her description of the healing value of her therapy with Dr. Miller is all the more impactful when she describes her experience of being with her therapist:

> She comes from the good people in the world, people who do not ren-der children government sexual automatons and leave blank darkened space where there should be a brain. People rooted in generations of rare normalcy. I feel the love her parents had and gave to each other and to her and her siblings. I feel that love pass through her to me and I know that that is what I never had, that I was a child my family didn't love and wouldn't let the outside world near. What Alison has and knows, she sends out. I didn't have and didn't know and that is the difference between us in these criminal cults and others in the world.
>
> (Hoffman, 2015)

When I start with a new client, I assume that I may be the first person in their life to care about them in a nonabusive way, especially if they are under 25 years old. Age does not have to define this experience, though. I have also seen clients in their 70s who are having their first real experience of being cared for in the therapeutic relationship. This is a great privilege and a great responsibility. What we do as therapists impacts people for the rest of their lifespan. We either foster love and trust or destroy it. We leave our clients in better shape at the end of a session, or in worse shape.

When I am not working with clients or writing books, I can often be found with my horses. I have had the pleasure of working with several horses in the kind of relational training called natural horsemanship. Natural horsemanship could be described as attachment-based horsemanship. Think horse whisperer. Horses travel in herds and are very social creatures. As with humans (and most mammals), attachment gives horses the ability to survive in the wild. They want to naturally attach to their humans and are capable of deep heart bonds. Because of this desire, they are very sensitive to their interactions with their riders. Horses attune to the moods of their people. We have a saying at our barn, "your horse is only as good as your last ride." The horse has such acute body memory and neurology that they will literally pick up where the rider leaves off. If the last ride was a power struggle, your next ride will begin with one. If you worked through your issues to a smooth flow of understanding, your next ride will be delightful.

I believe this same dynamic operates with our clients. Because people are more complicated than horses and can cover up these responses with placating behaviors or distractions, the dynamic is less obvious unless we work really hard to see it. As with horses, what we do in sessions deeply affects the neurology of our patients. Most of our clients are not so sensitive that an occasional error will torpedo the therapy (although it might if it is the beginning of working together), but toxic, unloving dynamics will definitely affect our clients adversely over the short and long term. Our clients, like every mammal on the planet, know instinctively if we care for them or if we don't. Unselfish love, agape, is as necessary to therapy as oxygen is to our ability to breathe. How else will our clients learn what love is and should be if not in the therapy hour?

But what if we are not confident at love yet, as therapists and as people? What if we did not, as Dr. Miller was described above, come from "people rooted in generations of rare normalcy"? So many therapists come to this profession to heal, to understand relationships, and to both give and receive love in a 'safe' container, yet so few of us are conscious of these motivations when we begin. As therapists we have to create the safety of the container as we discover our own capacity for compassion. Safety is not a given in the therapy hour; it has to be carefully created. Sure, there are legal and ethical parameters we follow, as well as good technique, but, in the end, the therapy container is only as safe and loving as we are. So, how loving are we really? How confident are we in our own ability to provide healing agape?

Grounding Ourselves in Love

To raise a child, as they saying goes, "it takes a village." It also takes a village to support a healer. To work in the depths of human suffering is no small task. None of us can do it alone. If we were unloved, ourselves, as children, we may be even more motivated to provide that missing love to others than if we were well loved. But we may lack the internal resources to do so.

In the five-element practice of traditional Chinese medicine, the element of earth connects to mother. Earth is literally the ground underneath our feet and the source all life, all resources. Look around you. Everything here is made from our mother, the earth. She gives to us unceasingly and humanity's job is to receive, cherish, and care for her. If we think about the symbolism of mother for a moment we realize that to mother is to open on every level. The egg opens at conception. Mothers' wombs enlarge and open to grow a baby. At birth the cervix and vaginal canal open to release the baby into the world. Breast ducts open and fill with milk and nipples open to feed the hungry baby. Mothers' hearts (ideally) open with every child and make room for that child in their family and their attention. Around the world the archetype of mother is one of abundance (Lakshmi, Pachamama), gentleness and merciful giving (Virgin Mary, Quan Yin, White Tara), and fierce protectiveness (Kali, Durga, Green Tara, Pele, Ixchel). To give is to open as mother, as earth element.

If we cannot get nourishment from mothering as a young child, the body will literally develop an imbalance in the earth element in our bodily systems. In Chinese medicine terms, the consequence to the body is problems with digestion and metabolism because the element of earth governs the stomach meridian. Psychological manifestations of earth (mother) imbalance manifest as worry and trouble with self-esteem; in an extreme imbalance there can be mania or severe anxiety. In modern psychology, we know that a person with a deficiency in mothering will become either too independent or too dependent; there will be difficulties in the arenas of attachment and love. For a person inclined to dealing with their earth deficiency through service to others (i.e., therapists), self-care can suffer and then may be compounded with overexertion on behalf of others. Most of the clients, including therapists, I have sent for acupuncture have a deficiency in the earth element, noticeable in the pulses. If the therapist is not held and supported in communities of love while giving in such a way, extreme imbalances can develop in the body and mind.

We need to learn how to receive in our hearts in order to give from our hearts. Some of us have had more opportunity for that than others. Because so many of us became therapists in response to what we were not receiving in our families of origin, we may need to retrain ourselves to ask for what we need to be able to give from a place of fullness rather than need. Remember the aphorism, "if mama ain't happy, ain't nobody happy." Therapists can practice with pristine technique, but if our hearts are hurting and our own love stores are low, our work will drain us, and we will struggle with the 'unconditional positive regard' so necessary to that holding environment our patients need. We need to put on our own oxygen masks first!

When I was receiving attunements and training for Reiki, a vision came to me about this dynamic. Somewhere along the line I had developed the idea that I was a channel for Reiki and healing to come through me, rather like a hose or a tunnel. The problem was that in that model I might have only a couple of drops left of that goodness for my own, as everything was passed through me to the client. In the vision, I was shown a new way to think about my practice. *I was to become a beautiful fountain, allowing myself to fill up with healing energy and only allowing the energy to flow to my patients once I had filled up first.*

This model works just as well for therapy as it does for Reiki. We must allow ourselves to fill up with the qualities that we want to share with our clients. It is not selfish to need to be filled with love in order to share love. If we want to be a presence of unconditional love for our clients, then we need to have at least one person in our lives who can be that source for us. We need to actively seek out teacher, mentors, peers, supervisors, and therapists who can embody those qualities for us, and those relationships need to be personal, to be specifically about us. I feel sad that there are therapists who are practicing without having had a truly caring therapist or supervisor in their corner. I don't know how we can offer what we have not received! All of us who take on the difficult and noble task of healing broken people need as much loving support as we can get. This work will take us to our knees, boggle our minds, and break our hearts. A mentor (supervisor, therapist, colleague) who can see us in our best self and elicit our best work is not a luxury for this work; it is a necessity.

Too many of us work in agencies where the human needs of the staff are ignored. I have seen a sad devolution of the practice of therapy in these agencies since the advent of managed care and ever-shrinking resources. Salaries have not gone up for therapists in decades. Staff are overworked, underpaid, and underplayed! For those of us who went into this field because of our love of connection and humanity, there is a sad irony in the levels of disconnection and disaffectedness that so many therapists are experiencing in the workplace. Thanks to the contribution of great minds and hearts in the field of therapy we know now, better than ever, how to help folks struggling with trauma, how to heal broken hearts. Yet, in so many agencies these techniques cannot get implemented due to financial procedures, liability concerns, and trauma-uninformed procedures. These environments become soul killing to developing therapists. More and more I hear stories of policies and procedures at agencies that are completely at odds with compassionate care and support of staff.

A 14-year-old boy has just been discharged following a rather serious suicide attempt and a hospital stay of a couple of days. He is weak but resolved to get help for himself and agrees to go into residential care. He is transported late in the day still woozy from his medical recovery to a facility for intake. At intake, the harried worker prepares him for the intake process, saying that she will need to go through 20 tabs of questions so that he may be admitted and perfunctorily informs him that he can refuse to answer any questions. He wants to be helpful and make a good start to his stay so he answers all of her questions, including a rather lengthy history of the trauma history of his family, which includes quite a bit of domestic violence and other traumas. By the end of the interview, it is late, the boy is exhausted, retraumatized, and shut down. He is walked over to his new residential unit in a state of shock, ill prepared for the task of entering a new environment.

This exact scenario was reported to me by a recent social work graduate in a supervision group. She was absolutely horrified that this was standard operating procedure for new admissions. She decried the priority of having the client answer questions for funding and administrative needs over a trauma-based approach. Watching this young teen get overwhelmed and shut down as he was about to move into a brand new setting for the evening created a mild traumatic response in her. She felt helpless to intervene in the situation. We talked about possible interventions that she could have done, such as gently challenging the need for 20 tabs of questions to be answered in that moment, or acknowledging out loud the potential traumatization of the youngster, especially in such a vulnerable state. But she was not sure of her rights or the child's rights, and she had gone into a mild state of shock herself at the disparity between what she felt was appropriate versus what was actually happening to this client. We discussed how an appropriate trauma-informed interview would never involve asking such intrusive questions of a person of any age before they were ready to discuss those things, much less of a young teen.

We need to do better. If any of our procedures are causing clients and staff to suffer and go into states of traumatic shock, we are doing it wrong! There is nothing kind, careful, or compassionate about such behavior. Funding needs is not a good enough answer. When did we decide to become so cold? I wish I could say this was an exception, but I do not believe that it is. Our mental health institutions have become very untherapeutic places, evidence-based procedures notwithstanding. When therapists are caught in these 'rock and hard place' scenarios, they have only a few choices to deal with their cognitive dissonance. They can actively resist and challenge business as usual on behalf of their clients risking censure, poor evaluations, and the perception of being a troublemaker, or they can knuckle down, give up, keep their job, and accept this mediocre way of practicing as legitimate even when their conscience says it isn't, or they can leave and try to find a job where they can keep their clinical and moral integrity. Why are we putting our most valuable therapeutic agents, our therapists, in such a position?

Choosing to be grounded in love for ourselves means staying true to ourselves. To surrender our integrity is ultimately an act of self-violence no matter what the reason. Pascal, the famous French mathematician, said, "the heart has its reasons of which reason knows nothing." No amount of bottom-line thinking can compete with what we know is good for our patients from our heart. No survival-level logic will compensate us for the plummet of our self-esteem when we find ourselves colluding with or being dominated by such a system. Our hearts will suffer when we cannot provide the care that we know we can give and long to offer.

Shadow Work

In order to protect our clients from the negative effects of mental health systems, we need to be vigilant about the negative aspects of ourselves and our practice, the Jungian shadow. The shadow encompasses hidden parts of the psyche that we would rather not see, the parts that remain outside of ordinary consciousness. If one is intent on doing and being good in the world, the shadow is comprised of the unloving aspects of the self—the 'dark side', as it were. Without understanding and accepting these selfish unloving aspects as part of every ego, the shadow gains power and can manifest in both the micro and macro aspects of treatment. How, then, do we protect our patients from the unloving aspects of ourselves, our unconscious sadism, our neediness?

The first step is to become aware that we have a shadow! When we discussed erotic countertransference, we were acknowledging a common shadow phenomenon in the therapy world, one that causes many clinicians to be sued or to lose their licenses. But there are many other shadows that get less publicity. Some of these are minimally acknowledged but common. All unacknowledged shadow is potentially dangerous to our clients and can cause us to act in ways that are unloving, unhelpful, and damaging or to participate in systems that are. None of us is immune to the shadow! Also, none of us really likes looking at the dark side of ourselves. When we look, we become vulnerable to intense feelings of shame and badness. As we go through the following list of toxic therapy's greatest hits, please keep in mind that shadow is an inevitable part of the psyche. In a weird way, even though the process of excavating shadow feels extremely personal, it is not personal at all, just an aspect of mind that all humans have in common. Just as we cannot eat food without having to pass feces, we cannot deliver loving service without dealing with shadow.

Sadism

I first heard sadism discussed overtly by the therapist Lynn Sanford, LICSW, author of the acclaimed book *Strong at the Broken Places* (Sanford, 1991). In a brave and brilliant talk, she called out her own and systemic sadism in her work with a teenaged male youth in residential treatment. I do not remember the exact details of the case, but I was struck by her description of staff behavior that was, in my previous experiences of residential care, quite common with a certain type of youth. Staff delighted in taking the 'obnoxious' youth's behavior down a peg or two without regards to the therapeutic or anti-therapeutic value of their comments. They felt entitled to their hateful comments because a child scared and horrified them. Sadism arises whenever we delight in another's suffering. We do not need to cause that suffering directly in order to 'enjoy' our sadism. Our sadistic pleasure at another's pain always becomes a further source of pain for our clients, whether we realize it or not.

Often we give ourselves permission to express sadistic feelings towards clients that are universally disliked, or have been labeled as villains either overtly or covertly in our practices. In the movie *The Thomas Crown Affair* (Brosnan, Trustman, & McTiernan, 1999), Faye Dunaway plays a therapist who is treating Thomas Crown, a wealthy narcissist who has tendencies towards antisocial personality disorder. Her dislike for this client is apparent in the first minutes of the movie and barely contained. The therapy devolves into a kind of cat and mouse game, a power struggle between two titanic personalities, lacking empathy or even kindness. In the following dialogue, we can see the therapist's anger escalate. It expresses itself first in condescension. By the end of the movie, she is openly mocking and sadistic, throwing any semblance of therapeutic neutrality to the wind.

TX: Has it occurred to you that you have a problem with trust?
CROWN: I trust myself implicitly.
TX: Yes, but, can other people trust you?
CROWN: What, you mean society at large?
TX: I mean women, Mr. Crown.
CROWN: Yes, a woman could trust me.
TX: Good. Under what extraordinary circumstances would you allow that to happen?
CROWN: A woman could trust me as long as her interest didn't run too contrary to my own.
TX: (eyebrows raised, fixed smile, brief roll of eyes) And society, at large? If its interests were to run counter to your own?
CROWN: (slight smile) Hmmm.

After finding that he is in love some weeks later . . .

TX: (laughing) Oh dear, Peter Pan decides to grow up and finds there's no place to land! The only sad part (still laughing) is if she's anything like you, she won't know what she's lost until it's gone.

The therapist's anger and sadism begins to emerge in sarcasm when she uses the unnecessary word 'extraordinary' in her question partway into the interview. She then rolls her eyes, an example of contempt, which she tries to hide with her smile. In the last line above, she openly mocks her client sadistically, calling him names and laughing at him.

Although the example is fictional, the dynamics are not. Sarcasm, eye-rolling, or other body language expression such as smirking, contempt, and mocking are all signs of sadism emerging in the therapy. This sadism can be mild, a mocking tone or turn of phrase. A therapist could respond, "wouldn't *you* like to know?" with an arched eyebrow in response to a personal question. More extreme versions of sadism in therapy can emerge when the therapists feel threatened by their client or judgmental towards them. Harsh humiliating confrontations of substance abusing clients are a classic way this dynamic can manifest.

There is a difference between unskillful interventions and sadistic acting out. We know it is sadism when there is a pleasurable release of tension after we have acted out with hostility towards a client, especially if we take satisfaction in 'making them squirm' or 'putting them in their place'. More extreme versions of sadism can take the form of retaliation, such as a psychiatrist holding a psychiatric patient in an institution longer than is necessary because they were personally offended by them or found them difficult. The use of unnecessary restraints or punishments by mental health staff would also fall into this category. After more than 40 years' experience in human services, I can tell you with sad confidence that sadism is common and ubiquitous in mental health care. Clients who have been in the mental health system for long periods have many tales to tell of the meanness of staff and therapists.

Like erotic countertransference, sadistic countertransference is a clear and present risk. It is normal to have sadistic feelings towards some patients, just as it is normal to have sexual feelings for some patients. Wise therapists accept these feelings as a matter of course in therapy and work with them consciously both to avoid acting them out and to use them to garner more information about the dynamics of the client. If we think we are too 'nice' to engage in such thoughts or behavior, we expose our clients and our practices to great risk. We need to get a handle on our own rage, our own desires to inflict pain, and the subtle gratification we get from seeing patients suffer when we loathe them. Some of our clients deserve and even seek our loathing. Pedophiles, cruel people, sex offenders, child abusers, and Machiavellian manipulators are easy to hate. It takes a great deal of insight, compassion, and self-control to deliver excellent services to these people without behaving sadistically towards them.

Neediness and Self-Gratification

All therapists go through needy phases of life, and it can happen at any age and stage of being a therapist. Maybe our lives have become boring or stressful. We may be going through a divorce or other profound loss in our lives. Maybe the people in our lives are angry with us, or difficult. Perhaps we are ill. We might be raising young children, or caring for our parents or both, which can be particularly ungratifying and exhausting. Our clients, on the other hand, need us, hang on our every word, and feel that they cannot live without us. In some cases, they fall in love with and idealize us. In a vulnerable time, we may find ourselves becoming addicted to that adulation and seeking unconsciously to preserve it at the expense of good therapy.

Neediness can be a particularly difficult area to navigate, as there is some component of the therapeutic relationship, as we have discussed earlier in this book, that encompasses limited personal sharing and transparency. We may want to show our vulnerability to our clients to close the power gap with our clients and enhance the connection with disaffected clients. We may let them see a tear in our eye, or share a story from the previous week. And these sharings need to be real in order to be effective. They also need to be relevant and ultimately focused on serving the client in order to be ethical.

We need to have some sort of personal review process, some quality assurance if you will, in place to ensure the safety of our interactions with our clients. So many of us work alone or do not have adequate supervision to address these issues. The shadow of neediness may sneak up on us after several years or decades of practice, when we have long since abandoned the idea that we need regular supervision or therapy. Like an older driver who has not had their driving skills tested in years, our abilities may have slipped, our boundaries subtly eroding without any real awareness that there is a problem until we crash.

Recently I heard from a client about a previous therapist who started sharing personal anecdotes, moved to asking her opinion about life situations, and then made overtures to meet outside of the therapy hour. It is not clear whether this was a grooming process or an inevitable erosion of boundaries. The client did leave this therapist, but did not report the therapist to a licensing board or make any type of formal complaint. It is not clear whether this therapist even knew the client was offended at these transgressions or knew they were crossing boundaries.

Ignorance is not an excuse. Therapists need to remain constantly on alert to their own very real and human needs and how these needs play out with clients in the therapy hour. It is one thing to take the occasional therapy hour to lighten things up, take a break from intensive work, and discuss current events or even tell jokes. It is another to find oneself confiding more and more in a particularly empathetic or entertaining client. Traumatized clients cannot, in many cases, defend themselves against these types of boundary violations. The pattern of rescuing or wanting to rescue abusive, needy parents appears so commonly in highly traumatized patients that we need to remain vigilant to our own needs. We need to make sure our clients are being appropriately served by helping them understand their unconscious need to caretake us as a transference dynamic while setting appropriate limits on ourselves and them.

Insensitivity and Neglect

By far the most common manifestations of shadow I observe lies in the emotional neglect of clients and oneself. This dynamic can play out through insensitivity. There can be many reasons why previously sensitive engaged and empathic therapists fall prey to insensitivity. The design of institutions and procedures often hinders sensitivity and creates compassion fatigue in caregivers. We can only bang our heads against brick walls so long before we are bloodied and exhausted trying to provide sensitive empathic services in a setting where we are not emotionally (and often not even financially) supported ourselves. Those are external factors. But there are also internal factors within the client-therapist relationship that can surface insensitivity and neglect.

A new client brings excitement, much like a new love or a new project. We are curious, engaged, and eager to help. Since therapists tend to practice in areas in which they need healing, there is the added excitement of self-discovery. Like any new relationship we may even get a subtle (or not so subtle) 'high' from the new developing connection. As treatment progresses, the patient starts to show their less desirable qualities. Treatment can hit impasses. Insurance and institutions throw up roadblocks to gratifying therapy. And, suddenly, ugh! We are no longer so enamored with our client (and they may not be with us, either!). The honeymoon ends, and the real work of treatment begins.

At this point, we are challenged to stay engaged in the face of much negativity and slow, painful progress. Depending on our own personal attachment style, we may be inclined to distance our clients even as they distance us. We can 'fall out of love' with them and start to indulge in judgmental and critical thoughts—much as we might do with a significant other in our life (spouse, child, etc.). It is at this point that the shadow rubber meets the road! Do we stay awake and aware of our negative tendencies, our self-protection through distancing, or do we lean into our own discomfort and theirs, learning as we go?

Neglect shows itself first in the little things. We are a little late for their appointments. We skip notes on them. We think of them and immediately feel a heaviness or resistance to wanting to see them. We start blaming them for everything that is not going well in the therapy ("if only they . . . would work harder, follow advice, were more compliant, etc.") Their complaints and suffering leave us cold. We become insensitive.

All of us do these things at some point in our practice lives. Heck, we do these things in our personal lives, why not our practices? Because this dynamic is so common, we can easily get colleagues to collude with us. We all love us some insensitive smack talk, or, to put it in millennial terms, it feels good to be salty! We are especially vulnerable to the emergence of neglect for our clients when we are being neglected by the institutions we work for. It takes great mastery to hold to our ethics when people, institutions, and governments around us are caving in to their negative tendencies and neglecting therapists. It feels *so* much easier to give into feelings of helplessness and apathy and jump in the neglect hole with everybody else.

But our job is to care. And if we are on a path of human development, a path of mastery and wisdom, we need to learn how to cleave to our own values even if everybody else around us is jumping ship. Even if our clients (apparently) don't care.[2] The shadow of neglect will try to manifest in our relationship to ourselves as well as with our clients. In other words, we need to become vigilant about how we are neglecting ourselves in order to refrain from neglecting our caseloads.

The key to dealing with all shadow phenomenon is *awareness*. Shadows cannot persist in direct sunlight. As soon as we become aware of neglectful tendencies, we can immediately begin repair through self-care and analysis of our malaise with our clients, which usually boils down to some counter-transference issue or other as is true with all shadow phenomenon. Engaging in these self-monitoring practices *is* love. We protect our clients against the shadow by staying vigilant for the proverbial wolf at the door. We may be the first in their lives to do so.

Unlocking Wisdom and Opening Hearts

To be a wise therapist, a master, is to practice wisdom in all aspects of our lives. We do not get there overnight or on a part-time basis. Knowledge must soak into our brains and our hearts that become soft with compassion over a long period of time. As younger therapists, we must 'fake it 'til we make it'. We practice wisdom and compassion in the therapy hour as best we can, integrating our left brain/right brain practice of theory and intuition. We examine our practice and our mistakes. We look at our attachment styles and the progress, or lack thereof, of our clients. We listen to our clients' feedback. If we can let go of our egoic defenses, our need to be right; if we can dance with our shadow, love all of our strange bits, heal our traumas, and do our due diligence, we have a shot at greatness.

I believe that humanity is at a crossroads of development. In yogic terms, we must move our consciousness from that of power and control, the little "I am," to our heart—our center of agape, of seva: service to others over service to self. Without this transition, we will doom ourselves to endlessly repeat every war, every mistake of the last several hundred years ad nauseam. We cannot get to wisdom and harmony through power and control either in therapy or in the world at large. Control is no substitute for love. The endpoint of such madness is species-wide suicide.

Every great spiritual teacher has taught the primacy of heart over power for a reason. Heart is the only way out of the negative spiral that clutches at humanity. We cannot fight for peace or think our way into higher states of consciousness. We must learn to dive deep into process, into the immense creative stores of the unconscious mind. We must heal our individual and then our collective traumas. As therapists, whether we realize it or not, we are major leaders of this task! We are the forerunners, the sine qua non of this evolutionary leap, at least here in the West.

The East has gurus, lineages of families that span dozens of generations and hundreds of years of wisdom passed down in an unbroken line. We do not have that legacy here; we lost it. In the West, in Europe, especially, we killed and tortured our healers and wise ones (largely women) for 300 years. Think about how long a period of time that is, how many generations. Entire lineages of wise people were lost to the genocidal Inquisition. A way of thinking that is suspicious of the deep places in the human mind emerged and with that loss of wisdom came war after war. Western nations spread this infection to the rest of the world through colonialism and religious conversion, disenfranchising cultures from their deep ways of knowing and calling it 'civilization'. Well, our 'civilization' has made us sick. We are more traumatized than ever and in need of people of wisdom to help right our course. And guess what? Tag! We are it! If we, as therapists, choose to be all that we can be and truly embrace the path of wisdom, we can create miraculous ripples of healing that spread from each individual treatment to communities, states, and then nations. In the meantime, we get to heal ourselves and become the person we dream we can be, the person we know we need to be in our hearts.

If we seek wisdom, becoming a therapist gives us the fast track, maybe the fastest available to us. Lucky us! We get a chance to practice the qualities of selfless love in a contained environment on a regular basis. We get a front row seat to watching the best of humanity emerge from the worst experiences. Attunement, compassion, empathy, caring, and presence are literally our bread and butter. Therapists are paid for developing soul qualities that, ironically, can only emerge in the presence of a suffering human being, our clients. As difficult as trauma work can be, we are rewarded with the chance to express our highest and best selves on a daily basis with people who truly need what we have to offer and who might perish without it. In return, our clients become attached to us; they develop the ability to form meaningful relationships and to be safe in those connections. Our love and wisdom sustains them, and their healing sustains us. When we realize our interdependence with our clients and reap the gifts of this arduous practice as a healer, we can truly embrace our own wisdom and love, embody it, and share it with the world.

Notes

1 Projective identification is the phenomenon whereby a patient projects qualities onto the treater so strongly that the treater starts to identify with the projected qualities and embodies them in the therapy, often to the detriment of therapy and against the therapist's conscious will. When the therapist can see how they are unconsciously taking on the patient's projection, they can help the client see aspects of themselves that they have disavowed in that projection.

2 And, of course, they do care. But they reach points of hopelessness at times where they feel that withdrawing and not caring is all they are capable of. If they are still coming into sessions, though, there is always hope!

References

Baur, S. (1997). *The Intimate Hour: Love and Sex in Psychotherapy*. New York, NY: Houghton Mifflin.

Brosnan, P. (Producer), Trustman, A. (Writer), & McTiernan, J. (Director). (1999). *The Thomas Crown Affair* [Motion Picture]. USA: MGM.

Hoffman, W. (2015). *White Witch in a Black Robe: A True Story About Criminal Mind Control*. London, UK: Karnac Books.

Online Etymology Dictionary. (n.d.). *Agape*. Retrieved October 30, 2017, from Dictionary.com: www.dictionary.com/browse/agape

Sanford, L. T. (1991). *Strong at the Broken Places: Overcoming the Trauma of Child Abuse*. London, UK: Virago Press.

Index